AD LAW

Breaking the mould
without breaking the rules

SECOND EDITION

Edited by
Marina Palomba and
Christopher Hackford

Published by the Institute of Practitioners in Advertising
44 Belgrave Square, London SW1X 8QS
Tel: 020 7235 7020 Fax: 020 7245 9904
Email: info@ipa.co.uk

IPA Regional Office
PO Box 85, Thirsk, North Yorkshire, Y07 2YQ
Tel: 01845 597878 Fax: 01845 597889

Scottish Office
Catchpell House, Carpet Lane
Edinburgh EH6 6SP
Tel: 0131 4677821 Fax: 0131 4670099

www.ipa.co.uk

A CIP catalogue record for this book is available from the British Library

ISBN 978 0 85294 133 1 2nd edition
ISBN 978 0 852941 132 4 (1st edition)

Cover advertisement reproduced by kind permission of Heineken Group
Agency: Collett Dickenson Pearce/Art Director: Alan Waldie/Copywriter: Mike Cozens/Illustrator: Paul Davis

'Ad Law' is used with the kind permission of Swan Turton, the UK member of Adlaw International and the proprietor of the 'Adlaw' UK registered trade mark.

Designed by Paul Barrett
Production services by Book Production Consultants Ltd
Printed and bound in Thailand by Kyodo Nation Printing Services

Contents

Preface

The UK is one of the world's most sophisticated advertising markets, and one in which its agency practitioners demonstrate a very high level of creativity and effectiveness on behalf of their clients. They are paid to develop strategies and communications campaigns for their brands, and this nearly always means challenging the conventions of a marketplace and 'pushing the envelope' in creative and media terms.

However, agencies also operate in the context of a dynamic dialogue between all stakeholders in society. As a result of this the UK market has one of the most elaborate and effective regulatory and self-regulation systems of advertising controls in the world, and a set of codes that are constantly under review in the context of technological developments, social change and the evolution of markets. Thus it is extremely important that agency people are fully aware of the codes, the law and their ethical responsibilities. This is why the IPA has introduced the mandatory 'LegRegs' exam-based qualification for everyone of Account Director or equivalent status in its member agencies.

In developing advertising and marketing communications of all kinds, the real skill is to 'break the mould without breaking the rules'. To do this, practitioners often need professional legal advice, and this book brings together expertise from leading law firms, and the IPA, as well as regulatory and trade bodies.

The book is a practical guide and covers the whole range of legal and regulatory issues facing agencies and their clients, with help in answering the sort of questions that might have arisen when the Humpty Dumpty execution in the famous Heineken 'Refreshes the parts other beers cannot reach' campaign was first mooted: Are the words 'Humpty Dumpty' a registered trademark? Is there copyright in the image? Will the use of a children's character for an alcoholic drink be in breach of the codes? If extracts from the nursery rhyme were to be used, is this also a breach of copyright? Can the strapline comply with the requirements of substantiation and rules on comparative advertising?

In their approach these expert authors are mindful of the nature of the creative endeavour, and approach problem solving with a 'glass-half-full' attitude and a desire to use their own creativity to make the most of an idea, and then protect it. If your creative idea looks broken, then their advice could help put it back together again.

Hamish Pringle
Director General, Institute of Practitioners in Advertising

Foreword

Advertising in Britain is an enormously important part of the creative economy. It nurtures and uses talent. It helps to oil the wheels of the economy as a whole. It is worth around £19bn a year. It adds to the spice and enjoyment of life. And on the whole, here in Britain, it's rather well done. Advertisements here tend to be witty, elegant, punchy, and often the best anywhere in the world.

I like to think that the self-regulatory system for advertising in the UK, headed by the Advertising Standards Authority, helps to reinforce this success. Overwhelmingly, advertising is accurate, responsible, and abides by the rules. It wouldn't be trusted by the public if it wasn't, or didn't. Sometimes, of course, creative teams will try to push the boundaries, but it's our job at the ASA to draw the line from time to time, to enforce the codes that have been agreed across the industry, and to keep the public's trust in place. We will continue to do this, as impartially as we possibly can.

The framework of codes and the legal restrictions and regulations that lie behind them can, however, be daunting and sometimes confusing. And that's where this up-to-date compendium becomes not just useful but essential: it sets out with real clarity – and in language the non-lawyer can understand – exactly what is covered and said by the self-regulatory codes and by the statutory provisions that also exist. It covers fundamental issues like copyright and trade marks and consumer legislation. It explains European directives, national laws, and voluntary codes. It includes an abundance of examples, many of them very recent, which bring the legal provisions to real life. And it touches on issues of ethics as well as practicality.

This book is, in other words, indispensable. The rules are there not to stifle creativity, but to help it to express itself as effectively as possible, and in as trustworthy a manner as possible. And this guide will, I know, help that to happen.

Rt Hon Lord Smith of Finsbury
Chairman, The Advertising Standards Authority

Bell Wedlake Bell Wedlake Bell Wedlake Bell Wedlake Bell Wedlake B
ke Bell Wedlake Bell Wedlake Bell Wedlake Bell Wedlake Bell Wedlake B
ke Bell Wedlake Bell Wedlake Bell Wedlake Bell Wedlake Bell Wedlake B
Wedlake Bell Wedlake Bell Wedlake Bell Wedlake Bell Wedlake B

1.1

Copyright

Copyright is so important in the context of the advertising world that, ideally, everyone who works in that world should have at least a basic understanding of the main principles.

Copyright is by far the most widespread of the 'intellectual property' rights that are covered in this book. For example, everyone reading this chapter will be a copyright owner, whereas relatively few will own trade marks or designs. The penalties for failing to have regard to copyright, whether it be one's own copyright or that of a third party, can be severe. More positively, the benefits of a greater understanding of copyright can be significant.

WHAT IS COPYRIGHT?

Copyright is a legal right which enables its owner to prevent others from copying or dealing with copies of the work which is protected by copyright. It differs from registered trade marks, patents and registered designs in two key respects.

Firstly, in the UK at least, the creation of copyright requires no registration or other formalities. It arises automatically whenever the conditions are met for the creation of a valid copyright work and provided the copyright work is recorded in some permanent form.

Secondly, it does not create a statutory monopoly over the copyright work. It protects only against the copying, or dealing with infringing copies, of a work.

For example, if someone has a valid registered design, no one else can make a product to that design, even if they were completely unaware of the registration when they made their own design and didn't copy the registered design. By contrast, a copyright owner cannot stop someone producing a similar work to the protected work if in fact it was their own original creation and wasn't copied.

There are a number of categories of copyright work. These cover virtually every type of creative material that is likely to be used for advertising – in whatever media. The following are just some examples:

- television or radio commercials;
- pop-up or banner adverts on the internet;
- PowerPoint presentations for new pitches;
- research reports, including charts, tables and supporting databases;
- bill-board advertising, posters, signs and point-of-sale materials;

- packaging and promotional material;
- media schedules.

In practice, there will often be different types of copyright work subsisting in the same type of advertising material.

In the UK, copyright law is governed by the Copyright Designs & Patents Act 1988 ('the CDPA'). This statute is 20 years old and has been extensively amended over the years, not least to cope with the onset of the internet and the digital age which has almost entirely grown up since the CDPA was enacted.

The CDPA is a complex piece of legislation which runs to over 300 sections. A detailed examination of all its provisions is beyond the scope of this book. In this chapter, an attempt will be made to summarise the most important points as they relate to those engaged in the advertising industry. What follows is not intended to be a comprehensive guide to the legislation.

WHAT TYPES OF COPYRIGHT WORK ARE THERE?

The CDPA sets out a number of different types of copyright work that can be protected. Many of these have their own particular rules governing such matters as the length of time the copyright protection will last and how it can be infringed, etc.

The different types of copyright works are:

- original 'literary works';
- original 'artistic works';
- original 'dramatic works';
- original 'musical works';
- sound recordings;
- films;
- broadcasts;
- typographical arrangements of published editions.

In addition to these types of copyright, the CDPA also provides protection for two further categories of rights: 'performers' rights' and 'moral rights'.

It is worth exploring in more detail some of the key aspects of the various types of copyright. This will help advertisers recognise the rights they have and avoid infringing the rights of other copyright owners.

LITERARY, ARTISTIC, DRAMATIC AND MUSICAL WORKS

The CDPA stipulates that in order to enjoy copyright protection literary, artistic, dramatic and musical works must be 'original'. What does this mean?

It is important to note that 'originality' for the purposes of copyright law does not have the same meaning as might be thought. In a copyright context it has nothing to do with the literary or artistic *merit* of a particular work. Rather, the concept of 'originality' means that a work must be the product of at least an investment of some independent skill and labour on the part of the author of the work. It cannot simply be a slavish copy of something.

For example, if someone makes an A4 photocopy of a picture in a book, the resulting copy will not enjoy any copyright protection. However, if that person photocopies several extracts from different books, cuts the copy extracts into squares, rearranges them into a pattern on another piece of paper and then photocopies the resulting compilation, he will probably have invested sufficient independent skill and labour to create a copyright work.

It is comparatively rare in copyright disputes for a claim to fail because there is insufficient 'originality' in the copyright work. However, the degree to which the work is the product of the original skill and labour of the copyright owner, rather than being derived from an existing work, is crucial when it comes to assessing infringement of copyright. This topic is dealt with in more detail in the section on copy infringement, page 6.

Literary works

A literary work means any work (except a dramatic or musical work) which is written, spoken or sung and includes, *inter alia,* a table or compilation, a computer program or a database.[1]

In relation to advertising, a 'literary work' could include the script for an advertisement, the text of a brochure, the text of a print advertisement and so on. But it would not cover single words such as a product or brand name – in spite of the fact that considerable research and investment often accompanies the choosing of a new brand identity.[2] It is also unlikely to protect simple slogans used in advertising. These would be better protected as registered trade marks (e.g. Tesco's slogan 'Every little helps').

Artistic works

These would include a graphic work (such as maps, drawings, charts etc.), photograph, sculpture or collage (again irrespective of artistic quality), works of architecture such as a building or a model for a building or a work of artistic craftsmanship.[3]

Whilst a brand name in the form of simple words would not be protected as a literary work, a stylised version of the brand name in the form of a logo could be protected by copyright as an artistic work (as well as a trade mark or design).[4]

Dramatic works

A dramatic work is a work of action, with or without words or music, which is capable of being performed before an audience. These include a work of dance or mime or a play. As a result of a case involving a disputed advertisement back in 2001, a film can itself now be treated as a dramatic work as well as being a recording of one.[5]

Musical works

This means a work of music – but excluding any words or action intended to be sung, spoken or performed with the music. So song lyrics, for example, are protected not by musical copyright but by literary copyright.

SOUND RECORDINGS, FILMS AND BROADCASTS

Unlike with literary, artistic, dramatic and musical works, there is no requirement for 'originality' in the copyright sense in relation to copyright in sound recordings, films and broadcasts. However, no separate copyright subsists in any of these works to the extent that they are merely copies of existing works.

Sound recordings

A sound recording is a recording of sounds from which the sounds may be reproduced or a recording of the whole or part of a literary, dramatic or musical work – regardless of the medium in which the recording was made.[6]

Obvious examples of sound recordings as copyright works are albums recorded on CD or recordings of radio programmes.

Films

A film means a recording on any medium from which a moving image may, by any means, be produced.[7] (As well as enjoying film copyright, a film can also be a dramatic work.)

Broadcasts

These cover television (including satellite television) broadcasts. Only certain broadcasts over the internet are included within the definition, such as where the broadcast is being made over the internet and via other means at the same time.[8]

TYPOGRAPHICAL ARRANGEMENTS

This type of copyright protects the appearance of the printed pages of published editions.[9] It subsists irrespective of originality. It is a totally separate copyright to any other forms of copyright.

For example, a book will contain literary copyright in the content of the text, but the appearance of the book and its pages will be protected by typographical arrangement copyright.

MORAL RIGHTS AND PERFORMERS' RIGHTS

The CDPA also provides for what are known as 'moral rights' for authors. These are limited rights that are personal to the creator of the copyright work in question. They can be waived or, in certain situations, enforced. This is looked at in more detail in the section on secondary infringement, page 9.

Performers' rights are another species of right created by the CDPA.[10] These rights protect the rights of performers and exist independently of other forms of copyright. Thus a recording of an album by a rock band would have protection as a sound recording for copyright purposes, and the performance of the band itself would attract performers' rights protection for their actual performance.[11]

OVERLAP OF COPYRIGHT WORKS

The various types of copyright work will often overlap with each other. A good example is a typical music CD incorporating a special video of the group in action.
This will contain the following copyright works:

- the sound recording of the music as recorded on the CD
- musical copyright in the music as recorded in the sound recording
- artistic copyright in the artwork on the booklet enclosed with the CD
- literary copyright in the lyrics of the songs (both as reproduced in the booklet and as recorded in the sound recording)
- typographical arrangement copyright in the appearance of the booklet
- film copyright and possibly dramatic work copyright in the video of the group
- performers' rights in the performances recorded.

DURATION OF COPYRIGHT

The duration of copyright protection varies according to the type of copyright involved.

The following table sets out the term of copyright applicable to each type of copyright work.

Type of work	Term of copyright protection
Literary, artistic, dramatic and musical works	• Life of author, plus 70 years from end of year of death. • Employer's copyright lasts the employee's life plus 70 years. • Assigned copyright lasts for the life of the original author plus 70 years from their death. • Joint authorship lasts for 70 years from the death of the last joint author to die.
Sound recordings	50 years after making, or 50 years after first release (if released within that time).
Broadcasts	50 years after first transmission.
Films	70 years after death of the last of the principal director, author of screenplay, author of dialogue or composer of soundtrack.
Typographical arrangements of published editions	25 years after first publication.

It should be noted that the CDPA came into effect in 1989 and there are various transitional provisions that deal with copyright works that were created prior to that.

OWNERSHIP OF COPYRIGHT

Generally speaking, the first owner of copyright in a protected work is the person who created it (i.e. the author).[12]

This does not apply where the work is created by an employee in the course of his or her employment. In such situations, the ownership of copyright automatically vests in the employer.

However, it is important to note that where a work is commissioned, it is the creator not the commissioner who retains ownership of the copyright in that work. This is very important and has caused problems in a number of advertising situations where an advertising or design agency has been asked to create something, but has not transferred title to copyright to the client.

It is crucial that in any contract between client and agency, or where work is sub-contracted, in contracts with third parties or freelancers, that they agree to assign or license their copyright adequately. Otherwise disputes can easily occur.

In many situations where a party has paid an agency to create artwork or advertising, the courts have been prepared to rule that the agency holds the copyright 'on trust' for the client and that it should transfer that ownership.[13]

But this should not be automatically assumed. The court will not invariably hold that title to copyright must be transferred, or imply a licence into an arrangement. In each case the particular circumstances will be taken into account. The case of *Robin Ray v. Classic FM* is an example of where the court was not prepared to go that far.[14]

Joint ownership may apply where more than one person contributes to the creation of a copyright work. This is unlikely to be much of an issue where several employees are involved since copyright will automatically belong to the employer anyway. But if different, independent contributors are making distinct contributions to the creation of something, care will be needed to ensure that copyright ownership is clearly dealt with.

COPYRIGHT INFRINGEMENT

As has been said, copyright cannot be infringed by the independent creation of a work that happens to be very similar to the protected work. Only if there has been copying or dealing with an 'infringing copy' can the infringement provisions of the CDPA be brought into play.

For infringement purposes, copyright is infringed if one of the prohibited acts set out in the CDPA is done in relation to the whole 'or a substantial part' of the copyright work, either directly or indirectly.[15]

What is a 'substantial part'?

In understanding what constitutes infringement, it is crucial to understand what is meant by 'a substantial part'.

Where the whole of a copyright work is copied (e.g. a complete photocopy of a report, or the recording onto an iPOD of a track from an album) the question of copying will be straightforward. However, very often there will not be a straight copy of the whole work. There might be copies made only of extracts from a copyright work. Or there may be what is known as 'altered copying' where the infringer copies the protected work but tries to put the material into his or her own words, or to mix it around so as to disguise the extent of the copying. Here, the concept of 'substantiality' becomes critical.

Unfortunately, there is no single test by which anyone can assess whether or not something is a copy of the 'substantial part' of a copyright work and so infringes it. This will always be a matter of impression for a judge to form on the available evidence.

'Substantiality' is primarily a 'qualitative' test and not a quantitative test. The key factor is not the quantity of the copying but whether what has been copied is a substantial part of the relevant original skill and labour of the copyright owner. This principle can be illustrated by means of a simple example.

Suppose that A publishes an annotated version of Shakespeare's *Hamlet*. The bulk of the book, say 75%, is made up of the play itself and about 25% of it is the annotations which are the original work of A. The book is published. It is a literary copyright work.[16]

Along comes B who, using A's book, copy types the whole of *Hamlet* from it into a book of his own, but not the annotations. In this situation, B has extracted and copied 75% of A's book. However, there is no infringement. Why? Because although in quantitative terms, B has copied the vast majority of A's book, the material he has copied is not the product of A's original skill and labour – it is the product of William Shakespeare's skill and labour.[17]

Meanwhile, C comes along and copies A's annotations into his own book. He has only copied 25% of A's book. But he has infringed A's copyright. This is because the material he has copied (i.e. the annotations) represent the original element of skill and labour that A contributed. So, although only 25% of the book was copied, C's book is still an infringing copy of A's work – there has been copying of a 'substantial part'.

In practice, most scenarios will not tend to be as straightforward as this rather artificial example. Things are more complicated where there is altered copying or copying of only various extracts from the protected work. In each case it is a question of examining what has been taken and determining whether it is a substantial part.

A good illustration of the 'substantial part' rule in action can be found in the High Court judgment in the 'Dr Brown's' case where the claimant successfully sued for, amongst other things, copyright infringement in relation to the copying of a substantial part of its logo. The competing logos are shown side by side in the judgment and demonstrate how infringement can occur even in relation to a relatively straightforward logo.[18]

In the advertising industry, as in other creative fields such as fashion, or journalism, there are all sorts of 'rules' which are bandied around about how much of someone's copyright work can safely be copied without penalty. For example, some designers are under the impression that if they make five differences between their work and a work they are copying, that will be enough to avoid infringement. Journalists often believe that they can take up to 30% and be okay. These rules have absolutely no foundation in law. They should be ignored.

The CDPA sets out various different ways in which copyright can be infringed. There are broadly speaking two categories of copyright infringement:

- primary infringement; and
- secondary infringement.

Primary infringement

This type of infringement is a 'strict liability' form of infringement. It does not matter whether the person committing the infringement realised that what they were doing was wrong. If they do the act giving rise to the infringement, they will be liable.

There are six categories of primary copyright infringement:

- copying the work;
- issuing copies of the work to the public;
- communicating the work to the public;
- performing, showing or playing the work in public;
- renting or lending the work to the public; or
- making an adaptation of the work or doing any of the above in relation to an adaptation of the work.

It is worth looking briefly at some of these.

Infringement by copying[19]

There are different rules for what type of copying is relevant depending on the type of copyright work involved.

For literary, artistic, dramatic or musical works, the copying can be in any material form. So photocopying, writing out by hand, scanning into electronic format, photographing or reading a literary work into a tape recorder could all infringe – provided either the whole or a substantial part of the original copyright work were to be taken. With an artistic work in two dimensions, the making of a three-dimensional copy could infringe and vice versa.

Copying in relation to a film or broadcast, however, requires a copy of the whole or any part of any actual image of the work and includes taking a photograph of the whole of a substantial part of any image forming part of the film or broadcast.

So, it cannot be an infringement of *film* copyright to shoot a new film incorporating identical subject matter to the original. This is because none of the images of the original film would have been copied.[20]

With typographical arrangements, logically enough, the copying must be by means of a facsimile copy of the work in order to infringe. But again, this must involve the copying of the whole or a substantial part of the published edition which enjoys typographical arrangement copyright.

For example, it would not be an infringement of typographical arrangement copyright in a newspaper to make photocopies of individual articles from the newspaper for use in a press-cuttings service. Generally, such photocopies of cuttings would not represent a substantial part of the typographical arrangement. There would need to be reproduction of much more of the page of a newspaper for that to be the case.[21] (However, there could still be infringement of the literary copyright in the articles themselves.)

Infringement by issuing copies to the public[22]

This is known as the 'distribution right'. It prevents anyone but the copyright owner from putting into circulation for the first time within the European Economic Area (EEA), originals of the copyright work or any copies (or substantial parts of them). This is the provision which enables rights owners to carve out separate territories in the world for CDs, books and DVDs.

In 2007, a number of record companies successfully used the distribution right in their legal action against the internet mail order company CD Wow which had been selling cheap CDs and DVDs to UK buyers from its base in Hong Kong.[23]

By the same token, once originals or copies of the copyright work have been put on the market in the EEA by the rights owner, he cannot exert any further control over those particular copies. So they can be freely traded. But of course any subsequent copying of them or a substantial part of them will, if done without the rights holder's permission, be an infringement.

Infringement by communicating the work to the public[24]

This form of infringement was introduced in part to update the CDPA to cope with the internet age. The legislators realised that it was no longer necessary for physical copies of records, videos, books, newspapers etc. to be put into circulation: they can now be put into circulation electronically at the touch of a button.

For example, if a company advertised its services over the internet but used the artwork of another company on its website, it could fall foul of this section by communicating the infringing copy to the public.

Infringement by adaptation[25]

If an advertiser were to take a literary work and without permission turn it, for example, into a script for a dramatised commercial this could amount to an infringement by adaptation. Another example of an adaptation would be a translation of the protected work.

Secondary infringement

Secondary infringement is another form of copyright infringement. It differs from primary infringement because the state of mind of the infringer is taken into account.

You can only commit an act of secondary infringement where you either know or have reason to believe that you are dealing with an infringing copy.

This is why it is always sensible, where possible, to place a copyright notice on any form of copyright work. Although not conclusive, it will usually be more difficult for a defendant to deny that he had the requisite knowledge or reason to believe where the material in question is clearly marked as a copyright work.

Secondary infringement prohibits anyone who has that state of mind from:

- importing into the UK;
- possessing in the course of a business;
- selling, letting for hire, offering or exposing for sale or hire;
- in the course of business, exhibiting in public, or distributing

an article which is, and which he knows or has reason to believe is an infringing copy of the work.[26]

For example, suppose that E, a prospective employee of N, an advertising agency, informs his interviewers at N that he will make copies of some pitch documents from his former agency and bring them with him when he joins.

E arrives at N's offices to start work and brings the copy pitch documents with him. They are placed on his desk at work. E has infringed his former employer's copyright by making unauthorised copies of the pitch documents. Due to what was said at the interview, his new agency N knows, or has reason to believe, that the pitch documents are infringing copies.

Result? N is committing secondary infringement of copyright merely by possessing the copy pitch documents in the course of its business.

Infringements of moral rights

Advertisers should also be wary of infringing moral rights of authors.[27]

Authors of copyright works can have the right to be identified as the author provided they assert that right.[28]

Authors who have not waived their moral rights have the right to object to the derogatory treatment or 'mutilation' of their work.[29] This could be an issue where an advertiser tries to make use of a protected work such as a film, or artistic work in say a TV commercial in another form of advertising.

For these purposes, a treatment is 'derogatory' if it amounts to distortion or mutilation of the work, or is otherwise prejudicial to the honour or reputation of the author (or director in the case of a film).

Authors also have the right to oppose false attribution of authorship. Again, this is something that could arise in an advertising context.[30]

Finally, quite apart from any rights they may have under privacy or data protection laws, a person may be able to object under the CDPA to the publication of photographs that were commissioned for private and domestic purposes – even if they themselves do not own the copyright in them.[31]

Infringements of performers' rights

There are various ways of infringing rights in performances. These mirror many of the ordinary copyright infringement provisions. They include primary and secondary infringements.

Advertisers should be aware of performers' rights if they are proposing to make use of recordings of performances such as musical performances, variety acts, recitations or other live performances.

DEFENCES TO COPYRIGHT INFRINGEMENT

There are a number of instances where the CDPA renders lawful what would otherwise be an unlawful infringing act. Unfortunately, these defences are not really that helpful to advertisers to justify the inclusion of copyright works without permission.

Fair dealing defences are available where the copyright work is being copied or used for purposes such as non-commercial research and private study, criticism or review, reporting current events or where the use is by an 'educational establishment'.[32] None of these is likely to apply to advertisers.

There is also a limited exception for 'incidental inclusion' of a protected work within a new work.[33]

Parodies

The world of advertising lends itself readily to using parody, caricature or pastiche.

For example, a few years ago Sony made a well-known television commercial for its BRAVIA televisions. This depicted slow-motion shots of tens of thousands of multicoloured rubber balls bouncing down the hilly streets of San Francisco to the accompaniment of a soothing Jose Gonzales soundtrack. The advertisement finished with the slogan 'Colour like no other'. Some time after the Sony campaign, the drinks company Tango ran a parody of this advertisement. The Tango advertisement showed what, on closer inspection, were pieces of fruit bouncing down the streets (of Swansea) in slow motion. The same soundtrack was used and the advertisement used the same visual details (such as a frog falling out of a drainpipe) which had featured in the original. The punchline to the advertisement was the slogan 'Refreshment like no other'. It showed a person emerging from a pile of fruit to the further slogan 'You know when you've been Tango'd'.

The mere fact that an advertisement may be intended to be a parody does not imbue it with any special status as far as the law of copyright is concerned. There is currently no special 'defence' available for such use of copyright works, partly because none is really needed, providing there is no substantial copying of a copyright work the parody will not infringe. Examples of such work are the 'New Mini Adventure' commercials including the *Lassie Comes Home* parody, and the use of *King Kong* and *Jaws* parodies in the Peugeot GTI advertisements. Other famous advertisements which pay homage to well recognised advertisements are the numerous copies of the M&S 'This is not just...' commercials and copies of the famous Honda 'Cog' advertisement, which itself was accused of copyright infringement.

If in doubt, permission can be sought and obtained from the rights holder of the advertisement or source material that is to be the subject of the parody. However, this can be expensive and sometimes it is not necessary. So what happens if the rights owner will not consent, or where the advertiser does not seek consent but goes ahead anyway?

In some cases the rights holder may object, but it is rare that legal action is taken, such as in the *Schweppes v. Wellingtons*[34] case where the defendant produced what it claimed was a parody of the claimant's tonic water bottle label and called it Schlurppes. As the judge commented, the purpose behind the adoption of this label (i.e. as a humorous parody) did not matter. What mattered was whether a substantial part of the work had been copied (which in that case it had). With the Sony BRAVIA advert, if permission had not been obtained by Tango, the sheer number of features copied from the original commercial would, in the author's view, have amounted to the copying of a substantial part of the original dramatic work.[35] However, most parodies are obvious, do not mislead and do not amount to a substantial copying. In most cases there is no real commercial benefit to the original rights owner taking action. Indeed, advertisement parodies may remind people of the original campaign and reinforce the message.

The *Gower's Review of Intellectual Property* has recently recommended that a new, specific defence be introduced for parodies. This would be an extension of the 'fair dealing' defences available in copyright infringement cases. However, this will not be an easy defence to introduce and reconcile with the rights of copyright owners and, in any event, such a defence is unlikely to extend to use in the commercial world of advertising.

COPYRIGHT AND COMPARATIVE ADVERTISING

As is discussed in Chapter 1.2 dealing with trade marks, at the time of going to press, it rather looks as though the European Court of Justice may be about to finally resolve some of the issues involving the use of trade marks in comparative advertising. However, the Comparative Advertising Directive[36] that is supposed to provide a comprehensive code for comparative advertisers says absolutely nothing about copyright and what the rules are about use of copyright works in comparative advertising.

The ASA Code of Practice, insofar as it deals with comparative advertising, precisely mirrors the relevant part of the Directive. So it is of no assistance on this point either.

Given that the prevailing EU policy is that comparative advertising is to be encouraged, it seems odd that the freedom of advertisers to use trade marks should be provided for, but not other forms of IP rights such as copyright or designs.

However, without any clarification from the courts on the point, on the face of it, there would appear to be no reason why the use of a copyright work belonging to another should be permissible in a piece of comparative advertising.

In the *IPC v. News Group Newspapers* case, News Group ran a piece of comparative advertising for its rival TV listings magazine. In its advertisement, it used a picture of the front cover of IPC's listings magazine. IPC sued News Group for breach of copyright. The court held that there was nothing in any of the legislation relating to comparative advertising to afford a defence to IPC's claim. The use by News Group of the copy of the front cover of IPC's magazine was an infringement.[37]

Care should therefore be taken when using material that could be protected by copyright in comparative advertisements.

CONSEQUENCES OF COPYRIGHT INFRINGEMENT

Copyright infringement is actionable in the High Court in the same way as most other intellectual property rights. A copyright owner can sue for a range of relief including an injunction to prevent further infringements and mandatory orders of the court requiring delivery up or destruction of infringing materials.

The remedies are discussed in more detail in Chapter 1.4 dealing with passing off.

Three additional points are worth making about remedies for copyright infringement.

First, copyright infringement is unusual under English law because it is one of the few instances where English law allows the imposition of damages on a 'punitive' rather than purely compensatory basis. Such 'additional damages', as they are called, can be ordered by the court where the infringements are flagrant in nature.[38]

Second, the CDPA contains a specific provision enabling copyright owners to obtain injunctions against internet service providers to stop people from using their services to infringe copyright.[39] This right applies once the service provider is on notice of the infringements.

Third, copyright infringement, like registered trade mark infringement, can be a criminal offence punishable in serious cases by a hefty term of imprisonment or an unlimited fine.

SUMMARY

Copyright is therefore a very important intellectual property right in the world of advertising. The breadth of copyright protection for everything from text to sound recordings means that there will be copyright in almost every piece of advertising – in whatever form it is.

It is vital for those in the industry to understand the importance of ensuring that copyright in the material they create is properly dealt with and that the infringement of other parties' copyright is avoided.

The old rules about what percentage of someone else's work can be copied and other similar guidelines should be ignored. Except in cases where the whole of a copyright work is copied, the correct test for infringement involves an analysis of whether a 'substantial part' was taken.

Copyright does not just protect against the act of copying. The distribution right protects against putting copies (and originals) into circulation in the European market without the permission of the copyright owner. Secondary infringement can apply to dealings with infringing copies.

Finally, there are some defences and exceptions to copyright infringement, such as fair dealing or through 'exhaustion of rights'.

Michael Gardner, Wedlake Bell

Notes

1   s3 CDPA
2   Although decided under the old legislation that pre-dated the CDPA, the case of *Exxon Corporation v. Exxon Insurance Consultants International [1982] RPC 69* is still regarded as authoritative on this point.
3   s4 CDPA
4   See for example the 'Dr Browns' logo referred to in *Handicraft Company & Anor v. B Free World Ltd & Ors [2007] EWHC B10 (Pat)*
5   See *Mehdi Norowzian v. Arks Ltd & Ors [1999] EWCA Civ 3014*
6   s5A CDPA
7   s5B CDPA
8   s6/6A CDPA
9   s8 CDPA
10 See CDPA Part II Rights in Performances
11 There is no suggestion in the authorities or textbooks that a studio recording does not qualify for performers' rights protection or that there must be a true 'live' performance.
12 s11 CDPA
13 e.g. *Pasterfield v. Denham [1999] FSR 168*
14 [1998] EWHC Patents 333
15 s16(3) CDPA
16 The book as published would also be a 'published edition' and so there would also be typographical arrangement copyright. This would not be infringed in the example because the text is copy typed from the book – only facsimile copying can infringe typographical arrangement copyright.
17 Besides which, copyright protection for the literary work *Hamlet* has long expired.
18 *Handicraft Company & Anor v. B Free World Ltd & Ors [2007] EWHC B10 (Pat)* – see in particular the appendix to the law report at www.bailii.org/cgi-bin/markup.cgi?doc=/ew/cases/EWHC/Patents/2007/B10.html&query="Dr+Browns"&method =boolean
19 s17 CDPA
20 *Norowzian v. Arks Ltd & Ors (No.1) [1998] EWHC 315 (Ch)*
21 *Newspaper Licensing Society v. Marks & Spencer plc [2003] 1 A.C 551*
22 s18 CDPA
23 *Independiente & Ors v. Music Trading On-Line (HK) Ltd [2007] EWHC 533 (Ch)*
24 s20 CDPA
25 s21 CDPA
26 s22 & s23 CDPA
27 Chapter IV CDPA
28 s77-78 CDPA
29 s80 CDPA
30 s84 CDPA – see also *Clark v. Associated Newspapers Ltd*
31 s85 CDPA
32 s29-30 CDPA
33 s31 CDPA
34 *Schweppes Ltd & Ors v. Wellingtons Ltd [1984] FSR 210*. Although this was a case decided under the 1956 Act rather than the current Copyright Designs & Patents Act, the principles remain the same.
35 But there would have been no infringement of film copyright because the Tango advert was a re-shoot and was not copied from the frames of the Sony original.
36 The Comparative Advertising Directive (97/55)
37 *IPC Media Ltd v. News Group Newspapers Ltd [2005] EWHC 317 (Ch)*
38 s97(2) CDPA
39 s97A CDPA

Trade marks

Trade marks are all around us. They are synonymous with brands and can become highly valuable assets for any business. A product bearing a well regarded trade mark can, irrespective of its relative quality, generally achieve a higher price than its unbranded competitor.

Trade marks are so important in the commercial world that special national and international systems of registration have grown up to protect them in almost every country in the world. Whilst it is still possible, even without registration, to enforce trade mark rights through such laws as passing off (in the UK) or unfair competition, registration is an essential measure for any serious business that wishes to protect its trade marks.

This chapter will focus on the law of registered trade marks. The protection of unregistered trade marks through passing off is dealt with in Chapter 1.4.

INTRODUCTION

A trade mark is a sign (which can be in the form of a name, logo, slogan, sound, colour or shape) which serves to distinguish the goods or services of one business from those of another.

For example, if you are driving along the high street looking to buy a mobile phone, you may see the Carphone Warehouse or Phones4U as possible places to buy one. When you enter the shop, the trade marks Nokia and Motorola will indicate which phones are made by these manufacturers. Meanwhile, you will be presented by the name and graphic trade marks of O_2, Orange, Vodafone, T-Mobile and Three to distinguish between the various mobile network operators.

Driving away with your new phone and listening to the radio, you may recognise the telephone dialing tune which accompanies adverts for Direct Line insurance. When you are driving along looking for a filling station, you may see the green colour of the signage denoting a BP garage. When you select a bottle of Coke from the refrigerator in the garage, the distinctive shape of the Coca-Cola bottle will reassure you that you are ordering the real thing.

WHAT ARE THE RELEVANT REGISTRATION SYSTEMS IN THE UK?

In the UK, the governing law of registered trade marks is derived from an EU Directive[1] and this is implemented here by the Trade Marks Act 1994 (TMA).

The TMA provides a system of national registration under which businesses can file UK trade marks and enforce them within the territory of the UK.

The UK legislation also recognises an international system of registration known variously as the Madrid or WIPO system. This enables trade marks filed in other countries to have their protection extended to cover the UK too, as though their trade marks were ordinary UK registered trade marks.[2]

Aside from UK registrations, the other most important type of registered trade marks are what are known as Community trade marks (CTMs). These are marks registered at the Office for the Harmonisation of the Internal Market (OHIM). Once registered as CTMs, they are enforceable in all countries of the EU.[3]

Fortunately, as far as the UK is concerned, the law applicable to UK registered trade marks, trade marks registered here through the Madrid/WIPO system and CTMs is essentially the same.

HOW DOES THE SYSTEM OF TRADE MARK REGISTRATION WORK?

Because there are an infinite variety of possible businesses that can be carried on, it is not necessary for a trader to register for trade mark protection in relation to every possible type of activity. Instead, trade marks tend to be registered in an appropriate 'class' (or classes) to cover the specific types of activities the business is involved with, or is likely to be involved with in the future.

In this way, the same trade marks can actually be filed and used by different companies without conflict.

For example, the trade mark Lloyds is part of the name of a famous banking group, Lloyds TSB. However, it is also the trade mark of the famous London insurance market

Lloyds. There is also a large retail chemist's chain called Lloyds Pharmacy. So there are three distinct, well known and quite separate businesses all sharing the same trade mark at the same time. Their registrations cover different classes.

A search of the trade marks register will reveal numerous similar examples.

So a business planning to file an application to register a trade mark will need to consider carefully what it is that they will be using the trade mark for and to tailor the specification of goods/services accordingly.

To discourage 'blocking' or tactical registrations for trade marks, there are various rules which enable challenges to be made to registrations on such grounds as bad faith or non-use.[4]

WHAT CAN BE REGISTERED AS A TRADE MARK?

As was stated in the introduction, trade marks are signs which serve to distinguish the goods or services of one business from those of another. It is essential, therefore, that the trade mark can fulfill that function. If it cannot act as a 'badge of trade origin' then it cannot function as a trade mark and will not be capable of registration.

The TMA contains a list[5] of types of signs that cannot be registered. Examples are as follows:

- signs which are devoid of distinctive character (unless by the time of the application for registration they had acquired such distinctive character through use);
- trade marks which consist exclusively of signs or indications which may serve in trade to designate the kind, quality, quantity, intended purpose, value, geographical origin or other characteristics of goods or services;[6]
- trade marks which consist exclusively of signs or indications which have become customary (e.g. 'escalator', 'aspirin' and other generic terms);
- signs consisting exclusively of a shape which results from the nature of the goods themselves, or which is necessary to obtain a technical result[7] or a shape which gives substantial value to the goods;
- trade marks contrary to public policy/morality;
- trade marks registered in bad faith;
- trade marks consisting of specially protected emblems (e.g. the Royal crown, national flag).[8]

It is also an essential rule of registered trade marks that in order to be registerable, they must be capable of being represented graphically[9] and in a manner that precisely identifies what they are.

In the UK and EU, the following types of signs are capable of registration as UK or Community trade marks: names, logos, shapes, sounds, colours and slogans.

Smells are one type of sign that cannot be registered as a trade mark.[10] The reason is that there is no practical method under which a smell can be represented graphically so as to precisely describe it and enable anyone searching the register of trade marks to identify it. Thus, whilst the name of a perfume such as Chanel No. 5 and the shape of its bottle can be registered, the smell of Chanel No. 5 remains unregisterable.

HOW DOES THE REGISTRATION PROCEDURE WORK?

In order to obtain a registered trade mark, an application is filed at the appropriate trade marks registry. This will include a graphical representation of the trade mark itself and a description of the goods or services for which it is to be registered (known as the 'specification'). A filing fee is paid too.[11]

Unless obviously flawed, the application will be advertised by the registry for opposition purposes. This is to enable any other trader affected by the registration to object to it. If formal opposition proceedings are filed then the progress of the registration is halted until the registry has decided whether or not the objections are valid.

If no successful opposition is made to the registration it will eventually achieve registration (within around six to eight months in the case of a UK registration and longer with a CTM).

It is important to note that once registration is achieved, the date on which the trade mark is deemed to have been registered is the date on which the application for it was originally filed.[12]

HOW LONG DOES A REGISTRATION LAST?

A registered trade mark will appear on the relevant register of trade marks and lasts for an initial period of ten years from the date of registration. However, it can be renewed for further periods of ten years at a time. In other words, once granted, a registered trade mark can last indefinitely.[13]

CAN A TRADE MARK BE CHALLENGED ONCE REGISTERED?

The fact that a trade mark achieves registration is not the end of the matter. It is always possible for another party to challenge the validity of the registration or to seek revocation of it.

If the party challenging it can show that the mark ought not to have been registered in the first place (e.g. because it is descriptive or describes the characteristics of the goods in question) it can be declared invalid. In those circumstances, it is deemed never to have been registered.[14]

Where the trade mark was validly registered but has since either not been used for a continuous period of five years, or as a result of the neglect of the proprietor has ceased to function as a trade mark, it can be revoked.[15]

CAN TRADE MARKS BE TRADED OR LICENSED?

Registered trade marks are items of property. They can be sold or licensed by the trade mark owner. It is quite common for companies which hold trade mark rights to license their rights to third parties to manufacture, market or distribute goods bearing the marks.

Licensees of trade marks have their own set of rights under the TMA (although these are subject to the terms of their licence agreements).

WHAT DOES A REGISTERED TRADE MARK PROTECT AGAINST?

Ordinarily speaking, and subject to possible defences discussed further below, the registered proprietor of a trade mark can sue for infringement in the following circumstances:

- where a party uses an identical sign to the registered trade mark in relation to identical goods or services to those for which the trade mark is registered;[16] or

- where because a party uses:
  - an identical sign to the registered trade mark in relation to similar goods or services to those for which the mark is registered; or
  - a similar sign to the registered trade mark in relation to identical or similar goods/services to those for which the mark is registered;

  there exists a likelihood of confusion on the part of the public.[17]

All trade mark holders are entitled to rely on the above infringement provisions of the TMA.

However, trade mark law is more generous to owners of better-known trade marks. Where the trade mark owner can show that its mark has a 'reputation' in the UK[18] there is a third type of infringement available.

This occurs where the use of the offending sign is without due cause and takes unfair advantage of, or is detrimental to, the distinctive character or repute of the trade mark.[19]

Such 'unfair advantage' infringement can apply irrespective of whether the sign used is identical or only similar to the protected mark. Moreover, unlike other types of infringement, it does not matter whether the goods or services for which the offending sign is being used are identical, similar or completely dissimilar to those for which the trade mark is registered. [20] Finally, for this type of infringement, it is not necessary to show confusion.

It is now standard practice for owners of famous trade marks to rely on this type of infringement in most cases involving their trade marks.[21]

However, at the time of writing, there remains some uncertainty over what exactly is meant by the term 'unfair advantage'. A pending case currently awaiting a judgment of the European Court of Justice (ECJ) may clarify this.[22]

TYPICAL INFRINGEMENT SCENARIOS

Where signs identical or similar to registered trade marks are used without the proper consent in relation to goods or services, there may be trade mark infringement.

'Use' for these purposes covers use in advertising, importing or exporting goods under the offending sign, affixing the sign to goods or selling/offering goods for sale by reference to the sign.[23]

There are a variety of scenarios which can lead to trade mark infringement. In assessing whether or not there is infringement, it is necessary to analyse whether the particular circumstances are capable of amounting to infringement and then seeing whether or not any defence applies.

There might also be a question mark over the validity of the trade mark that is being relied on in the infringement case.

Identical sign/identical mark and identical goods

This is the most straightforward type of infringement. It will apply where a sign is being used in the course of trade and that sign is identical to the registered trade mark and being used in relation to identical goods or services to those for which the mark is registered. There is no need to show confusion, unfair advantage or anything else.

For example, Arsenal football club registers its name as a registered trade mark in Class 25 for football shirts. An independent trader starts manufacturing his own shirts bearing the name 'Arsenal' on the front and selling them outside Arsenal's ground. Result? Trade mark infringement.

An independent retailer registers the internet domain name 'www.tesco.net' and starts using it to promote an online grocery delivery service. Result? Trade mark infringement.

Similar sign/identical goods or identical sign/similar goods or similar sign/similar goods + likelihood of confusion

Sometimes, traders will avoid using an identical sign to a registered trade mark but will instead adopt a sign that is only *similar*. In assessing whether or not a mark is similar, it is important not to take too narrow-minded an approach.

For example, just because a particular registered trade mark may be in the form of stylised words or a combined word and artistic logo, doesn't mean that it will be okay to use words alone. Words alone (such as an internet domain name) can be treated as sufficiently similar to a logo where the words of a logo are its dominant characteristic.[24]

But for this type of infringement, similarity between the offending sign and the trade mark, and between the goods or services for which the mark is registered are not enough. There must be a likelihood of confusion between the sign and the registered trade mark.

Where a sign is used in conjunction with other words, even descriptive words, this can be enough to dispel the likelihood of confusion and so render the sign non-infringing. For example, the use on the internet of the sign 'Reed Business Information' by a well-known publishing company to promote its job search services did not infringe the 'Reed' trade mark registered by the employment company Reed Executive plc.[25]

Although the requirement to show confusion for this type of infringement is similar to one of the requirements of passing off, unlike with passing off, it isn't necessary for the holder of a registered trade mark to show that the mark has been used so as to build up goodwill and reputation. In the case of a registered trade mark (as opposed to one that is unregistered) the court must assume that the mark has been in use and developed a basic reputation and goodwill for the specification of goods or services.[26]

Unfair advantage/detriment

This type of infringement is only available to those trade marks which really have acquired a 'reputation' in the UK (or in the case of a CTM, in the EU). In practice this means that only reasonably well-known brands will qualify.

In some cases, this kind of infringement adds little to the case (for example, in a counterfeiting case where an identical sign is used in relation to identical goods to those of the trade mark holder). However, it can be useful in other scenarios, including where the mark is being used in relation to dissimilar goods or services.

The boundaries of this type of infringement are still being explored by the courts. However, there have been a few cases where the courts have held that the actions of infringers have taken unfair advantage of, or been detrimental to, the distinctive character or reputation of a registered trade mark.

In *L'Oréal v. Bellure*[27], the well-known cosmetics company succeeded at trial in proving that a maker of cheap 'smell-alike' perfumes had taken unfair advantage of certain of its trade marks by trading off the goodwill associated with those products.

This arose from the similarity, both visual and conceptual, of the packaging of the defendant's products when compared to the registered trade marks, even though they were not sufficiently similar to cause a likelihood of confusion. This decision has been appealed and is now before the ECJ.[28]

In *Tesco v. Elogicom*, the supermarket giant successfully argued that a company had taken unfair

advantage of the Tesco trade mark. The use complained of was via the registration of domain names incorporating the word 'Tesco' in them, which were then used to route consumers to Tesco's own website via an affiliate marketing scheme.

DEFENCES

A complete blanket prohibition on the use of trade marks without the permission of the trade mark holder in all situations would be undesirable for a number of reasons. Therefore, the TMA provides that there will be no infringement where certain uses are made of the trade marks – provided that such use is in accordance with honest practices in industrial and commercial matters.

Statutory defences in the TMA

The most important of these defences applies where the use being made of the mark is purely descriptive, or to indicate the characteristics of the goods or services involved.[29] However, to qualify for this defence, the use made of the mark must be in accordance with 'honest practices in industrial or commercial matters'.

For example, the rock group 'Wet Wet Wet' had registered their name as a trade mark for, amongst other things, books and printed matter. The group sued for trade mark infringement when an unauthorised book about them was published. The court ruled that although the mark Wet Wet Wet was being used as a trade mark, it was being used in an honest manner to describe what the book was about. That use was permitted by the TMA.[30]

'Honest' for these purposes is an objective test.

Non-trade mark use and comparative advertising

Although there have been some rather unsatisfactory rulings on the issue by both the ECJ and the English courts, it is now clear that no question of trade mark infringement can apply unless the offending sign is being used 'as a trade mark' (i.e. to denote trade origin).[31] Pure descriptive use will not be actionable.

However, one of the areas that the courts have struggled with concerns the use of trade marks in comparative advertising.

In a comparative advertising scenario, there is no question of the advertiser seeking to indicate that there is any connection between it, its goods or its services and those of the party whose goods are being compared. On the contrary, the very essence of a comparative advertisement is that the reader knows that the goods of two different companies are being compared. The comparative advertiser wants the public to see the differences between the two companies and to highlight that his own goods or services are better/cheaper by comparison.

There have been many cases over the years involving comparative advertising scenarios in which the courts have struggled to reconcile trade mark law with an EU Directive on comparative advertising.

It had been hoped that a long-running case which reached the ECJ might have finally answered many of these unanswered questions. The case arose from a long-

running battle between mobile phone companies O_2 and Hutchison Telecom. The English Court of Appeal had taken the stance that the infringement provisions of the TMA should have no place in relation to cases of comparative advertising.[32] This view was shared by the Advocate General of the ECJ who published an opinion agreeing with the Court of Appeal's view.

However, in the end, the ECJ pulled back from this and held that trade mark law does still apply to comparative advertising.[33] Comparative advertisers can therefore still be sued for trade mark infringement if their adverts are in breach of the criteria set out in the Comparative Advertising Directive, or otherwise infringe the trade marks.

Comparative advertising is looked at in more detail in Chapter 3.2.

Parallel imports

The European Union is supposed to promote the free movement of goods between Member States. Allowing trade mark owners to place restrictions on the onward trade in goods bearing their trade marks within the EU would be at odds with this. So the TMA provides for a concept known as 'exhaustion of rights'. This means that once goods bearing registered trade marks have been placed on the market in the European Economic Area (EEA) by, or with the consent of, the trade mark owner, the trade mark rights in those goods are 'exhausted'.[34] In other words, trade mark rights can generally no longer be used to inhibit trade in those particular goods.

So if a trader from the UK purchases a consignment of Nike T-shirts that have been put on sale by Nike in Germany, there is nothing to stop him importing them into the UK and advertising them for sale over here.[35]

From an advertisers perspective, just as the trader would be entitled to sell those Nike goods in the UK irrespective of whether or not Nike objected, so he would also be entitled to use the Nike trade marks in the ordinary course of trade to advertise the goods for sale.[36]

However, it is important to note that this 'exhaustion' principle applies only to goods placed on the market within the EEA by, or with the consent of, the trade mark owner. It does not apply to goods from outside the EEA, unless the trade mark owner has given clear consent to their importation.[37] This is so, even if the goods in question are genuine and exactly the same kind as those normally sold officially in the EEA.[38]

Since such goods from outside the EEA will be infringing, any advertising or promotion of those goods using the trade marks will also be infringing.

If, for example, a consignment of Lee jeans is bought in the US and imported into the UK without the permission of the trade mark holder and advertised under the slogan 'Lee jeans – direct from the US to save you money', that would be an infringement.

An advertising or printing company that prepared such advertising might itself be in danger of committing trade mark infringement along with the trader if it knew, or had reason to believe, that putting the trade mark on the advertising material was not authorised.[39]

TRADE MARKS AND LEGAL PROCEEDINGS

The owner of a registered trade mark is entitled to bring infringement proceedings against those who are infringing or threatening to infringe the trade marks.

The scope of relief available for trade mark infringement and the types of injunctions that can be sought are very similar to those available for infringement of other IP rights such as copyright, designs and passing off. They are dealt with in more detail in Chapter 1.4 relating to passing off.

One aspect of the UK law of registered trade marks that is worth noting is the fact that if a party issues unjustified threats of trade mark infringement proceedings, these can themselves be actionable by the party threatened.[40] So, when confronted by a trade mark claim, it is always worth seeing whether a 'groundless threats' response is appropriate.

SUMMARY

Registered trade marks can be powerful and invaluable business assets. They have a number of advantages over trade marks that are unregistered. These are:

- because they show up on searches at official registers it is easier for other traders to avoid clashing with them and this may deter other traders from adopting the same or similar trade marks;

- they make it easier to monitor attempts to register marks that could be in conflict with the registered mark and so make it easier to prevent them being adopted in the first place;

- they are items of property whose ownership is certain, and that can be transferred or licensed to others;

- they can be enforced more easily and cheaply than unregistered trade marks in some circumstances;

- in some scenarios passing off will not be available at all (e.g. where there is no goodwill or trading history), but registered trade marks can still be enforced;

- the Community trade mark and the Madrid/WIPO systems enable protection to be obtained in other territories far more easily than with unregistered trade marks;

- there are limits to the effect of registered trade marks due to statutory defences and in fields such as comparative advertising or parallel imports.

Michael Gardner, Wedlake Bell

Notes

1   Council Directive 89/104/EEC
2   s35 TMA
3   Council Regulation 40/94/EEC
4   See for example s46 of the TMA
5   s3 TMA
6   A trade mark will fall foul of this rule if at least one of its possible meanings designates a characteristic of the goods or services concerned (see *OHIM v. Wm Wrigley Jr. Company C-191/01P*).
7   To breach this rule it is not necessary that the shape be the only means of achieving that result. It is sufficient that it is one of a number of ways of doing so (see *Koninklijke Philips Electronics NV v. Remington Consumer Products Ltd & Anor [2006] EWCA Civ 16*
8   s4 TMA
9   s1(1) TMA
10   *Ralf Sieckmann Case C-273/00*
11   s32 TMA
12   s40(3) TMA
13   s42 TMA
14   s47 TMA
15   s46 TMA
16   s10(1) TMA
17   s10(2) TMA
18   Or in the EU in the case of a CTM
19   s10(3) TMA
20   *Adidas Salomon AG & Anor v. Fitnessworld Trading Ltd C-408/01*
21   For recent examples see *Tesco Stores Ltd v. Elogicom Ltd & Anor [2006] EWHC 403* and *L'Oreal SA & Ors v. Bellure NV & Ors [2006] EWHC (Ch) & [2007] EWCA Civ 968*
22   Reference *C487/07 L'Oreal v. Bellure ante*
23   s10(4) TMA
24   See for example the comments of Lord Justice Jacob in para 80 of his judgment in *Phones4U Ltd & Anor v. Phone4u. co.uk Internet Ltd & Ors [2006] EWCA Civ 244*
25   *Reed Executive & Anor v. Reed Business Information Ltd & Ors [2004] EWCA Civ 159*
26   This is another advantage of having a registered trade mark rather than having to rely purely on passing off, where the claimant must prove they have acquired the necessary goodwill and reputation through use of the mark.
27   *L'Oréal v. Bellure [2006] EWHC 2355 (Ch)*
28   *L'Oréal v. Bellure [2007] EWCA 968*
29   s11(2) TMA
30   *Bravado Merchandising Services Ltd v. Mainstream Publishing (Edinburgh) Ltd [1996] FSR 205*
31   See *R v. Johnstone [2003] UKHL 28* and *Arsenal Football Club plc v. Matthew Reed [2003] EWCA Civ 696*
32   O_2 *Holdings Ltd & Anor v. Hutchison 3G Ltd [2006] EWCA Civ 1656*
33   O_2 *Holdings Ltd & Anor v. Hutchison 3G UK Ltd Case C-533/06*
34   Article 7(1) of Directive 89/104/EC/ s12(1) TMA
35   There are exceptions to this rule, such as where there is repackaging or other changes made to the goods before they are resold. These exceptions are beyond the scope of this work.
36   *Parfums Christian Dior & Anor v. Evora BV C-337/95*
37   *Zino Davidoff SA v. A&G Imports Ltd C-414/99*
38   *Case C-173/98 Sebago and Maison Dubois*
39   s10(5) TMA
40   See s21 TMA or in relation to CTMs reg 2 of the Community Trade Mark Regulations 2005

ke Bell Wedlake Bell Wedlake Bell Wedlake Bell Wedlake B
ke Bell Wedlake Bell Wedlake Bell Wedlake Bell Wedlake Bell Wedlake B
ke Bell Wedlake Bell Wedlake Bell Wedlake Bell Wedlake Bell Wedlake B
Wedlake Bell Wedlake Bell Wedlake Bell Wedlake Bell Wedlake B

1.3

Design rights

Design law can be relevant in the context of advertising. It can apply to the products which are the subject of advertisements, but also to the advertising itself. Design laws are no longer concerned exclusively with three-dimensional objects. They can cover graphics, packaging, logos and a host of other features. It is worth being aware of these design laws.

INTRODUCTION

In the same way that trade marks are capable of enjoying protection with, or in some cases without registration, so the same applies to designs.

But as a result of the significant changes introduced in 2002 by new EU design laws,[1] it is fair to say that designs have increased in importance. They are capable of protecting a much larger variety of designs than was formerly the case, including two-dimensional designs. One area, for example, where they have made a significant difference is in relation to the world of clothing and fashion.

Unfortunately, the design regime in the UK is now rather complicated. There are four different types of design protection:

- registered Community designs;
- registered UK designs;
- unregistered Community designs; and
- unregistered UK designs.

Mercifully, there is a considerable degree of overlap between the rules applicable to the first three in that list. Unregistered UK designs is the odd one out.

In addition to these specific design laws, it should also be borne in mind that copyright law can also be relevant, particularly where 'artistic works' are involved. It is also possible to register trade marks for shapes.

COMMUNITY DESIGNS

What is the scope of Community design protection?

Community registered designs and Community unregistered designs protect the following:

'the appearance of the whole or a part of a product resulting from the features of, in particular, the lines, contours, colours, shape, texture and/or materials of the product itself and/or its ornamentation.'[2]

'Product' for these purposes is very widely defined indeed and includes 'any industrial or handicraft item, packaging, get-up, graphic symbols and typographic typefaces'.[3]

In other words, the scope of what can be protected by these design laws is very wide indeed.

For example, the following products have been held to enjoy protection: the shape of an air freshener canister[4], the mesh of a bag for fishing bait[5], a poncho[6], the zip and piping for the expander of travel luggage and a designer handbag[7].

However, it is not just three-dimensional objects that are relevant. The wide definition of design includes surface decoration and colours. This means that two-dimensional designs can also be protected. Thus a logo, or some artwork for packaging, can attract protection as UK or Community registered design and as a Community unregistered design.

A Community design protects against any other design which does not produce on the informed user a different overall impression compared to the protected design.[8]

The design owner has the exclusive right to use the design and to prevent any third party from using it (or a design which doesn't create a different overall impression) without his consent.[9]

'Use' for these purposes covers making, offering, putting on the market, importing, exporting or using a product in which the design is incorporated, or to which it is applied, or stocking such a product for those purposes.[10]

However, it should be noted that in the case of unregistered Community designs, the design owner can only prevent such use if it is the result of the copying of the protected design. So it is only a registered Community design that gives the design owner a true monopoly on the design in question.

Community designs cannot protect features of appearance of products which are solely dictated by their technical function, or which are contrary to public policy, or immoral.[11]

Designs must be 'new' and have 'individual character'

In order to qualify for protection, designs must be 'new' (i.e. they must not be identical to any earlier designs) and they must be of what is termed 'individual character'.

In assessing whether or not a design has 'individual character' the test that is applied is essentially whether the new design creates 'a different overall impression on the informed user' when compared to previous designs 'made available to the public' prior to the relevant date.[12]

Some important points need to be made here.

Firstly, the previous designs against which novelty and individual character must be assessed *exclude* designs which could not reasonably have become known in the normal course of business to the circles specialised in the sector concerned, operating within the EU.[13]

In other words, if someone were to challenge the validity of a Community design on the basis that it lacked novelty or individual character, they would have to produce evidence of a prior design (i.e. 'prior art') that could reasonably have become known to the relevant sector operating in the EU.

Secondly, although an application for a Community design registration will specify the product to which the design has been applied, the protection of that design is not limited only to products of that type or in that design 'sector'. If, for example, you register a Community design for the handle of an umbrella and a third party later uses the same design in a handle on a piece of office furniture, the latter will infringe the design. The fact that the defendant has applied the design to a different product in a different sector is irrelevant.

Thirdly, as is noted under the first point, in assessing whether or not a design is new or has individual character, you ignore designs which 'could not reasonably have become known in the normal course of business to the circles specialised in the sector concerned, operating in the EU.' However, when assessing novelty and individual character the 'sector concerned' is the sector of the prior art, which may not be the same as the sector in which the design owner is using the design.

For example, A claims Community design protection for the appearance of spiky balls which are sold as accessories to help improve the performance of tumble dryers. However, it turns out that before A's new design application was filed, another company, B, had been marketing very similar spiky balls for use in massage therapy. Also, B's design could have been known about in EU design circles specialising in the health/massage products sector.

In that scenario, even though A's Community design was being applied to products in a different sector to B's prior design (i.e. the laundry products sector as opposed to the health/massage sector) and was new in that sector, if A's design does not have individual character when compared to B's design, the design will be invalid.[14]

How are Community designs protected?

In the case of a Community unregistered design, as with copyright, the protection is automatic.

If the designer wishes to protect his design as a registered Community design, he must file an application to do this at the Office for Harmonization in the Internal Market (OHIM). The filing procedure is fairly simple. The application must include a graphic representation of the design and a relatively modest fee must be paid.

The applications for registration are not subjected to particular scrutiny by OHIM at the time of filing. So the mere fact that they are accepted for registration does not mean that they will necessarily survive if challenged.

How long do Community designs last?

Unregistered Community design protection lasts for three years from the date on which the design was made available to the public.[15]

Registered Community design protection lasts for five years from initial filing and can be extended for further periods of five years up to a maximum of 25 years in total.[16]

Who owns title to Community designs?

As with copyright, the first owner of the Community design is the creator (i.e. the designer), unless the design was created by an employee in the course of his employment in which case title to the design automatically belongs to the employer.[17]

The governing legislation is silent as to what happens where a design is commissioned. So, unlike with UK designs, even if there is a commission the title to the design remains with the designer – unless there is a contract to the contrary.

Those commissioning advertising or design agencies should therefore take note.

Can Community designs be challenged – even after registration?

In the same way that registered trade marks or other registered rights such as patents can be challenged, so too can Community designs.

It is common in design infringement cases for the defendant party to deny that its design creates the same overall impression compared to the claimant's design, and at the same time to argue that the claimant's design ought never to have been registered.

This is what happened in the important *Procter & Gamble v. Reckitt Benckiser* case.[18] This concerned allegations of Community registered design infringement in relation to the design of two competing air freshener spray canisters. P&G accused Reckitt Benckiser of infringing its design for the Air Wick air freshener. Reckitt counterclaimed for P&G's registered design to be declared invalid.

At the original trial, the judge rejected the attack on the registered design, but held that there was infringement. However, on appeal, although the court agreed that the design was valid, it overturned the finding of infringement. The Court of Appeal held that the Reckitt design did not create the same overall impression on the informed user as the P&G design.

How is infringement assessed?

The 'overall impression' test is conducted through the eyes of the 'informed user'. This mythical person is not a technical expert, but nor is he an ordinary consumer. Rather, he is someone in between, a person who is familiar with the designs of products in the area concerned.

When comparing two conflicting designs, the correct approach is to consider them carefully having regard to their various features. However, it is not correct to go by the overall impression that is left in the mind after they have been viewed. The overall impression test must be conducted differently to the approach in a trade mark case. A more careful scrutiny of the competing designs is needed. You continue to look at them in deciding whether or not the disputed design infringes. The concept of 'imperfect recollection' does not apply.

Another relevant factor is 'the freedom of the designer'. This must be taken into account when assessing infringement[19] (i.e. the more freedom there is to design a product, the more importance the court is likely to attach to design features which are very similar in the disputed design).

What remedies are available in infringement cases?

In effect, the same remedies are available in Community design cases to other intellectual property rights cases. These include injunctions, delivery up/destruction of infringing materials, damages (or an account of profits) and orders for costs.

These remedies are looked at more closely in Chapter 1.4 dealing with passing off.

Are there many Community design infringement cases being brought?

There have been a number of such cases threatened or brought. Some of the more high-profile disputes have involved designers bringing claims against retailers for selling clothing and other accessories which are alleged to be copied from protected Community designs. The phenomenon of cheap high-street 'chic', where look-alike designer clothes are sourced cheaply by ordinary retailers using designs copied from more exclusive originals, has led to a spate of law suits and disputes. Among the well-known brands involved have been Chloe, Monsoon and Jimmy Choo.

UK REGISTERED DESIGNS

The legislation covering UK registered designs was significantly amended at the same time as the introduction of the new Community design regulation. Much of the relevant law is now the same for both design regimes. However, some differences remain and are worth pointing out.

Firstly, as has been said, under the UK legislation, where a design is commissioned by someone the title to the design vests in the commissioner. This differs from the Community design system.

Secondly, if a UK registered design is infringed, an infringer may not need to pay damages if he can prove that at the date of the infringement he was not aware, and had no reasonable ground for supposing, that the design was registered. This contrasts with the position with Community designs where there is no such get-out for innocent infringers.[20]

Thirdly, UK registered designs, as their title suggests, apply only to the UK. Applications for filing such designs have to be made at the UK Intellectual Property Office.

UK UNREGISTERED DESIGNS

What are the main features of UK unregistered designs?

Otherwise known as 'design right', UK unregistered design protection is available under the Copyright Designs & Patents Act 1988 (CDPA). It arises automatically without the need for registration.

UK unregistered design protection lasts for up to 15 years from the end of the year in which the design was first recorded in a design document, or an article was first made to the design. But where a product to the design is made available for sale or hire, the term lasts for ten years from the end of the year in which that first occurred.[21]

The scope of what can be protected by a UK unregistered design is more restrictive than for a Community or UK registered design. UK unregistered designs protect the original designs of 'any aspect of the shape or configuration (whether internal or external) of the whole or part of an article'.[22]

Such rights do not apply to methods or principles of construction or features of a shape or configuration of an article which enable it to be fitted to another article (i.e. like spare parts).[23]

Also, 'surface decoration' is excluded from protection. So again, this is much narrower than Community designs which extend protection to colours and ornamentation.

Designs must be 'original' to qualify for protection. They will not be original for this purpose if they were commonplace in the relevant design field at the time of creation.[24]

As with UK registered designs, for UK unregistered designs the person commissioning such a design becomes the first owner of design right in the design.[25]

One final point of interest is that with UK unregistered designs, in the last five years of the term of protection, the designer is obliged to grant a licence to anyone who wants to use the design. If the licence fee cannot be agreed, there is a mechanism in the CDPA for the fee to be determined by an independent party.[26]

How are UK unregistered designs infringed?

The owner of a UK unregistered design has the exclusive right to reproduce the design (or a document embodying the design) for commercial purposes.

Reproduction covers reproduction of articles exactly or substantially to the design. As with copyright, infringement of UK unregistered designs is divided up into:

- 'primary infringement' (i.e. copying the design for commercial purposes so as to produce articles exactly or substantially to that design);[27] and
- 'secondary infringement' (i.e. importing or possessing for commercial purposes or selling, letting for hire, advertising for sale or hire an article which the infringer knows, or has reason to believe, is an infringing article).[28]

In the same way that UK registered design law allows an innocent infringer to avoid paying damages or an account of profits, so too does the UK unregistered design law. Again, this differs from Community designs.[29]

The same remedies are available to owners of UK unregistered designs as per any other intellectual property right.

GROUNDLESS THREATS

As with registered trade marks, the legislation governing designs includes provisions which enable a party aggrieved by threats of design infringement proceedings to launch legal action for unjustified threats. This applies to threats made in respect of either forms of Community design,[30] UK registered designs[31] and UK unregistered designs[32].

Relief for groundless threats includes injunctions and damages. Accordingly, as with registered trade marks, care should be taken before issuing any communication that could be construed as a 'threat'. There are some exceptions to the situations under which the groundless threats provisions will apply. If framed correctly, it may be safe to make a threat of design infringement proceedings without risking a groundless threats counterclaim.[33]

DESIGNS AND COMPARATIVE ADVERTISING

As is noted in Chapter 1.1 dealing with copyright (see page 13), the extent to which designs can be used in comparative advertisements remains rather unclear. In the same way that the relevant part of the Comparative Advertising Directive[34] says nothing about copyright, neither does it mention designs. Yet it is perfectly possible that a logo or other sign used in a comparative advertisement could be a Community design rather than a registered trade mark.

The interface between trade marks and comparative advertising may be about to be clarified by the European Court of Justice in the O_2 case.[35] However, somewhat illogical though it is, parties who wish to dispute comparative advertisements may still be able to rely on other IP rights such as designs.

SUMMARY

UK design law is complicated by the existence of a number of different types of design protection regimes. These are community registered and unregistered designs, UK registered designs and UK unregistered designs. Copyright and trade mark laws may also overlap in part.

Unregistered design protection arises automatically, and in some cases a design can attract protection under both the UK and Community design regimes. Registered design protection requires registration within specified time limits.

Registered designs can be more straightforward to protect, since the registrations are proof of the design, and there should be no need to delve into the background and design history when taking cases to court. However, like many patent cases, where design infringement is relied upon, the party threatened by proceedings will very often seek to attack the validity of the claimant's design.

Michael Gardner, Wedlake Bell

Notes

1   Council Regulation 2/2002/EC ('the Regulation')
2   Article 3 (a) of the Regulation
3   Article 3 (b)
4   *The Procter & Gamble Company v. Reckitt Benckiser (UK) Ltd [2007] EWCA Civ 936*
5   *Reginald John Bailey & Ors v. Graham Haynes & Ors [2006] EWPCC 5*
6   *Walton v. Zap Ltd, Designs Registry, 22 January 2007*
7   *Landor & Hawa International Ltd v. Azure Designs Ltd [2006] EWCA Civ 1285*
8   Article 10 of the Regulation
9   Subject to the usual EU exhaustion of rights principles – see Article 21 of the Regulation and the parallel imports section of Chapter 1.2 in this book on trade marks (see page 25)
10 Article 19 of the Regulation
11 Articles 8 and 9 of the Regulation
12 For registered designs the date is the date of filing or priority date, for unregistered designs it is the date on which the design was first made available to the public (see Article 6(1) of the Regulation)
13 Article 7(1) of the Regulation
14 *Green Lane Products Ltd v. PMS International Group plc & Ors [2008] EWCA Civ 358*
15 Article 11 of the Regulation
16 Article 12 of the Regulation
17 Article 14 of the Regulation
18 *The Procter & Gamble Company v. Reckitt Benckiser (UK) Ltd [2007] EWCA Civ 936*
19 Article 10(2) of the Regulation
20 See *J Choo (Jersey) Ltd v. Towerstone Ltd & Ors [2008] EWHC 346 (Ch)*
21 s216 CDPA
22 s213(2) CDPA
23 s213(3) CDPA
24 s213(4) CDPA
25 s215 CDPA
26 s237 CDPA
27 s226 CDPA
28 s227 CDPA
29 s233 CDPA
30 Regulation 2 of the Community Design Regulations SI 2005/696
31 s26 of the Registered Designs Act 1949
32 s253 of the CDPA
33 See for example, in the case of UK unregistered designs, s253(3) & (4)
34 The Misleading Advertising Directive (84/450) as amended by the Comparative Advertising Directive (97/55)
35 *O$_2$ Holdings Ltd & Anor v. Hutchison 3G Ltd [2006] EWCA Civ 1656*

ke Bell Wedlake Bell Wedlake Bell Wedlake Bell Wedlake
Bell Wedlake Bell Wedlake Bell Wedlake Bell Wedlake B
ke Bell Wedlake Bell Wedlake Bell Wedlake Bell Wedlake B
Bell Wedlake Bell Wedlake Bell Wedlake Bell Wedlake B

1.4

Passing off

The law of passing off protects the goodwill and reputation of a business against unfair exploitation by others. It often overlaps with other intellectual property rights, especially registered trade marks, although it can be relied on in its own right. Passing off is not the product of any statute – hence it is often referred to as a 'common law' right (i.e. it has been evolved over the years by the courts rather than through an Act of Parliament).

This chapter examines the elements that are required to bring a successful passing off claim and looks at the different variants of passing off that can occur. It also deals with the remedies that are available against traders who have committed passing off.

INTRODUCTION

Passing off protection does not depend on registration or any other formalities. But as is illustrated below, not all traders will be able to rely on passing off. This is because in order to get a passing off case off the ground, a number of requirements must be satisfied first. In many cases, these conditions will not be satisfied.

So although passing off is a very useful form of protection, it is not always the most straightforward way of protecting a brand from unfair competition. Wherever possible, therefore, traders should look to bolster their protection through the registration of their trade marks and designs.

It should also be noted that ignorance of the law is no defence to a claim of passing off. It doesn't matter whether an advertiser or other passing off defendant knows, or has reason to know, that they are doing it. Also, even where a party tries consciously to avoid committing passing off, judges can still be influenced by the degree to which that party has been prepared to 'sail deliberately close to the wind' in promoting itself or its products with similar branding or get-up to an established competitor.

Advertisers must be particularly wary of passing off since, by its nature, it often occurs in the context of the advertising, promotion or marketing of goods and services.

HOW DOES THE LAW OF PASSING OFF WORK?

Each passing off case will depend on its own particular facts. But advertisers should be aware that there are three basic requirements to every passing off claim.[1] Generally speaking, unless all three of these elements are established on the facts, the claim will fail. In a nutshell, for a claimant to bring a successful passing off case, it must show that:

- it has a sufficient goodwill and reputation in the UK by reference to a relevant identifying name, logo or 'get-up'; and
- that there has or will be a misrepresentation by another trader using the identifying name, logo or get-up (or something confusingly similar) which deceives or threatens to deceive the relevant public; and
- that damage has resulted from, or will result from that misrepresentation.

These three core elements of passing off are explained in more detail below.

Goodwill and reputation

In order for a passing off case to reach the starting block, the claimant must first be able to show that it has sufficient goodwill and reputation in the UK. There are two important points to note about this 'goodwill and reputation' requirement.

Firstly, there must be goodwill and reputation in the *UK market*. It is no good if the claimant has such goodwill and reputation in Spain or Japan. Some kind of trading record in the UK will therefore be essential.

Secondly, the goodwill and reputation must be relevant to the facts of the case. It is not enough that people have heard of the claimant or know what business it is in. They must generally identify the claimant, or its goods or services, by reference to some kind of distinctive sign or identifier. This 'identifier' can be anything. It could be the company's corporate or trading name, the name of a particular product or service it promotes, the get-up of a product or its packaging, or a logo. But that identifier must itself be so distinctive that it has a trade origin significance in the minds of the relevant trade or public.

Famous, well-established brands such as Sony or Ford will have no difficulty demonstrating that they have sufficient goodwill and reputation by reference to their trading names and logos. Most people have heard of those brand names.

Similarly, given their big budget marketing and sales operations, they will quickly build up goodwill and reputation by reference to other identifiers such as product names. For example, Sony has extensively advertised and promoted its BRAVIA range of televisions. As a result, the term 'BRAVIA' used on its own in relation to televisions may itself have sufficient goodwill and reputation attached to that name for passing off purposes.

The model names of Ford's range of cars such as KA, Focus, Mondeo etc. are so well known in their own right that again, even without mention of the name Ford in the same breath, a significant portion of the public know that a Mondeo is a type of car made by Ford.

However, suppose that an entrepreneur is about to launch a new business start-up under a carefully chosen name. Before it has started using the name, it will have no protectable goodwill and reputation in the UK by reference to that name. Therefore, it cannot use passing off to protect itself against rival traders adopting the same or similar names. By contrast, if it had registered a UK or Community trade mark for the name, it would have rights from day one – irrespective of whether it had traded or built a reputation in that name.

The same would be true of a successful foreign company with a brand that is well-known in its home country, but which has yet to be introduced to the UK. Without any UK goodwill and reputation there would be no chance to bring a passing off claim here.

In practice, many instances of passing off will involve neither iconic brands like Sony or pure start-ups that no-one has heard of. Instead, they will involve ordinary companies which, though perhaps not household names, have nevertheless been trading and promoting their businesses sufficiently to have the necessary goodwill and reputation for passing off purposes. Just as Sony and Ford can, such ordinary companies can use passing off too to protect their goodwill.

Misrepresentation

The second element of passing off requires that a third party be making (or threatening to make) a misrepresentation involving the use of something identical or confusingly similar to the claimant's own identifier (e.g. logo, name, get-up etc.).

By way of a simple example, suppose that a clothing retailer decides to advertise its summer sale on a local radio station. To promote the sale it announces in the advertisement that it is cutting the price of its Ralph Lauren polo shirts by 20%. In fact, unbeknown to the retailer, the Ralph Lauren polo shirts it is selling are actually counterfeit.

The result? The retailer is making a misrepresentation to consumers that it is selling Ralph Lauren clothing when in fact the clothing is fake. For passing off purposes, it does not matter whether the retailer knew they were fake or not. The result is the same: passing off.

Instances involving counterfeiting are very obvious forms of misrepresentation. By their very nature, such cases involve the use of identifiers that are identical to those of the goodwill owner (e.g. the name Ralph Lauren as per the example above). However, misrepresentations for passing off purposes can take many other forms and be more subtle. By recognising in more detail how passing off can occur, advertisers can learn to steer clear of situations that might otherwise expose them to allegations of passing off.

Use of confusingly similar identifiers

Most passing off cases occur where one party believes that the other has been using branding that is too similar to theirs in order to promote their business.

In the *United Biscuits v. Asda* case[2], the makers of the well-known Penguin chocolate biscuit sued supermarket retailer Asda for passing off when the latter began marketing a chocolate biscuit of its own under the name of another seabird, Puffin. The judge held that the name and packaging of the Puffin products were deceptive and likely to cause sufficient confusion among consumers. Whilst he did not think

the public were likely to mistake the Puffin biscuits for Penguin biscuits, he did think that they would mistakenly conclude that the two were products of the same manufacturer.

So, it isn't necessary that people be deceived into thinking that a particular product is product A when in fact it is product B. It is enough that they are deceived into thinking that product A, though different to product B, is none the less made by the same company.

Interestingly, *United Biscuits* was a case where the judge was plainly influenced by the fact that there the creators of Asda's product had been well aware of the possible risks they ran. He said:

> *'I cannot escape the conclusion that, while aiming to avoid what the law would characterise as deception, they were taking a conscious decision to live dangerously. That is not in my judgment something that the court is bound to disregard.'*

Although it is not necessary in passing off cases to show that the defendant intended to pass off its goods as those of the claimant, the state of mind of the defendant can nevertheless be an influential factor, as the judge's reasoning in *United Biscuits* indicates.

False endorsement

It is not necessary that a trader should hold its products or services out as actually being those of someone else or made under licence from them. In some cases, a trader will seek to gain commercial advantage by wrongly claiming that it, or its products/services, are *endorsed* or *recommended* by the goodwill owner.

For example, suppose that a manufacturer of dishwasher tablets claims on its packaging that its products are recommended by Bosch, a well-known dishwasher brand, when that is not the case. In this instance, no misrepresentation is being made as to who makes the dishwasher tablets, but the goodwill associated with Bosch's name as a dishwasher brand is being exploited by the tablet manufacturer. This is passing off.

Another common scenario in advertising where this type of passing off occurs is where there has been, at some point in time, a genuine endorsement or recommendation, but one that is later exaggerated or used out of context.

Suppose that the magazine *Practical Photography* tests and reviews a particular model of digital camera in 2006 and gives it a glowing review. The manufacturer of the camera then decides to run an advertising campaign in 2008 under the strapline 'Our cameras are recommended by *Practical Photography* magazine'.

This would again amount to passing off. Just because the magazine had concluded that one particular model of camera was good in 2006 does not mean that it had recommended the whole range, or that this recommendation would be applicable to the 2008 range. Such an advertising strapline would be a misrepresentation, unfairly exploiting the goodwill and reputation of the magazine to help drive camera sales.

Passing off by means of false endorsement/recommendation is particularly relevant in an age where the culture of celebrity has become so important. TV, film and sporting celebrities can make a lot of money by endorsing products and services. The courts have recognised this and adapted the law of passing off to protect them.[3] This topic is dealt with in more detail in Chapter 3.1.

Instruments of fraud

The internet is big business. Internet domain names are the addresses used to access websites. They have become extremely valuable commodities. Well over ten years since the internet really took off, the activities of so called 'cyber-squatters' continue to pose a major headache for brand owners. The continued release of ever more domain name extensions has exacerbated the problem.

Cyber-squatters are people who register internet domain names incorporating brand names and trade marks in the hope they can sell them on at a profit. This kind of activity is another form of passing off (and in some cases, trade mark infringement).

The courts have held that in the case of famous brand names such as BT, Virgin or Marks & Spencer, internet domain names incorporating those brand names will invariably give rise to passing off if they are ever used by a third party. Such domain names are, therefore, in effect, 'instruments of fraud' in the hands of anyone but the brand owners themselves and an injunction will be granted to stop anyone from equipping themselves with such domain names. So even registering domain names without making any active use of them can still amount to passing off.[4]

It would also be passing off to use such well-known trade marks in domain names to earn 'affiliate' income on the internet by routing customers to the websites of the trade mark owners themselves.[5]

The champagne cases and others

As most people know, champagne is the name given to sparkling wine produced in the Champagne region of France. There are many producers of champagne and many brands on the market, e.g. Moet, Krug, Piper Heidschieck, Verve Cliquot, etc. No single producer has a monopoly on the use of the word 'champagne'. But again, the courts have adopted a flexible approach to the law of passing off and held that it prevents anyone but a wine grower from the Champagne region from describing their wine by reference to the mark 'champagne'.

The rationale for this is that champagne has a distinctiveness and cachet (i.e. goodwill and reputation) attached to it that would be diluted if other wine growers or traders from other regions were to be able to use the term to describe their own products. So an attempt by a UK drinks company to market a sparkling drink under the name 'Elderflower champagne' was prevented by an action for passing off.[6]

It is not merely champagne that is the beneficiary of this variant on passing off. The English courts have applied similar principles to other classes of goods having particular geographical origin. In one case, the court granted an injunction to certain Swiss chocolate manufacturers to prevent Cadburys from marketing chocolate under the name 'Swiss Chalet'. As with champagne, the courts were persuaded that Swiss chocolate had a goodwill and reputation in the UK that needed to be protected and that allowing non-Swiss chocolate to be called Swiss Chalet risked damaging that goodwill.[7]

False attribution

Although comparatively rare, there is a form of passing off which arises where an attempt is made to use another's goodwill to attract interest in a product or service. This type of passing off overlaps with copyright law. It is known as false attribution of authorship.

A classic case of such passing off occurred when the *Evening Standard* newspaper was successfully sued by a Tory MP, the late Alan Clark.

Alan Clark MP had achieved considerable commercial success with the publication of his colourful and entertaining political diaries. The *Evening Standard* started running a regular 'Alan Clark Diaries' column written by one of their journalists in Mr Clark's style. They claimed it was intended to be a parody of Clark's diaries.

Clark, however, sued the publishers of the *Evening Standard* for passing off. He claimed – successfully – that they were unfairly profiting from his success by making readers think that their 'Alan Clark Diaries' were really being written by him.[8]

Reverse passing off

Where a party falsely presents the goods or pictures of goods belonging to another party in order to promote their own goods, this is known as 'reverse passing off'.

An example would be where a company selling conservatories produced a brochure showing pictures of newly built conservatories. In fact the conservatories had been built by a rival company and were not the defendant's work at all. The court held that this was nevertheless passing off – even though potential customers had no idea about the identity of the real builder of the conservatories.[9]

Damage

The third and final element that must be proved in order to win a passing off case is that there is, or will be, damage caused to the goodwill owner by the activity complained of.

In the vast majority of cases it will not be necessary to produce much evidence of actual damage, since damage will naturally be inferred as an inevitable consequence of the passing off.

In a counterfeiting case, the brand owner may claim that it has lost like-for-like sales. It will also be able to say that it has suffered damage to its goodwill by the release onto the market of products which are of poor or inconsistent quality and whose image will damage the quality image associated with the brand.

Another type of damage recognised by the courts in false endorsement cases is what is loosely termed 'dilution' damage. This is a more subtle type of damage. For example, suppose that a sports radio station runs a press advertisement showing a photo of a sports celebrity which suggests the celebrity is endorsing the radio station. This could reduce the ability of the celebrity to exploit his goodwill and reputation by endorsing other similar businesses. It would be damage recognised for passing off purposes.[10]

A word about disclaimers

Some traders believe they can avoid the consequences of passing off by using disclaimers in advertisements, on packaging, on websites or point-of-sale material. Such disclaimers may say: 'Please note that we have no connection with company X or any of its products'.

There are three problems with such disclaimers.

First, they may be ineffectual because many customers may simply not read them at all.

Second, they may even be counter-productive by causing confusion that would not otherwise have occurred. This will happen if consumers do not read them fully or catch only a fleeting glimpse of them. Very often consumers will only notice the presence of the brand name being disclaimed and will come away thinking that there is actually a commercial link between the brand featured in the disclaimer and the advertiser.

Third, if legal action is taken for passing off, the fact that a disclaimer was thought necessary can actually damage a party's case. After all, why was a disclaimer necessary? The obvious answer is that the advertiser must have thought that without it there was a risk of customers being misled.

So disclaimers should be approached with care. They are not necessarily going to inoculate an advertiser against passing off. To be effective, they may have to be far more prominent than most advertisers would wish. Small print disclaimers can be counter-productive.

WHAT ARE THE CONSEQUENCES OF PASSING OFF?

Legal action

If passing off occurs, or is about to occur, the goodwill owner can take legal action against the party at fault. It can issue legal proceedings in the High Court seeking a range of remedies. These can be draconian and can include similar relief to that available in a copyright or trade mark case. The relief would include:

- a permanent injunction to prevent further acts of passing off from occurring again in the future;
- an order that the party committing the passing off deliver up or destroy all materials and/or products which if used would cause passing off to occur (e.g. unsold stocks of products, marketing and advertising materials);
- an order requiring the defendant to disclose the identity of the entity that supplied it with the offending goods;
- financial compensation for the damage caused by the passing off, or an enquiry into the profits made by the party from the acts complained of;
- an order that the defendant pay the claimant's legal costs.

Injunctive relief cannot easily be ignored because the penalty for breaching injunctions is contempt of court. This can result in serious fines or even imprisonment.

Interim injunctions

In some cases, the claimant will wish to stop the passing off in its tracks, or even prevent it occurring before the party concerned can start its activities. This may lead to an application being made for an interim injunction so that the status quo can be protected until the court is able to finally rule on the case at trial. (It may take many months to bring the case to a full trial.)

On an interim injunction application, the court will be asked to decide whether it should impose a temporary or interim injunction for this purpose before all the facts can be tested at trial. In making its decision it will be guided by a number of factors:

- the strength or otherwise of the claimant's case;
- the 'balance of convenience' (i.e. the practical factors that weigh for or against the grant of an injunction, such as the degree of disruption or harm that would be caused to each party by granting an injunction, over not granting one);
- the ability of the claimant to compensate the party injuncted should the latter suffer damage and it later turn out that the injunction ought not to have been granted.

Interim injunctions can be granted at very short notice by the courts depending on the circumstances. They also put third parties on the spot. Where a third party is made aware of an interim injunction, they must be careful not to do anything that would impede the administration of justice.[11] So if an advertising agency were to be shown an interim injunction under which its client was ordered not to use or promote itself by reference to a particular brand name, the agency would be potentially at risk of being in contempt if it were to actively help its injuncted client to frustrate the interim injunction.

Interim injunctions and human rights

It might seem surprising, but commercial advertisers are now entitled to rely on parts of the Human Rights Act 1998 (HRA) to help resist interim injunction applications. Under the HRA, where the court is being asked to make an interim order that could affect a party's 'right to freedom of expression' under Article 10 of the European Convention on Human Rights, the court must impose a higher hurdle on the party applying for the injunction.

The courts have held that advertising is a form of 'freedom of expression' for these purposes. Accordingly, a party seeking an interim injunction in such a case to prevent a piece of advertising, must show that it is 'likely' to succeed at trial, rather than showing only that it has a real prospect of success.[12]

Evidence

In any legal action, the court will need to see evidence to prove that the three elements of passing off are present (i.e. goodwill and reputation, misrepresentation and damage).

The claimant will be expected to show that it has engaged in sufficient promotional and trading activities to build up sufficient goodwill and reputation by reference to the appropriate identifier. Examples of advertising and details of promotional spends are often cited. Sales figures are also important.

Companies should therefore, wherever possible, keep a dossier containing examples of advertisements, exposure in the press and media and other marketing activities.

The best evidence of misrepresentation is the unsolicited and spontaneous evidence from members of the trade or public who have been confused or deceived by the defendant's activities. However, this is very often in short supply, especially where the offending activity may only recently have started.

Sometimes it will be necessary to undertake surveys by market research companies to help convince the court. Surveys are expensive and are often treated with scepticism by the court. They should be approached with great care. Sometimes, survey evidence will be undermined in court.[13]

SUMMARY

The right to sue for passing off can be a valuable tool for businesses against competitors and others who may try to exploit their success. However, there are situations where it will not be of any assistance (e.g. situations where no goodwill and reputation has yet been acquired, such as new businesses start-ups and where parties spike new product launches).

Trade mark and/or design registration should always be considered wherever businesses want to protect their goodwill. Passing off should be seen as a supplement, not a replacement, for such registered rights.

Advertisers should remember that there are a number of different ways in which passing off can occur: straight passing off of one party's products for those of another, false endorsements/recommendations, instruments of fraud, geographical indications of origin such as the 'champagne cases', false attribution and reverse passing off.

The consequences of passing off can be serious, because the court has wide powers to grant relief against the guilty party in the form of injunctions and orders for delivery up and damages. Finally, neither innocence nor ignorance is any defence.

Michael Gardner, Wedlake Bell

Notes

1   See for example *Reckitt & Coleman Products Ltd v. Borden Inc. [1990] RPC 341*
2   *United Biscuits (UK) Ltd v. Asda Stores Ltd [1997] RPC 513*
3   See for example *Irvine & Ors v. Talksport Ltd 2003 EWCA Civ 423*
4   *British Telecommunications plc & Ors v. One in a Million Ltd & Ors 1998 4 All ER 476*
5   *Tesco Stores Ltd v. Elogicom Ltd & Anor 2006 EWHC 403*
6   *Tattinger SA v. Albev Ltd 1993 FSR 641*
7   *Chocosuisse Union des Fabricants Suisses de Chocolat & Ors v. Cadbury Ltd. [1999] EWCA Civ 856 [1999]*
8   *Clark v. Associated Newspapers 1998 EWHC Patents 345*
9   *Bristol Conservatories Ltd v. Conservatories Custom Built Ltd [1989] RPC 455*
10   See *Irvine & Ors v. Talksport Ltd* ante
11   *Attorney General v. Times Newspapers Ltd [1992] 1 A.C. 191*
12   *Boehringer Ingelheim & Ors v. Vetplus Ltd [2007] EWCA Civ 583*
13   See for example *Weight Watchers UK Ltd & Ors v. Tesco Stores Ltd 2003 EWHC 1109*

Turton Swan Turton Swan Turton Swan Turton Swan Turton Swan Turton
Turton Swan Turton Swan Turton Swan Turton Swan Turton Swan Turton
Turton Swan Turton Swan Turton Swan Turton Swan Turton Swan Turton

1.5

Defamation and malicious falsehood

CLEARING COPY – ASSESSING THE RISK

Unlike editorial material there is generally less to be gained commercially from advertisements that are either defamatory or borderline, which might generate the threat of legal action which would undermine the commercial value to the agency of the work. But perhaps more importantly, the relationship between the agency and the client, which might be the most serious casualty if a campaign generates litigation.

Practically, advertising copy checks involve a two-stage process. The first is determining whether the image(s) and/or text are defamatory of an identifiable prospective claimant. If the answer to that is no then there is no need to worry. If the answer is yes, then the second question is: Will the prospective claimant sue? The answer to the second question might be no because there is a viable defence which would deter the prospective claimant(s), or there may be other non-legal reasons why a claim would be unlikely.

Sometimes an advertisement which is intended to be controversial, and for which the answer to the first question is yes and the second question is no, will be the basis of a good campaign, for example Major Charles Ingram who was found guilty of cheating on *Who Wants To Be A Millionaire?* was used in an easyJet advertisement with the headline 'Need a cheap getaway?'. As he was guilty of fraud the comment was unlikely to be defamatory.

Obviously the second question is not always solely a legal one, but it should be asked. A specialist in this field should have sufficiently comprehensive knowledge of the media and entertainment industry to be able to at least make an intelligent judgement as to the likelihood of any prospective claimant investing legal fees in mounting a claim.

Need a cheap getaway?

(No Major fraud required!)

Lowest fares to the sun:
Alicante • Barcelona • Bilbao • Ibiza
Madrid • Majorca • Malaga • Nice

easyJet.com
the web's favourite airline

Generally however, the lower risk that can be achieved when looking at advertising copy the better, and so we will look first at the law of defamation, where most problems are likely to occur. Defamation is a *strict liability* tort, so it does not matter that you do not intend to libel anyone in the advertisement. Malicious falsehood is different and the requirement of proof of malice (i.e. bad faith) creates a substantial hurdle to bringing such a claim.

DEFAMATION

When any marketing communication refers to a living individual or a company you should always consider whether there is a defamation risk. The law of defamation protects reputation, and since most advertisements (apart from comparative advertisements which fall outside this chapter) do not threaten the reputation of others this is not an area of law that arises frequently in the marketing context. It can, however, arise if any living individual or company is referred to, either expressly or implicitly, in a derogatory manner.

What is defamation?

A defamatory statement about a person or company is most commonly defined as one that lowers the reputation in the minds of 'right-thinking people'. Many libel trials still take place before a jury which represents 'right-thinking people'. Alternative formulations have been: words which expose the claimant to 'hatred, ridicule or contempt', or which cause others to 'shun or avoid' the claimant. Statements that an actor is hideously ugly or an actress has a large bottom, or portraying an actress without teeth in an advertisement for a dentist, have all been judged to have been defamatory.

What is libel?

A defamatory statement in writing or other permanent form, including statements on broadcast radio, television, film and new media, is called libel. The law looks at the words and/or images and if they are defamatory, it will assess the gravity of the allegation and synthesise out of the totality of the material published a defamatory meaning or 'sting'. A defamatory statement is only actionable if:

- it is untrue or if one of the libel defences does not apply. If a defamatory statement about a person, even in an advertisement, is true or substantially true that person cannot successfully sue for libel no matter how extreme or unflattering the statement is; or

- it is published to a third party in a 'permanent' form, as is the case in virtually all marketing communications, and it refers to the claimant.

What is slander?

Slander is the mere oral or non-permanent form of defamation. It is therefore unlikely to arise in the advertising context and the rules relating to slander are not covered in this book.

Can you libel somebody by implication?

Intention is irrelevant in libel (except to some extent in assessing the measure of damages), which means it is possible to libel someone inadvertently. It is also possible to include sufficient information in an advertisement to identify a prospective claimant without actually including a name. Words which are not inherently defamatory, or do not name any individual or company, may also still be actionable when they are read by people who know information supplemental to that conveyed by the words/images, which information when combined with those words/images creates a defamatory implication or innuendo.

This is a particular danger where marketing material is targeted at a specific industry or profession. Visual representations of a person may convey an imputation defamatory of him either by their content or their context. The same applies to a representation of a product or of a person in a cartoon or a caricature.

Picture libels are particular traps for the unwary. If a general allegation is made in a soundtrack or in subtitles accompanying images of individuals or specific premises, the net result can be defamatory. For example, if the voiceover in a television advertisement makes a general statement that some banks treat their customers badly, but the accompanying pictures show the premises of a specific bank, the general statement could be treated as referring to that bank which could sue for libel.

By contrast, sometimes words that are associated with a picture may remove the otherwise defamatory sting which might arise from the publication of the picture alone. A court will always look at an advertisement as a whole, and decide on that basis whether or not it carries a defamatory sting.

Can endorsements and testimonials cause problems?

If endorsements or testimonials used in an advertisement are critical of a rival product, service or its provider, or if they falsely suggest that an advertised product or service has been endorsed by another company or person, particularly a celebrity, there is potential for a claim of defamation.

Many of the defamation cases in the marketing context are old but remain good examples of what can constitute libel in an advertisement. For example, describing a house erected by a builder as 'Jerry built'[1] and a claim that the kitchen of a famous chef was dirty were both found to be defamatory.

It is not of itself defamatory to merely use a person's name without their authority or publish their picture without consent, but in an age when celebrities increasingly seek to protect their 'image', any endorsement of a product or service without a celebrity's consent could be subject to an action for passing off (see Chapter 1.4).

However, there may still be a risk of a claim for defamation where the unauthorised endorsement carries some negative implication about the complainant. For example, in a New Zealand case, it was held that an advertisement using a reputable trader without his consent was defamatory as it implied the trader was exploiting his regular customers by selling the same product as that advertised for a higher price.[2]

It may well also be defamatory to imply endorsement of a product or service by a celebrity in cases where the endorsement adversely affects the alleged endorser's reputation. Thus an inferior but recognisable voiceover was held to be defamatory as it implied the actor's career had deteriorated to such an extent he was reduced to making anonymous commercials.[3] In another case a caricature of an amateur golfer showing a packet of the advertised chocolate in his top pocket was held to undermine his status as an amateur sportsman.[4]

It may also be defamatory to link a politician or other high-profile individual in an advertisement to a product that might as a consequence of that association reduce his or her professional standing. This might either be because the product itself carries some stigma or because a commercial endorsement of any kind would be inappropriate or even unlawful for that individual. Likewise a high-profile performer, photographer or artist who has said publicly that his/her work would never be used for advertisements might be accused of hypocrisy by implication if that work is used in an advertisement.

Beware, also, if you quote in marketing communications defamatory remarks made by someone else. The well established 'repetition rule' in our law of defamation requires you to defend those remarks as if you had made them yourself. That means you will either have to prove the truth of the allegations or show that some other defence applies, e.g. it is a legitimately expressed opinion (see the defence of 'fair comment' page 55). Even if the remarks are not defamatory, it might be possible for the subject of those remarks to sue for malicious falsehood (see page 56).

Can look-alikes be used?

It is not of itself defamatory to use a photograph of an individual in an advertisement which closely resembles a celebrity or high-profile individual. However if the 'look-alike' is depicted undertaking an activity or in a setting which would cast that celebrity/individual in a bad light, and the public was unaware that a 'look-alike' had been used, then the impersonated individual may be able to sue for libel. If this were done deliberately so that a person could be identified, especially a celebrity, they may have a claim for malicious falsehood or passing off (see 'Malicious falsehood' page 56 and Chapter 1.4 on the law of passing off).

An example of this was the use of a George Michael look-alike standing outside a public convenience in an advertisement for a radio channel, no action was taken.

You can libel someone without meaning to, so ignorance of a possible claimant is no defence (although it may mitigate the damages). With all marketing communications it is therefore important to follow clearance procedures to check that any fictional characters or companies referred to do not have real-life namesakes who might become claimants.

However, it is not actionable to deploy in an advertisement a photograph of an individual who has consented to its use when coincidentally that photograph closely resembles someone else. In one case, a newspaper published an advertisement for an adult internet service provider that featured a well-known glamour model. The advertisement invited readers to join the service to see pictures of her, although she was not named. The model in the photograph happened to look identical to the claimant, with the result that she was associated with the pornography industry. She sued for libel because she had no such connection. Although the court accepted that anyone seeing the advertisement who knew the claimant would reasonably assume she was the woman featured, it said it would impose an impossible burden on publishers if they had to check whether a true picture of a person resembled someone else who might be defamed, and it would be an unjustifiable interference with the freedom of expression of commercial advertisers.

What is the time limit for bringing a libel action?

A libel action must generally be started within one year after the date of publication or broadcast; otherwise the claimant will be barred from bringing a claim in the courts unless exceptional circumstances can be shown. For newspapers, magazines, television or radio advertisements, press releases and other print marketing communications, the date of publication is deemed to be the day on which it was published or broadcast. Do bear in mind, though, if the defamatory material is re-published in another broadcast or issue that will constitute a new publication and a new limitation period will start.

The situation is slightly different for books and the internet:

- *Books* – a new 'publication' will be deemed to have taken place on each day the book is on sale to the public, and therefore a new one-year limitation period starts each day until the book is withdrawn from sale.

- *Internet* – each day a marketing communication is accessible on a website will be treated as a fresh 'publication' and therefore the one-year limitation period will start again each day. This is equally true of material which is no longer on the main website but has been stored on the website's archive, as long as the archive can be accessed and read by third parties.

Who can sue?

- *Any living individual* – a claimant cannot claim from the grave, his estate cannot claim and neither can his family or relatives. Individuals do not have to prove that their reputation has been damaged or that they have suffered distress. This is assumed to exist in libel, though the claimant can adduce evidence of damage and distress to increase their prospective recovery in damages.

- *Companies* – can sue in relation to their business reputation, but not for hurt feelings or for distress caused by the publication. A director of a company can sue if he or she is so closely associated with a company that a defamatory allegation against that company amounts to an allegation against one or all of its directors – who can recover damages for distress. It is not enough, however, simply to criticise a company's products or services, an allegation has to go beyond that to suggest some kind of incompetence or lack of skill or judgement in order to be defamatory. For example, to say a fast food company's products were harmful to health would be defamatory; but for a critic to say a wine merchant had for sale a vintage that was not good wine would generally not be held to be defamatory as it would merely be an expression of opinion. A company can recover 'special' damages if it can show that it has suffered financial loss as a direct consequence of a defamatory advertisement. The easiest way for a company to demonstrate that it has suffered damage to its business reputation would be to show that its profits have declined or that it has, for example, lost a particular contract, as a result of the publication.

- *Partnerships* – can sue in the name of the firm as a whole. The individual members of the partnership can also sue if the advertisement identifies them sufficiently.
- *Non-profit making organisations* – can sue in respect of statements which adversely affect their financial position. This would include charities.
- *Groups* – can bring actions if the group is small enough for the individuals to be identifiable. For example, an allegation that a regional CID officer had committed an offence without naming the officer entitled all 12 CID officers in the region to sue and receive damages. Therefore, not naming someone in respect of a particular allegation will not always prevent a libel action being brought.

Unincorporated associations and governmental bodies such as the departments of central government of the UK and local authorities cannot sue, nor can political parties. However, if defamatory statements are made in an advertisement which reflect badly on individual officers of such bodies, they may sue in their personal capacities.

Who can be sued?

A claimant could sue any or all of the following:

- the author of a defamatory statement;
- the publisher of a defamatory statement;
- anyone having editorial or equivalent responsibility for the content of the statement or the decision to publish it. This could include the advertiser, the publisher and/or the broadcaster and also the advertising agency, the distribution company and the media owner.

This means that anyone involved in the publication of a defamatory advertisement is potentially liable to be sued.

What must the claimant establish?

All the claimant must prove is that:

- the words and/or pictures in the advertisement were defamatory; and
- the words referred to the claimant.

It is then up to the defendant to prove on the balance of probabilities that the words were true, or that another defence is available.

Is advertising covered by the right to free speech?

It is now established by the European Court of Human Rights and our own courts that advertisements are covered by Article 10 of the European Convention on Human

Rights, the right of free expression. However that right is restricted in certain circumstances, one being where the rights of others are impinged – principally the right to privacy and reputation guaranteed by Article 8 of the same convention.

What defences are available if a claim is made?

Not many defences are of much assistance in the marketing context, where the issues are most likely to be whether the advertisement is defamatory and/or whether it refers to the claimant. Below is a summary of the defences which may be available in a claim about advertising copy – the burden being on the defendant to prove one of them if the advertisement is found to be defamatory and to refer to the claimant.

- *Justification* – if you can prove the defamatory sting borne by the advertisement is true this is an absolute defence however defamatory it is.

- *Consent* – it is an absolute defence if the claimant has consented to the publication of the defamatory advertisement.

- *Fair comment on a matter of public interest* – fair comment is an honest belief concerning a set of facts depicted expressed in the form of defamatory comment (rather than defamatory assertions of fact). The term 'public interest' is interpreted widely, but the defence of fair comment will be defeated if the claimant can prove malice on the part of the defendant; malice in libel being either an improper motive or no genuine belief in its truth. If the comments were honestly made then an accusation of malice will fail. It should be borne in mind that simply inserting a phrase such as 'in my view' or 'it seems to me' will not on its own offer complete protection. It is a vital part of this defence that the underlying facts on which the comment is based must be true and should be known to the 'author' of the advertisement when it was made. This will be particularly relevant if testimonials are being given, or comparisons between products or services are being made.

- *Absolute and qualified privilege* – certain defamatory publications attract absolute or qualified privilege. It is difficult, however, to conceive of any circumstances in which such defences would be available for advertisements, so they will not be dealt with here.

What remedies can a claimant seek?

- *Injunction* – this is an order that can be granted by a court to prevent any further publication of the same or similar defamatory words. Claimants sometimes try to obtain an interim injunction to prevent publication before a trial takes place. But this is notoriously difficult to achieve, particularly if the defendant argues that the defamatory publication is true or can otherwise be defended. If, however, a libel claimant wins at trial, a permanent injunction will normally be granted.

- *Damages* – the amount of damages is usually decided by a jury at trial, but the courts' current view is that £200,000 is generally accepted as the maximum amount which should be awarded.

Can a claimant sue a UK-based defendant over something published abroad?

Yes, if the law of the foreign country in which the marketing communication is circulated allows it. This is a real concern with regard to the internet, as anything posted on a website is often accessible globally and in theory legal action could be taken in any country.

In an Australian case a claimant sued the US news organisation, Dow Jones, in Australia for libel in respect of material published on its website. The Dow Jones organisation argued that as the material was uploaded onto its website in the US, the claimant should sue for libel in the US. The Australian courts disagreed and allowed the claimant to sue in Australia, where he had a much higher profile. It took the view that publication had taken place in Australia because the website was accessible and the material complained of was read in Australia. This same approach has been taken in the UK, and it is likely also to be applied to electronic mail.

Can foreign claimants sue for libel in the UK?

Foreign claimants can bring claims in this jurisdiction against UK defendants if:

- the marketing communication complained of was published in the UK; and
- (in the case of non-EU claimants) the claimant can show that he has sufficient connection with, and reputation, in the UK.

MALICIOUS FALSEHOOD

Marketing communications that make statements about another company's products or services in comparative advertising, which are untrue and which are published maliciously, can be the subject of a claim of malicious falsehood. The statement must also either have been calculated to cause pecuniary damage to the claimant or must have actually caused such damage. Some claimants use this as an alternative to libel claims, or in cases where false statements are made which are not necessarily defamatory.

Malicious falsehood is a useful and more frequently used tool than defamation in the advertising context. It is often referred to as trade libel or disparagement of goods.

How is it different from libel?

- The words complained of do not have to be defamatory.
- In malicious falsehood, the claimant must prove both that the words were false and that they were published with malice. In libel the burden is on the defendant once the words have been shown to be defamatory. To show malice, it is not enough to show that the defendant was pursuing his own business interests; it must be shown that the statement was made with the direct intention of injuring the claimant's business.
- The claimant has to prove actual monetary damage – probably general loss of trade or possibly loss of customers.
- An action for malicious falsehood survives the death of either party.

How is it similar to libel?

- The statement must be understood to refer to the claimant.
- There must be publication of the statement to a third party.
- The same remedies are available – an injunction and damages.

How is it relevant to marketing communications?

In marketing communications, care should be taken to avoid making inaccurate disparaging claims about rivals' products or services. A distinction should, however, be drawn between 'advertising puffs' and false representations about rival products or services.

'Advertising puffs' which extol the virtues of a particular product or service over that of a rival, will not be actionable. For example, simply saying that one trader's goods are better than another's (or, indeed, any other) would not be actionable. If, however, inaccurate factual claims are made which criticise or disparage a rival's products or services, those could be actionable if the test for malicious falsehood is satisfied.

In one case, the claimant manufactured and marketed a natural diamond abrasive and the defendant manufactured and marketed a synthetic diamond abrasive.[5] The defendant circulated at an international trade market a pamphlet purporting to report the results of laboratory experiments comparing the two products and contained statements reflecting adversely on the claimant's product. The court held that as this purported to be a proper scientific test carried out by proper laboratory experiments, a reasonable man would take it as a serious claim and would not dismiss it as mere 'idle puff'. In another case, Vodafone sued Orange for malicious falsehood over the slogan 'On average, Orange users save £20 every month' for a big advertising campaign in late 1995.[6] The saving was expressly stated to be in comparison with Vodafone's or Cellnet's 'equivalent tariffs'. Here, the court said:

> 'This is a case about advertising. The public are used to the ways of
> advertisers and expect a certain amount of hyperbole. In particular the public
> are used to advertisers claiming the good points of a product and ignoring
> others, advertisements claiming that you can "save £££££ …" are common,
> carrying with them the notion that "savings" are related to amount of spend,
> and the public are reasonably used to comparisons – "knocking copy" as it
> is called in the advertising world. This is important in considering what the
> ordinary meaning may be. The test is whether a reasonable man would take
> the claim being made as one made seriously … the more precise the claim
> the more likely it is to be so taken – the more general or fuzzy the less so.'

In this case, the court found that the advertisement was not misleading and consequently that malice was not established, so the claim failed.

SOME LITIGATION TIPS

If you receive a claim letter it is important to make a comprehensive assessment of the prospect of the claim succeeding at a very early stage. If necessary you should seek the assistance of a specialist solicitor, and if the claim is a potentially expensive one, or it is a very difficult risk to assess, then a specialist barrister's opinion can be sought.

The assessment of whether a set of words and/or images is defamatory can be very difficult, as often there can be two respectable opinions either way which means that even judges might disagree.

The issue of whether the advertisement carries a defamatory meaning can be dealt with by a court as a preliminary issue. It is sometimes worth either seeking the consent of the claimant, or an order from a judge that this be dealt with as a preliminary issue which can be a relatively inexpensive way of resolving a dispute of this sort.

If the claim looks to be bad because of the clear lack of a defamatory meaning, you can apply to a specialist judge for a determination of whether the advertisement is *capable* of bearing either the defamatory meaning contended by the claimant or any defamatory meaning at all. This is also sometimes a quick and relatively inexpensive way of dealing with a defamation claim.

One of the reasons why there is little modern case law on advertisements is that most claims will settle when an expert opinion is sought on advertisements and a pragmatic view is taken on a prospective claim. One other option if you are faced with a pragmatic opponent is to agree to expert mediation, or that you will jointly instruct a leading libel barrister to give his/her opinion, and agree that you will be bound by that.

More information can be found about comparative advertising in Chapter 3.2.

Jonathan Coad, Swan Turton

Notes

1   *Erasmus v. Scott (1933)*
2   *Mount Cook Group Ltd v. Johnstone Motors Ltd (1990) 2 NZLR 488*
3   *Lahr v. Addel Chemicals 76 HLR1685*
4   *Tolley v. J S Fry and Sons (1930) 1 KB 467*
5   *De Beers Abrasive Products Ltd v. Int. General Electrics Co of New York Ltd [1975] 1 WLR 972*
6   *Vodafone Group plc v. Orange Personal Communications Services Ltd [1997] FSR 34*

Regulation

INTRODUCTION

The nuts and bolts of advertising regulation in the UK rely not on the law, rather on self- or co-regulation on the basis of codes drawn up by the advertising industry itself through the Committee of Advertising Practice (CAP), administered by the Advertising Standards Authority (ASA). There are other industry specific regulators. The Financial Services Authority regulates financial promotions. PhonepayPlus (formerly ICSTIS) regulates premium rate telephone lines. The Proprietary Association of Great Britain has a code for the marketing of over-the-counter medicines. The Direct Marketing Association has a code on direct marketing. But the bodies which advertisers are most likely to come across are the ASA and CAP.

SOME HISTORY

CAP started life as a committee of the Advertising Association (AA), the umbrella trade association for the advertising industry. In 1961 it set up the ASA which has regulated non-broadcast advertising ever since, on the basis of codes written by CAP. In 1975, under threat of legislation, the financing of the ASA was put on a more secure footing with the establishment of the Advertising Standards Board of Finance (ASBOF). ASBOF raises a percentage levy on the cost of space in paid-for media and Royal Mail mail-sort contracts. In 1976 the ASA survived a review of the UK self-regulatory system of advertising control by the Office of Fair Trading (OFT) which dismissed the possibility of converting the ASA into a statutory body with statutory powers.

The regulation of broadcast advertising has had a different history. Advertising on television was regarded with some suspicion when independent broadcasts first began in 1954, and was subject to statutory regulation under broadcasting legislation from the outset – by the ITA, ITC and finally Ofcom. The justification for continued statutory control of broadcast advertising is a concern that television in particular is a very powerful medium (see for example the 2008 judgment of the House of Lords in *Animal Defenders International v. Department for Culture, Media and Sport*[1]). Nevertheless, the Communications Act 2003 provides for the broadcast media regulator, Ofcom, to have regard to the desirability of self- or co-regulation, and in November 2004 the regulation of broadcast advertising was contracted out by Ofcom to the newly established broadcast arms of ASA and CAP.

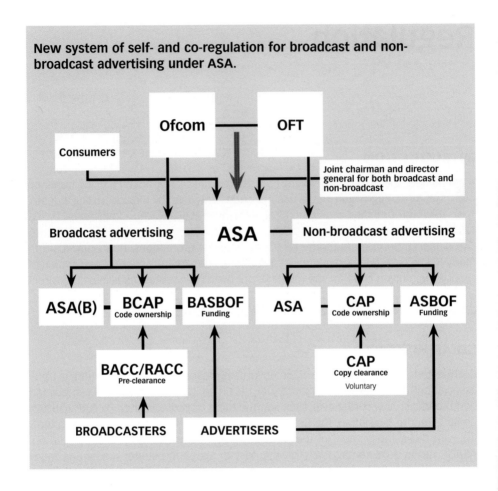

New system of self- and co-regulation for broadcast and non-broadcast advertising under ASA.

WHY SELF-/CO-REGULATION?

Advertisers and the media sometimes question the need for CAP and ASA, particularly given that there is now so much law governing advertising. Most advertisers however, recognise that self-regulation maintains higher standards in advertising in the UK than the law alone could. If consumers grow too cynical about claims made in advertising they will pay less attention to it. There are some areas better suited to self-regulation, such as matters of taste and decency. The law is a blunt instrument, and less swiftly adaptable to changing moral and cultural standards, and changing technology. Statutory regulators (primarily trading standards authorities) are insufficiently resourced to enforce the huge range of laws that exist. The EU recognises the benefits of self-/co-regulation (it is referred to in consumer protection directives), and self-regulatory systems inspired by the ASA have been set up in many other jurisdictions.

NON-BROADCAST STRUCTURE: CAP/ASA

CAP is an unincorporated association whose members comprise:

Advertising Association
Cinema Advertising Association
Direct Marketing Association
Direct Selling Association
Directory & Database Publishers Association
Incorporated Society of British Advertisers (representing most significant advertisers)
Institute of Practitioners in Advertising (representing agencies)
Institute of Sales Promotion
Internet Advertising Bureau
Mail Order Traders Association
Mobile Broadband Group
Mobile Marketing Association
Newspaper Publishers Association (national newspapers)
Newspaper Society (regional newspapers)
Outdoor Advertising Association
Periodical Publishers Association (magazines)
Proprietary Association of Great Britain
Royal Mail
Scottish Daily Newspaper Society
Scottish Newspaper Publishers Association
Clearcast (formerly BACC)
Radio Advertising Clearance Centre

CAP draws up and revises the British Code of Advertising, Sales Promotion and Direct Marketing ('the Code'). It provides copy advice to advertisers and publishes Help Notes and advice online on various areas on which the industry needs particular guidance. It assists in enforcing ASA adjudications including publication of 'Ad Alerts' to the media where an advertiser has published, or is about to seek to publish, an advertisement in breach of the Code or an ASA decision. CAP member organisations agree to comply with the Code, and members of these organisations in turn agree to comply with the Code. This covers much of the UK advertising industry and media through which advertisers place their advertising. Newspapers, magazines and other publishers will ordinarily include in their terms and conditions for acceptance of advertising a requirement that the advertising complies with the Code. It is a requirement of signing up to a mail-sort contract with the Royal Mail that direct marketing complies with the Code, and the other licensed postal operators have a similar arrangement. So, one way or another, the majority of advertisements published in the UK should be under a requirement, often contractually binding, to comply with the Code. That said, the Code does not at present cover advertisers' own websites, save to the extent they carry sales promotions or other paid-for advertising, and there will be other ways in which an advertiser can convey a marketing message without being under any legal obligation to comply with the Code.

The ASA is a company limited by guarantee. It considers complaints about breaches of the Code. Those which it investigates formally are adjudicated on by a Council made up of approximately 12 members, the majority of whom are independent of the advertising industry. Their names appear on ASA notepaper and on the ASA's website: www.asa.org.uk. ASA Council adjudications are published on their website. ASA decisions are subject to review by an independent reviewer of ASA adjudications (who can refer matters back to the Council for reconsideration on certain grounds), and ultimately by the courts on judicial review.

Enforcement of ASA decisions

The ASA asks an advertiser against whom a complaint has been upheld to sign an assurance that the relevant claim will be changed and not repeated, and the ASA and CAP monitor to ensure compliance. In addition, CAP seeks to ensure that other advertisers abandon similar contentious claims, so ensuring a level playing field. But the ASA has no power to fine advertisers for breaches of the CAP Code, unlike the Financial Services Authority (which fined Axa Sun Life £500,000 in 2004 for misleading advertisements) or Phonepay Plus (up to £250,000 under the Communications Act 2003 s.123). So why, apart from peer pressure, do advertisers comply with the Code and ASA decisions?

- ASA decisions may attract significant adverse publicity, which may affect turnover and reverse the beneficial impact of any campaign. Sometimes an ASA adjudication appears higher on a Google search result than an advertisers' own website. Agencies are named in adjudications.

- Media and other carriers will not usually publish an advertisement against which complaints have been upheld, although advertisements already booked for publication may be allowed to run their course. They may be reluctant to publish future similar advertisements unless the CAP Copy Advice Team has approved them, so delaying publication for an advertiser.

- CAP may require an advertiser to refer copy to the CAP Copy Advice Team for vetting prior to publication where an advertiser has a history of non-compliance. This applies particularly in the case of posters where poster site owners do not want disputes about liability for lost revenue when a poster is pulled down.

- Regulators and others on whose goodwill the advertiser may rely may have regard to ASA rulings. Thus the Charity Commission's Guidance on Campaigning and Political Activity by Charities[2] states that a serious breach of the Code, or persistent breaches by a charity, might be an indicator of underlying mismanagement or maladministration of the charity's affairs, such as to require the Charity Commission to take regulatory action.

- An advertising agency against whose advertisement an adjudication has been upheld will not be able to win an award for it.

- In the case of misleading advertising or impermissible comparative advertising, an advertiser can be referred to the OFT for action under the Consumer Protection from Unfair Trading Regulations 2008 or the Business Protection from

Misleading Marketing Regulations 2008. The OFT will seek undertakings against advertisers and others involved in publication, and if need be seek an injunction and an order for publication of a corrective statement by the advertiser. In the first such referral, under predecessor regulations, Mr. Justice Hoffman stated that:

'It is in my judgement desirable and in accordance with the public interest to which I must have regard that the courts should support the principle of self-regulation. I think that advertisers would be more inclined to accept the rulings of their self-regulatory bodies if it were generally known that in cases in which their procedures had been exhausted and the advertiser was still publishing an advertisement which appears to the court to be prima facie misleading, an injunction would ordinarily be granted.'

Director General of Fair Trading v. Tobyward[3]

That referral concerned advertising of a slimming product, Speedslim, made from guar gum, in the *Sunday Sport*. Subsequent referrals have included MagnoPulse Limited and Magna Jewellery Limited (in respect of health claims for magnet products), Tower House Promotions (in respect of claims to be raising money for charity), the *Daily Sport* (for running a front-page flash suggesting that the newspaper cost 10p when this referred to a magazine inside) and Ryanair (for failure to make clear in advertisements significant limitations on advertised offers).

BROADCAST STRUCTURE: BCAP AND ASAB

The Broadcast Committee of Advertising Practice (BCAP) is a company limited by guarantee. Its members comprise:

Advertising Association
British Sky Broadcasting Limited
Channel 4 Television Corporation
Channel 5 Broadcasting Limited
Direct Marketing Association
Electronic Retailing Association UK
GMTV Limited
Incorporated Society of British Advertisers
Institute of Practitioners in Advertising
ITV plc
RadioCentre
S4C
Satellite & Cable Broadcasters' Group
Teletext Limited
Virgin Media TV
Clearcast
Radio Advertising Clearance Centre.

BCAP exercises duties contracted out to it by Ofcom under the Deregulation and Contracting Out Act 1994, the Contracting Out (Functions Relating to Broadcast Advertising) and Specification Relevant Functions Order 2004, and subsequent authorisation as envisaged in an earlier Memorandum of Understanding with Ofcom. The primary contracted out duty is to set and revise codes containing rules which set standards for broadcast advertising, under sections 319 and 324 of the Communications Act 2003. The most relevant standards are that *'the inclusion of advertising which may be misleading, harmful or offensive in television and radio services is prevented'*, that *'persons under the age of eighteen are protected'* and that *'the international obligations of the UK with respect to advertising included in television and radio services are complied with'*. These obligations include the advertising and scheduling requirements of the Television Without Frontiers Directive[4], as now amended by the Audiovisual Media Services Directive[5]. BCAP is required to consult interested parties if it reviews any standards. The independent Advertising Advisory Committee advises BCAP from the consumer perspective. The codes are the Television Advertising Standards Code, the Radio Advertising Standards Code, Rules on the Scheduling of Television Advertisements and the Code for Text Services ('the Codes'). Ofcom retains direct responsibility for Rules on the Amount and Scheduling of Advertising, and the Ofcom Broadcast Code includes rules on sponsorship.

Ofcom standard form licences for television and radio services require licensed broadcasters to comply with the Codes. Because it is the broadcasters (as opposed to advertisers) who will be sanctioned by Ofcom for non-compliance, and because of the commercial problems caused if an advertisement has to be taken off air mid-booking, the major broadcasters require advertisements to be cleared as compliant, prior to acceptance, by Clearcast in respect of television and the Radio Advertising Clearance Centre (RACC) in respect of radio. Clearcast is owned and funded by ITV; GMTV; Channel Four; Five; Sky; IDS (Virgin Media); Viacom and Turner. It publishes its own detailed guidance notes.

The Advertising Standards Authority (Broadcast) (ASAB) mirrors the ASA. It is a company limited by guarantee. There is a Council of approximately 12 members, of whom the majority are independent of the advertising industry. To assist with consistency, the majority of the ASAB Council members also sit on the ASA (non-broadcast) Council and vice versa. Like BCAP, ASAB derives its powers from Ofcom. Ofcom has contracted out to ASAB its complaint investigation function and enforcement powers under section 325 Communications Act 2003.

Enforcement of ASAB decisions

ASAB has the power under the Communications Act (as contracted out) to give a direction to broadcasters with respect to (a) the exclusion from a licensed service of a particular advertisement or its exclusion in particular circumstances and (b) in respect of misleading advertisements, the descriptions of advertisements and methods of advertising to be excluded from the service (whether generally or in particular circumstances). Broadcasters are required by their licences to comply with ASAB directions. If a broadcaster fails to comply with ASAB directions, or if the breach of the Codes is a particularly bad one, the broadcaster can be referred to Ofcom for further sanctions. Ofcom has the power to levy fines and in extremis to withdraw a broadcasting licence. Ofcom threatened Auctionworld, a teleshopping channel, with withdrawal of its licence and fined it £450,000 in 2004 following numerous complaints about misleading guide prices for jewellery, delays in delivery and poor customer service. The company subsequently went into liquidation.

Given that the main purpose of contracting out, as far as the advertising industry and consumers are concerned, is to have a 'one-stop shop' for advertising standards and complaints, why are there still different rules? BCAP and ASAB were set up as parallel organisations so that if things do not work out Ofcom can take back the broadcast functions relatively easily, and also to meet non-broadcast media concerns that Ofcom should not be allowed to creep into the regulation of non-broadcast editorial matters. In addition, broadcasting has always been viewed as a more powerful medium (see page 59) and the nature of the medium requires different rules.

Remit: what advertising do the Codes cover?

In the case of broadcasting, remit is determined by the Communications Act 2003, to which all television, radio and text services licensed by Ofcom are subject. So the BCAP Codes cover:

- television (the most complained about medium in 2007);
- radio;
- teletext;
- teleshopping;
- interactive TV.

Television advertising is that which takes place in advertising slots distinct from other parts of programming, as required by the Television Without Frontiers Directive. It defines advertising as *'any form of announcement broadcast whether in return for payment or for similar consideration or broadcast for self-promotional purposes by a public or private undertaking in connection with a trade, business, craft or profession in order to promote the supply of goods or services including immovable property, rights and obligations, in return for payment'*. The European Court of Justice has ruled that a prize game offered by means of dialling a premium rate phone number in a television broadcast of ostensibly editorial content could constitute teleshopping or advertising (*Komm Austria v. ORF*[6]). Television advertisements broadcast from other EU member states should generally be subject to home authority control in their country of origin.

In the case of non-broadcast advertising, remit is governed by the wording of the CAP Code, which does not define precisely what constitutes advertising. The CAP Code covers advertising appearing in UK media (plus the Channel Islands and Isle of Man) in:

- national press (the third most complained about medium in 2007);
- regional press;
- magazines;

- posters, including digital;
- cinema and video commercials;
- catalogues, brochures, leaflets, whether by direct mail or otherwise;
- promotions, competitions, special offers;
- emails and text messages;
- banners and pop-ups;
- some virals (advertiser generated);
- sponsored search online;
- electronic games.

The following are outside remit of the Codes:

- advertisements in foreign media, although direct marketing from outside the UK may be subject to the Code if no appropriate cross-border complaint system operates;
- packaging and price lists;
- point-of-sale displays, including in shop windows except sales promotions and advertisements in paid for space;
- website content;
- live oral communications, including telephone calls;
- flyposting;
- private classified advertisements;
- statutory/public notices;
- press releases;
- political advertisements (widely defined by the Communications Act 2003) in broadcasting;
- political advertisements in non-broadcast media whose principal function is to influence voters in local, regional, national or international elections or referendums;
- editorial content.

There are two particularly difficult issues.

What constitutes editorial as opposed to advertising?

The Press Complaints Commission will generally regulate editorial material with a lighter touch as far as accuracy is concerned (given free speech concerns), but sometimes what appears to be editorial is, or is near to being, advertising. In 1999 Charles Robertson (Developments) Limited, proprietors of some department stores in Cornwall, sought to challenge in court a decision by the ASA that a full page paid for in regional newspapers which mostly advertised products for sale in the stores, but also included an editorial column (in which the company's founder held forth on issues of concern to him – such as Europe, homosexuality, Cornish planning officials) constituted advertising. Both the advertising and the editorial column were nationalistic in tone. Mr Justice Moses said that the fact that the page was paid for by Charles Robertson was not of itself determinative, and that *'that which plays no part in the promotion of a product, however widely product is defined, cannot be said to be part of the advertisement'*. But he held that the ASA had been entitled to take into account not just content, but also the visual impact of the column, and its position and the fact that the advertising itself was of a similar tone. In contrast, in 2007 the ASA received complaints from children's charities about an article in *OK!* magazine featuring the model Jordan feeding her three-week-old baby daughter with a branded bottle of formula milk, which by law cannot be advertised. The adjacent page carried an advertisement for SMA Nutrition's follow-on milk, for older babies, which can be advertised. The ASA took the view that despite the juxtaposition and product placement the article featuring Jordan was editorial and that it could not investigate. Trading Standards and the Food Standards Agency looked at the case instead. In television and radio there are strict rules on the separation of advertising and editorial content, although product placement and sponsorship (which the Audiovisual Media Services Directive will permit to a greater degree if Ofcom accepts a relaxation in the rules) may blur the distinction.

What to do about website content?

About 12% of complaints to the ASA in 2007 were about internet advertising, the second most complained about medium. The vast majority were about the content of websites and as such fell outside the ASA's remit. Clearly it is not satisfactory that a rapidly expanding medium for advertising is not subject to effective regulation. The Advertising Association's Digital Media Group (DMG) is looking at how regulation might extend to advertisers' own websites, how sanctions might work, and who would fund a wider role for the ASA; for example would internet service providers (particularly Google) collect a levy on paid-for search advertisements? A recommendation will be made by the DMG to the industry as a whole by the time you read this. It is not doubted that an extension of the CAP Code to commercial promotions on the internet will happen, but many issues need to be resolved prior to the Code being enforced in previously unregulated areas on corporate websites.

Difficult areas include consumer generated content, classified advertisements on, for example, eBay and television advertisements delivered as part of 'on demand' content to internet services and mobiles. The Audiovisual Media Services Directive[7], which amends the Television Without Frontiers Directive, came into force on 19 December 2007 and must be implemented by the UK by 19 December 2009. It will extend the requirements of the original Directive to audio-visual-type broadcasting including television viewed via the internet.

COMPLAINTS

In general the ASA acts on complaints, although it may add its own challenge to an existing complaint, or act on apparent breach of the Code identified by monitoring by CAP. The ASA received 24,192 complaints in 2007 about 14,080 advertisements.

The complaints were spilt roughly evenly between non-broadcast and broadcast. Less than 10% were from competitors or others with a trade interest in the outcome of their complaint. Such complainants are identified in any formal investigation. Consumer complainants are not identified.

A typical complaint investigation in relation to a broadcast or non-broadcast advertisement runs as follows.

1. Complaints received are assessed against the Codes. A complaint should ordinarily be made within three months of appearance of the advertisement.

2. If there is a case to answer an informal approach is made to the advertiser.

3. If necessary (because the advertiser disputes the issue, or the complaint raises a matter which is not minor and clear cut) a formal investigation is launched.

4. The ASA asks for written evidence to substantiate claims. In the case of broadcast advertisements, the clearance centre (Clearcast or RACC) is also involved, given the broadcasters' responsibility as licensees.

5. On receipt of the advertisers' response, ASA staff draft a ruling that goes to the advertiser and to the complainant for comment. The ASA may take advice from an independent expert, or from another regulator with expertise in that area.

6. The draft ruling may be amended in the light of comments received, and goes to the ASA Council who may adopt it or come to a different decision.

7. Council's decision is published online on the ASA's website (usually on Wednesdays).

In cases where significant harm is likely to result from continued appearance of the advertisement, ASA procedures may be truncated or the ASA may take interim action, for example requiring suspension of publication of the advertisement pending the outcome of an investigation.

Code rules and how the ASA adjudicates

Guiding principles

- *Free speech* – advertising should not be restricted unless there are good grounds for doing so, and then only in a proportionate manner.

- *Context* – conformity with the Codes is assessed according to the advertisement's probable impact when viewed as a whole and in context. So, in the case of non-broadcast media, an advertisement featuring a near naked woman is more likely to offend if placed on a poster near a school than if featured on the inside pages of a glossy magazine. The advertisement in 2000 for Opium perfume, featuring Sophie Dahl, attracted three complaints about its appearance in women's magazines (which were not upheld) and 730 about the posters (which were upheld). Similarly, a contentious claim for a product may require more detailed explanation of the product characteristics if featured in a consumer magazine than if featured in a trade magazine. Consumers'

expectations of an internet advertisement may differ from those of an advertisement in a newspaper or magazine. In the case of broadcast media the likely expectation of the audience as to an advertisement's content will change depending on the nature of the surrounding programmes, and time of day.

- *Substantiation* – CAP Code clause 3.1 provides that '*before distributing a marketing communication, marketers must hold documentary evidence to prove all claims, whether indirect or implied, that are capable of objective substantiation*'. This is common sense. The regulatory system would quickly break down if the ASA had to prove challenged claims to be untrue. The rule mirrors the language of EU directives. Directive 2005/29/EC on Unfair Commercial Practices (Article 12) provides for courts or administrative authorities to require a trader to furnish evidence as to the accuracy of factual claims, and to consider such claims inaccurate if the evidence is not forthcoming or is inadequate. The advertiser has the specialist knowledge on which it based the claim, and should be in a position to prove it. There are similar provisions in the Broadcast Codes (rule 5.2.1 in the TV Code, rule 3.1 in the Radio Code), and the Broadcasting Acts 1990 and 1996 give ASAB the power to require from the advertiser evidence relating to the factual accuracy of any claim, and to deem a factual claim inaccurate if such evidence is not provided. In December 2007 Ryanair published an advertisement headed '*January Sale 2 million seats from £10 one way, taxes & charges included Travel Monday – Sunday*'. The small print at the bottom stated '*Book until midnight tonight.*

Subject to availability, terms & conditions'. A consumer challenged availability of discounted seats on Fridays and Sundays. Ryanair produced evidence of a couple of successful bookings for each, but declined to offer more until the ASA told it exactly how many bookings it would expect. The Council upheld the complaint. Given the number of previous upheld adjudications and Ryanair's publicly proclaimed lack of interest in complying with the CAP Codes, the ASA referred the matter to the OFT.

Legality

All the Codes contain a requirement that the advertisements and the products which they advertise should be lawful. The appendix to the Codes contains a list of relevant legislation, rapidly expanding (well over 200 measures) and much of it EU inspired. Scotland, Wales and Northern Ireland may have separate legislation, although consumer protection is not a devolved power. The ASA does not generally make findings in relation to the law but in some cases, for example in respect of the advertising or promotion of a lottery which is unlawful under the Gambling Act 2005, it may do so if the appropriate regulator is not taking action.

In addition, the Broadcast Codes prohibit the advertising of certain categories, including escort agencies, pornography, political advertising, prescription-only medicines, and services offering individual advice on personal or consumer problems. Political advertising is very widely defined by the Communications Act 2003 section 319 and section 321 to include advertisements from a body whose objects are wholly or mainly of a political nature (e.g. Greenpeace, Amnesty) or advertisements whose content is aimed at influencing law reform or government policy, the policy or decision of any public authority or body acting under international agreements, or public opinion on a matter which in the UK is a matter of public controversy. For example, the RSPCA's campaign to secure a ban on hunting with dogs was permitted by the Charity Commission but not on TV or radio.

Truthfulness and misleadingness

About half of all complaints about advertising in 2007 concerned misleading advertising, with advertising on the internet being particularly well represented. Advertising should not mislead, or be likely to mislead, by inaccuracy, ambiguity, exaggeration, omission or otherwise.

JANUARY SALE

2 MILLION SEATS

FROM **£10**

ONE WAY, TAXES & CHARGES INCLUDED

TRAVEL MONDAY · SUNDAY

WWW.**RYANAIR**.COM

AVIONIC MECHANIC VACANCIES APPLY ON WWW.RYANAIR.COM

Book until midnight tonight. Subject to availability, terms & conditions. Flights direct from London (Stansted).

The Codes have been amended to take into account the provisions of Directive 2005/29/EC on Unfair Business to Consumer Commercial Practices, implemented in the UK by means of the Consumer Protection from Unfair Trading Regulations 2008 (CPRs), which came into force on 26 May 2008. CPRs concern commercial practices directly connected with the promotion, sale or supply of a product to consumers, 'product' being defined as *'any goods or services including immovable property, rights and obligations'*. There is a parallel Directive 2006/114/EC which deals with misleading advertising directed at traders. This is implemented in the Business Protection from Misleading Marketing Regulations 2008, which also came into force on 26 May 2008.

Certain advertising is regarded under CPRs and the Codes as always likely to mislead consumers, including:

- false claims as to endorsement by a public or private body or other bodies;
- bait advertising;
- bait and switch advertising;
- false claims to very limited time of availability;
- presenting what are in reality legal rights as distinctive to that trader;
- using editorial content in the media to promote a product where the trader has paid for the promotion without making that clear;
- materially inaccurate claims as to the personal security of the consumer or their family if they don't purchase the product;
- promoting a product similar to one made by a particular manufacturer so as to deliberately mislead;
- falsely claiming that a trader is about to close or move;
- claiming that a product is able to facilitate winning games of chance;
- falsely claiming a product is able to cure illness, dysfunction or malformations;
- giving materially inaccurate information on market conditions or supply, with intent to sell on less favourable terms;
- offering a competition prize promotion without awarding the prizes or reasonable equivalent;
- describing products as free etc. if the consumer must pay other than the unavoidable costs in responding to the advertisement and collecting or paying for delivery; and
- creating the false impression that the advertiser is not a business.

CAP has published Help Notes on some of these areas, including advertisement features, free claims, and compulsory holiday insurance, and the ASA has ruled on all of them in the past. So, for example, the ASA upheld a complaint against TalkSport in 2006. A blog on a football-club related website suggested that readers should go to the TalkSport website and register in the hope of becoming a representative for their local premiership or football league club on the radio station. The blogger was exposed as a TalkSport member of staff. TalkSport said he was on a frolic of his own. The ASA upheld the complaint on the grounds that the advertisement was misleading and not properly identified as marketing. It was treated as being within the ASA's remit because it was an online sales promotion.

'Buy one get one free offers' may not be prohibited, but an advertisement which involves payment for more than the legitimate and unavoidable cost of participation in a promotion, or otherwise overstates what is 'free' will be. So, in 2006 the ASA upheld a complaint against Yes Mobiles trading as Express Mobiles for a text message which said *'ORANGE CUSTOMER, YOU HAVE BEEN SELECTED FOR A FREE PHONE. 1ST COME 1ST SERVED. CALL NOW ON [XXX]'*. The phone may have been available at no extra charge, but the consumer had to take up an 18-month contact on a new tariff to get it. The message also contained no information on the identity of the sender and no information on how to opt out. It was unclear how the advertiser had obtained the Orange customer database. The complaint was upheld, the use of text messaging could not justify the omission of such information. Carphone Warehouse's TV and press advertisements and CD promotion for a new TalkTalk telephone package with *'free broadband forever'* resulted in 145 complaints to the ASA in 2006. The ASA found that the broadband element was not 'free' because it was only available as an option to people who paid a connection charge to sign up and who continued to pay a monthly charge. Nor could it be described as 'free forever' because it would become an inclusive part of the package paid for by consumers.

Other potentially misleading business-to-consumer advertising practices require a case-by-case analysis, the issue being whether they are likely to cause the average consumer to take a transactional decision which he/she would not have taken otherwise. A transactional decision is defined as being *'whether, how or on what terms to purchase, make payment for…, retain or dispose of a product or exercise a contractual right in relation to the product, whether the consumer decides to act or refrain from acting'*. So, if the advertisement is unlikely to cause consumers to take a decision about a product there may be no breach of the Codes. Given that the aim of most advertisements is to change consumers' spending decisions such cases are likely to be rare. A transactional decision includes a decision not to buy a product.

Advertisements which do not concern a commercial practice or the promotion of goods or services do not require assessment of whether the advertisement would prompt a transactional decision. This would include most charity or 'political' advertisements. So, for example, an International Fund for Animal Welfare (IFAW) advertisement in 1995 called for a boycott of Tesco until it stopped selling Canadian tinned salmon under the heading *'Every tin of Canadian Salmon Tesco sells is another blow Sir Iain'*. The advertisement was found to be in breach of the CAP Code because it misleadingly implicated Tesco (of which Sir Iain MacLaurin was chairman) in the killing of seals by associating the salmon (fished off Canada's west coast) with seal culling thousands of miles away off Canada's east coast, and implied that the Chairman had taken a hypocritical stance on the issue.

The average consumer is described as being *'reasonably well informed, reasonably observant and circumspect'*, account being taken of social, cultural and linguistic factors. The test is not a statistical test. If there is a clearly identifiable group the advertisement should be assessed from the perspective of that group, and if there is a clearly identifiable vulnerable group (because of mental or physical infirmity, age or credulity) the advertisement should be assessed from the perspective of the average member of that group. So, an advertisement in *Saga Magazine* offering magnets as a cure for arthritis will need to be assessed from the viewpoint of someone who may well be elderly and suffering from arthritis.

An advertisement can be misleading if the advertiser indicates in advertising that he is bound by an industry code of conduct (e.g. British Bankers Association Code of Conduct for the advertising of interest-bearing accounts, or Direct Marketing Association Code of Practice), but fails to comply with that code.

An advertisement may also be misleading if it omits, hides or provides in an unclear, unintelligible, ambiguous or untimely manner 'material' information the average consumer needs to take an informed transactional decision, or fails to identify the commercial intent of the advertising. Regard should be given to all the circumstances, limitations of the medium and other means to make the information available. In 2008 the ASA upheld a complaint about a radio advertisement for CC Automotive Group trading as Carcraft, for new cars purchased under a finance package. The terms and conditions for the offer were delivered too quickly and at a much lower volume than the rest of the information in the advertisement, and were thus not clearly audible. The advertisement was likely to mislead. In 2006 the ASA upheld complaints about television and press advertisements for Wanadoo which claimed *'up to 8 Meg broadband'*. In fact the unbundling of local exchanges was proceeding slowly and at the time the advertisements were published less than 5% of the population would obtain broadband at a speed of 8 meg, and the remainder would obtain only a 2 meg connection. 'Up to' was insufficient. In addition, the advertisement failed to make clear whether uploading or downloading speeds were involved. In 2008 most telecoms companies offering broadband services signed up to a new voluntary code on broadband speeds under the auspices of Ofcom, backed up by mystery shopping exercises to check on speed in practice.

'Material information' includes information required by other EU laws. In addition an advertisement *'which indicates the characteristics of the product and price, and thereby enables the consumer to make a purchase'* is treated as an *'invitation to purchase'*. Material information that must be included in such an advertisement includes:

- main characteristics of the product;
- geographical address and identity of the trader/his principal;
- price inclusive of taxes, or how the price is calculated if it cannot be ascertained in advance, plus additional charges;
- payment, delivery, performance and complaint handling details if they depart from the requirements of professional diligence;
- any withdrawal and/or cancellation rights.

An advertisement does not necessarily need to feature a direct response mechanism in order to be an 'invitation to purchase'. The basic position is that all information that is likely to affect significantly a consumer's decision must be included. The Yes Mobiles advertisement referred to earlier is an illustration of that.

It is to be hoped that the accuracy of most advertisements will continue to be considered without the need to consider too closely complicated tests. In 2007 the ASA upheld a complaint about a TV and press advertisement for L'Oréal's new mascara which claimed *'up to 60% longer... Take your eyelashes to telescopic lengths'*, with close-ups of Penelope Cruz's eyelashes. In fact Penelope Cruz had some individual false lashes added to her real ones, and the evidence was that the mascara would make the lashes appear up to 60% longer rather than actually being up to 60% longer. The complaint was upheld, the fact that Ms Cruz was wearing some false lashes and that the claim related to appearance should have been made clear.

Advertisements addressed to other traders may be considered for misleadingness, applying normal common sense as to what is likely to mislead.

Comparative advertising

Complaints about comparative advertising are more often resolved through the ASA than through court action, particularly given the difficulties of taking action successfully for defamation, malicious falsehood or infringement of registered trade mark (see *O$_2$ Holdings Limited v. Hutchison 3G*[8], which reached the Court of Appeal in 2006 and European Court of Justice in 2008). If the advertisement explicitly or by implication identifies a competitor or their goods or services then it must comply with certain rules which reflect those in the Business Protection from Misleading Marketing Regulations 2008[9]. In particular such an advertisement is permitted only when it:

- is not misleading, including by omission;
- compares goods or services meeting the same needs or intended for the same purpose;
- objectively compares one or more material, relevant, verifiable and representative features of those goods and services, which may include price. The requirement that a comparison be objective rules out expressions of opinion. And the requirement that a comparison be verifiable means that it should be verifiable by consumers and competitors based on information in the advertisement or accessible relatively easily from it. In 2008 the ASA upheld a complaint against national press advertisements for the supermarket Asda which compared the cost of a weekly shop at Asda with that at Morrisons on the basis of a trolley with 44 or 48 items. The ASA noted that Asda had not indicated in the advertisements how the cost claims could be verified and had declined to provide such information to Morrisons when requested. In addition it was not clear how the items had been selected and, in some cases, items on temporary promotion in Asda appeared to have been selected;
- does not create confusion amongst traders between the advertiser and a competitor or their trade marks, trade names, goods or services;
- does not discredit or denigrate the trade marks etc., activities or circumstances of the competitor. Robust price comparisons and robust extolling of the virtues

of the advertiser's own product are acceptable, but an advertisement is likely to discredit or denigrate if it contains potentially damaging, untrue information about the competitor or its products, includes gratuitous abuse, or constitutes an attack on the competitor's trading practices;

- for products with an EU designation of origin (primarily certain foods), relates to products with the same designation;
- does not take unfair advantage of the reputation of the trade mark etc. of the competitor;
- does not present goods or services as imitations of a competing product.

There are a number of CAP Help Notes in this area including on retailers' price comparisons, price claims in utilities marketing and price claims in telecommunications marketing.

Harm and offence

The rule across all three Codes is that advertisements must not cause serious or widespread offence. This can be to the public generally or to a particular group, including on grounds of religion, race, sex, sexual orientation or disability. CAP has a Help Note on religious offence. There are also rules on causing distress and on condemning or encouraging violence or irresponsible behaviour.

The likelihood of an advertisement causing offence depends on context and medium as well as content, with television, posters and direct mail more likely to cause concern than internet or press or magazine publication.

The use of offensive or shocking advertisements in a commercial context is unlikely to be acceptable. The requirement for possible mandatory pre-publication vetting of posters, after an adverse ASA adjudication, was introduced in the 1990s following a number of adverse adjudications against Benetton for using shocking images, and the difficulties this caused for poster-site operators. In 2005 the ASA upheld a complaint about an online video clip for a computer game, 'Mortal Combat', supplied by Midway Games. It appeared in paid-for space on a website aimed at 18–40-year-olds, which included a warning that viewers should be 18. The advertisement on the video clip featured a stabbing, the ripping out of a heart, and a decapitation by a flying hat, which the advertiser said was intended to be humorous. The ASA was concerned that the advertisement glorified violence, some scenes could be emulated and the advertisement was likely to cause fear or distress and widespread or serious offence.

Even for advertising by charities or the Government in press advertising on serious issues, there are limits. In 2003 national press advertisements for Barnardo's showed a new born baby with various items in his mouth, including a syringe and a cockroach. The text stated *'Baby Greg is one minute old. He should have a bright future. Poverty is waiting to rob Greg of hope and spirit and is likely to lead him to a life of squalor... Don't let poverty destroy a future. Call us...'*. Barnardo's had received favourable CAP copy advice. Charity advertisers can be tempted to use shock tactics, partly because they are dealing with social issues that may require a dramatic

The average smoker needs over five thousand cigarettes a year.

Get unhooked. Call 0800 169 0 169 or visit getunhooked.co.uk

SMOKEFREE

message, partly because they need to make an immediate impact with a limited budget. The ASA acknowledged the serious message of the Barnardo's advertisements, but considered that the images were likely to cause serious or widespread offence.

An advertisement by the Department of Health in 2007 to encourage smokers to stop smoking showed people being dragged along with hooks in their faces, to symbolise addiction. It attracted 774 complaints. Complaints that the advertisements were likely to cause fear and distress to children were upheld in respect of the television and poster advertisements, but rejected in the case of press, magazine and internet advertisements. An 'ex-kids' restriction had been imposed by the BACC for the television advertisements, but they were likely to distress older children too, so there was a breach of the scheduling rules. And although the posters had not been placed near schools, they were otherwise untargeted and were likely to be seen by children. On the other hand, all the complaints about offensiveness were rejected, because adults would understand the seriousness of the message.

Environmental claims

Numerous advertisers have made unsubstantiated misleading green claims for products, and green campaigning groups have likewise on occasion exaggerated the risks to the environment of certain conduct. A 2008 advertisement for Shell headed *'Don't throw anything away there is no away'* showed an oil refinery with flowers coming out of its chimneys, and stated *'we use our waste CO_2 to grow flowers, and our waste sulphur to make super-strong concrete'*. Readers were directed to the Shell website for *'real energy solutions for the real world'*. The ASA upheld a complaint on the basis that only a tiny proportion of Shell's output was recycled in this manner.

A 2007 advertisement for campaigning groups Airportwatch and Enoughsenough headed *'Just cut down on the flying, that's all we ask'*, showed a barren African landscape with cattle skeletons, aircraft trails above, and made a number of claims about the impact of climate change and aviation's responsibility for it. The ASA upheld complaints about some of their claims on the basis that they had in effect portrayed measurements in relation to aviation emissions as generally agreed when there were no internationally agreed figures, and presented as fact a worse-case scenario concerning temperature rise without making that clear.

Food and drink

Restrictions were introduced in 2007 to ensure that advertisements do not condone or encourage poor nutritional habits or unhealthy lifestyles in children. There are differences between the Codes. The TV Code has scheduling restrictions whereas the Non-Broadcast Code is solely a set of content restrictions. The TV Code adopted the Food Standards Agency's Nutrient Profiling Model to restrict products assessed as HFSS (high in fat, salt or sugar) from being advertised to children whilst the CAP Code and Radio Code apply to advertisements for all foods except fresh fruit and vegetables. Restrictions were placed on the use of licensed characters and celebrities popular with children, and measures to curb advertisements that prompt excessive consumption of food or drink were tightened.

Clearcast's enforcement of the restrictions, and advertiser awareness of continuing public and regulatory concern about the issue, means that there were few investigations in the period after the new restrictions were introduced. In 2008 the ASA rejected 26 complaints about a television advertisement for Kellogg's Coco Pops and milk as *'a bowl full of chocolaty fun even after school'*, which showed two children asking their mother for Coco Pops after returning home from school and ended with the on-screen text *'as part of a healthy balanced diet and active lifestyle'*. Coco Pops are an HFSS food because they contain 34 grams of sugar per 100 grams, so Clearcast had imposed restrictions ensuring that the advertisement was not broadcast in or adjacent to programmes made for children under 16 or programmes commissioned for, directed at, or likely to appeal to children under ten, or appeal particularly to children under 15. The ASA noted that Coco Pops with milk were low in fat and contained several vitamins, calcium and iron, that a typical serving (30g) would contain only 10g sugar and that viewers were unlikely to infer that children should eat Coco Pops for both breakfast and after school. The advertisement was unlikely to encourage excess consumption or poor nutritional habits in children.

Several investigations into food advertisements have concerned health claims for foods, where the advertisers have not been able to substantiate the claims made. Flora's claim that adding Flora margarine to sweetcorn made it healthier was found to be misleading. Polyunsaturated spread was likely to be a healthier alternative to butter, but it was not the case that adding additional fat to a plain vegetable was better for health than eating the vegetable on its own. Cereal Partners UK's TV advertisement for breakfast cereals stated that experts had in effect recommended that people eat three servings of Nestlé's wholegrain cereals per day for health benefits. There was no consensus among experts, and the fibre found in wholegrain was available in other foods, including fruit and vegetables. Complaints about Ferro UK's claims for the nutritional benefits of Nutella were also upheld in part as misleading because of the high sugar and fat content of Nutella.

Health claims

Prescription-only medicines may not be advertised to the general public. Other medicines should have a marketing authorisation from the Medicines and Healthcare products Regulatory Agency (MHRA) before they can be marketed, and claims made must conform with the authorisation. The Codes contain a number of rules about the advertising of medicines which reflect those in the Medicines (Advertising) Regulations 1994.

All claims about the efficacy of health related products must be backed by proper evidence, which will often need to include full reports of proper trials on humans including a control/placebo, accepted for publication in peer-reviewed journals. Breakthrough claims will require particularly robust evidence.

The average reader of a health claim may often be more vulnerable than the average consumer, and more susceptible to exaggerated claims, and advertisers need to remember that when creating advertisements for products for slimming, baldness, arthritis and so on. The first case to be referred by the ASA to the OFT under the legislation dealing with misleading advertising concerned unsubstantiated slimming claims (*Director General of Fair Trading v. Tobyward*[3]).

The more stark, categorical or absolute the claim, the greater the evidence required. Poster and magazine advertisements by SmithKline Beecham for Ribena Toothkind in 1999 were headed '*There is only one soft drink accredited by the British Dental Association*' and showed bottles of Ribena as bristles on a toothbrush. The magazine advertisement described the dangers of dental erosion from soft drink consumption, and stated that in a study by a leading university dental school Ribena Toothkind was found to be almost as kind for teeth as water. A trade press advertisement also stated that '*Ribena Toothkind does not encourage tooth decay*'. The ASA concluded, partly on SKB's own expert evidence and the basis of their own expert evidence, that the carbohydrate content of the drink had been lowered but not eliminated. The product did appear to be less damaging to teeth than other soft drinks, but the poster was misleading in implying that the product actively benefited oral health, and the magazine advertisement was misleading in claiming that the drink did not encourage tooth decay because this was an absolute claim whereas the evidence justified only a comparative claim. SKB's challenge to the ASA's decision in judicial review proceedings failed, amid much publicity.

Primary Care Trusts and Strategic Health Authorities deal with breaches of a new Code of Practice for the Promotion of NHS-funded Services (2008), where the rule in that Code is additional to rules in 'the Codes'.

Alcohol and gambling

The aim of the rules is to prevent harm, particularly to children and young people, by ensuring that advertising does not make alcohol or gambling strongly or particularly attractive to them. The alcohol rules were tightened in 2005, and new rules on gambling were introduced in 2007. In both areas advertisers appear conscious of the need to comply with the rules, and there have been relatively few breaches.

In 2007 and 2008 the ASA rejected complaints about Coors Brewers' use of the slogan 'Belong' in TV and poster advertising for Carling beer. One television advertisement featured astronauts in space suits trying to get into a venue in space. One astronaut wearing trainers is refused admittance, and the astronauts all agree to stick together. The poster is on a similar theme, under the heading '*You know who your mates are*'. The ASA considered that the advertisements did not associate alcohol with daring or toughness, or suggest that consumption could help overcome social problems. The advertisement did no more than associate Carling with a spirit of togetherness.

In contrast, the ASA found in 2008 that a press advertisement for Paddy Power showing a short man in a stretch limousine holding champagne and a cigar and flanked by two glamorous women, with the text '*Who says you can't make money being short*', did breach the rules on associating gambling with sexual success and social esteem.

Children

All the Codes have special rules aimed at the protection of children, generally defined in the Codes as those under 16. The requirement in the TV Code that advertisements should not make a direct appeal to children to buy advertised products or persuade their parents or other adults to buy advertised products for them, was extended in 2008 to radio and non-broadcast media. The Codes have specific rules in respect of food and alcohol. The ASA has upheld complaints about women who were portrayed as, or looked young enough to be under 18, in advertisements with sexual overtones for FCUK and Ryanair.

Many complaints concern the use of inappropriate media. In the case of television, 'ex kids' (not transmitted during or either side of children's programmes or between 4pm and 5.45pm and not before the 9pm watershed) restrictions are enforced by Clearcast and the ASA, along with other scheduling restrictions. Television companies have a system of indexing audience composition, with an index of 120 meaning that a programme is substantially more popular with children. In 2005 the ASA upheld 298 complaints about television advertisements for Jamba! GMBH's Jamster 'Crazy Frog', 'Sweetie the Chick' and 'Nessie the Dragon' ringtones, on the grounds that it was unclear that the advertisements were promoting a subscription service (rather than a one-off payment) and that the style of the advertisements were of particular appeal to children. The ASA ordered a post-9pm restriction to be imposed on the advertisements in future. Jamba!'s attempt to obtain an injunction against publication of the ASA's decision failed, but the Council did partially revise its ruling following a recommendation by the Independent Reviewer to remove a ruling that the advertising would cause social, moral or psychological harm to children.

Privacy

The Codes contain different rules concerning the portrayal of individuals in advertisements. The TV Code requires (with a few exceptions) advertisers to have the written permission of a living person before broadcasting an advertisement that features, caricatures or refers to that person. The Radio and CAP Codes simply urge advertisers to obtain permission, but complaints will only be upheld if the individual is featured in an adverse or offensive way, as in the IFAW advertisement referred to on page 72.

The fact that an advertisement is acceptable under the Code's rules does not necessarily mean that an individual will not have a legal right of action against the advertiser, either in the UK or abroad where privacy or image rights may be stronger. The ASA rejected in 2007 complaints about a press advertisement by Ryanair featuring Martin McGuiness and Ian Paisley. But the French court in 2008 awarded Carla Bruni damages in respect of a Ryanair advertisement featuring her and her husband, Nicolas Sarkozy.

Another important area is the privacy of individuals in relation to database and direct marketing. There are detailed rules in the CAP Code, and this is covered in Chapter 3.10.

Similarly, advertisements for financial services and price claims in advertising are dealt with in more detail in Chapter 3.5, Financial promotions.

Copy advice and clearance

Copy clearance is required by broadcasters for television advertisements. Most television advertisements are cleared by Clearcast although regional advertisements may be cleared locally (e.g. for ITV). For Clearcast clearance the advertiser will need to provide at the outset the evidence to substantiate factual claims. A substantive response is likely within a few days, but actual clearance will take longer if expert input is required. Certain categories of radio advertisement must be cleared by the RACC, others are cleared locally by the radio stations.

Note that advertisements are cleared for a limited time period. In 2008 the ASA upheld a complaint about a radio advertisement claim *'state of the art trains'* for South Eastern Trains. The RACC's clearance of a similar script had expired, and neither the broadcaster (LBC) or advertiser spotted that. The claim was misleading.

In the case of non-broadcast advertisements, the media may insist on clearance if the ASA Council or CAP advise it, where the advertisements are contentious or the advertiser has a troublesome history. CAP copy advice is advisable if the campaign involves high-risk areas such as children, comparisons, alcohol, food or health. It is generally prompt (95% of requests for copy advice received advice within 24 hours in 2007), and free.

Other hints for Code compliance

- Know the Codes.
- Open and maintain a dialogue between the marketing department and compliance/regulatory/legal.
- Explore commercial issues, particularly in sales promotions, to ensure that, for example, demand can be fulfilled (and avoid another Hoover).
- Assess the content of the advertisement as though you were an ordinary, reasonable reader of it – are the key messages included so that it does not mislead?
- Is the artwork included likely to cause any difficulties? (NB the Codes do not cover intellectual property issues such as trade marks, copyright and passing off.)
- Check ASA Council decisions, but remember that each case depends on the facts.
- Check Clearcast Guidance, CAP Help Notes and AdviceOnline (CAP's database of advice, with links to appropriate code clauses, and the more significant adjudications) but remember that this does not bind the ASA Council.
- If the advertisement is likely to be contentious, is alternative copy available if it has to be pulled quickly?
- Can the advertiser substantiate all claims, if necessary with expert evidence? Do not make absolute claims for a product if an expert's report says that test results are positive but further research is required. For health claims, tests on humans will invariably be required. Tests on rats will not do. Do not try to extrapolate too far (example of St Ivel Advance Omega 3 milk endorsed by Lord Winston).

Responding to complaints

If the advertiser has a good previous record, and the issue is minor and clear cut, can the ASA be persuaded to deal with the matter informally if the advertiser puts its hand up quickly and is not going to be publishing the advertisement further?

The sort of arguments that will/will not work include the following:

- *'Look at my disclaimer'* – in general it is no good making a misleading claim and then trying to put matters right in the small print. In 2008 the ASA decided that a British Gas television claim *'zero carbon'* and associated images implied that the advertiser supplied carbon-free gas. The disclaimer *'relates to offsetting schemes'* in superimposed text contradicted the overall impression and the advertisement would be likely to mislead.

- *'We give a money back guarantee'* – this does not excuse misleading claims.
- *'I am just repeating what someone else said'* – if testimonials give the impression that a product has been found to work then the advertiser will be required to produce proper evidence that the product does actually work. The Office of Fair Trading took action and obtained undertakings from MagnoPulse in respect of such claims in 2006.
- *'I am on the web, it is unregulated'* – much website advertising is unregulated by the ASA at present, but not all. And the ASA may refer the case to trading standards or the OFT.
- *'It would be contrary to the free movement of goods and services under the EU Treaty to stop me advertising'* – advertisers of medical devices often deploy this argument but the Medical Devices Directive does not harmonise EU law on advertising in respect of such devices. There are other Directives which do harmonise EU law, e.g. Directive 2001/83/EC on the Community Code relating to medicinal products for human use (see *Gintec International v. Verband Sozialer Weltbewerb*[10]), Directive 2004/24/EC regarding traditional herbal medicinal products, Directive 2005/29/EC on Unfair Business to Consumer Commercial Practices, and Regulation 1924/2006 on nutrition and health claims made on food. Regulations, which are directly effective, give the least scope for manoeuvre.
- *'You are infringing my right to free speech'* – all adverse ASA adjudications may do that, but free speech can be subject to limitations, including for the protection of rights of others.
- *'I do not believe anyone could possibly complain about my advertisement, the complainant must be a competitor, I want to see the letter of complaint'* – the identity of members of the public who complain is kept confidential, the outcome of an investigation rarely depends on any disputed factual evidence from such complainants, and the ASA is experienced in spotting obvious competitor complaints.
- *'My substantiation evidence is too confidential to disclose'* – ASA procedures provide for substantiation evidence to be treated in confidence by the ASA (and any expert instructed) where it is genuinely confidential, but if an advertiser is going to make claims to the world he needs to anticipate that such claims may be subject to external scrutiny.
- *'I must have an oral hearing'* – the ASA Council does not provide oral hearings, and the law does not require that it should.
- *'Council must see all my substantiation material'* – this is wholly impractical. Council has delegated the investigation of complaints to the ASA executive, and all that is required to be put to the Council is a fair summary of the advertiser's position and the advertisement. In exceptional cases the Council may consider additional material.

- *'Your expert is biased'* – this is another argument that is often run. In a relatively narrow field or in relation to a controversial subject it may be very difficult to find an expert that does not have an existing opinion, but that does not mean that the expert cannot seek to approach the matter afresh, or that the expert's alleged bias will render any subsequent ASA decision unfair. The court said as much in *SmithKline Beecham v. ASA*[11].

- *'There has only been one complaint'* – this is relevant, but not determinative under any codes' rules, and is particularly unlikely to be persuasive in the case of misleading advertising. As Mr Justice Etherton put it in *Office of Fair Trading v. The Officers Club*[12]: *'It is in the very nature of a misleading or deceptive advertisement that the consumer is left unaware of the true facts. Further, many consumers, even though aware of the deception, and even though aggrieved, may not have the time, ability, personality or inclination to make a complaint'*. On the other hand, the most complained about advertisement in the ASA's history resulted in a 'not upheld' adjudication. A television commercial for the KFC zinger crunch salad in 2005 attracted 1,671 complaints from viewers who said it encouraged bad manners in children. The ASA did not uphold complaints, reasoning that it takes time to instil good manners in children and that this television advertisement would not adversely affect their behaviour in the long term.

- *'My competitor makes similar claims'* – of course the ASA must seek to ensure a level playing field, but the fact that one advertiser is publishing advertisements in breach of the Code does not justify any other advertiser doing it.

- *'I've been doing it for years'* – this may be relevant, but not determinative.

- *'It works on mice'* – generally not good enough.

- *'F… off you toothless watchdog'* – behaving like an outlaw may work for certain advertisers for a while, but in the end the advertiser is likely to encounter difficulties with the media, other regulators and the public.

Complaining about competitor campaigns

The ASA generally treats competitor complaints in the same way as complaints from members of the public, save that the competitor will be identified, and may be required to spell out exactly why the challenge is being made. In addition, competitors will be asked to confirm that they are not intending to litigate the same issue. It is worth noting that competitor complaints are often hard fought and can take longer to determine than consumer complaints; and that once a formal investigation has commenced the ASA will not generally allow withdrawal of a complaint simply because it looks as though the complaint is likely to be not upheld.

What if an advertiser (or complainant) does not agree with the ASA's decision?

The advertiser (or complainant) may use the Independent Review Procedure which is in similar terms for both broadcast and non-broadcast. A request for a review of a decision by the ASA Council can be made to the Independent Reviewer of ASA adjudications either:

- where additional relevant evidence becomes available (and an explanation is provided as to why it was not submitted previously); or
- where there is a substantial flaw in the Council's adjudication or in the process by which that adjudication was made.

An application for an independent review should be made within 21 days of the date on the ASA's letter of notification of an adjudication. The ASA will not delay publication of the relevant adjudication pending the outcome of a review, save in exceptional circumstances. Debt Free Direct plc sought to obtain an injunction against publication of an ASA decision in May 2007, pending the outcome of its application for permission to bring proceedings for a judicial review of a decision by the ASA upholding complaints about DFD's television advertising for debt management services offering individual voluntary arrangements. Mr Justice Sullivan ruled that it would require the most compelling reasons to prevent a regulatory body such as the ASA from publishing its adjudications, and that DFD should exhaust its available remedies (i.e. the independent review procedure) before seeking to involve the court.

The Independent Reviewer may refer the case back to the Council with a recommendation to reverse or revise its previous decision. In 2005–2007 the Independent Reviewer reviewed 74 adjudications, of which 23 were sent back to the Council. Council asked the ASA executive to reopen an investigation in one case, and reached a revised or different decision in the remaining cases.

If the party seeking the review still does not like the outcome, they may be able to seek permission to bring proceedings for a judicial review of the decision of the Council or Independent Reviewer, seeking an order quashing the disputed decision. An application for judicial review must be made promptly and at most within three months of notification of the decision in question. Any application should be preceded by a letter before action complying with the Pre-Action Protocol for judicial review, setting out the potential claimant's case, in a final attempt to resolve matters without litigation. The court will not substitute its own views for that of the decision maker. Generally damages are not claimed or awarded even if a judicial review challenge is successful.

The grounds for judicial review are:

- *Illegality* – if the ASA has acted beyond its powers.
- *Procedural impropriety* – this includes breach of the principles of natural justice, for example because the advertiser has not been told the substance of the case against him, has not had his case put fairly to the Council (see *R v. ASA ex parte Insurance Service*[13]), has not had his case considered fairly under the relevant procedural rules or because of bias by the decision maker. Advertisers often ask the ASA to ensure that Council sees all the correspondence and substantiation material, but that is not what the law requires. Challenges to ASA decisions on grounds of bias have been rejected by the courts. In *International Fund for Animal Welfare v. ASA*[14], the IFAW argued that two Council members were biased. In fact one of those members had even voted in the advertiser's favour.

- *Irrationality* – where the decision is so outrageous in its defiance of logic or accepted moral standards that no sensible person who applied his mind to the question to be decided would have arrived at it. This is a high threshold, but if the advertising is 'political' advertising, widely defined, the court may subject the decision maker to greater scrutiny.

- *Lack of proportionality* – where the action taken is disproportionate to the harm to be corrected. Given that the ASA has no power to fine (let alone imprison) and does not impose complete bans on an advertiser, this is rarely an issue.

- *Failure to provide a 'fair trial'* – pursuant to Article 6 of the European Convention on Human Rights, including a public hearing before an impartial tribunal. It is questionable whether the ASA determines civil rights and obligations such that Article 6 of the Convention can be invoked, but even if it does its decisions are generally judgemental rather then fact finding and the availability of judicial review means that the process as a whole satisfies Article 6 (*Stephen Buxton trading as The Jewellery Vault v. ASA*[15]).

- *Unlawful restriction on freedom of expression* – Article 10 of the European Convention on Human Rights. Article 10 provides that *'everyone has the right to the freedom of expression… without interference by public authority…'*, but it may be *'subject to such restrictions… as prescribed by law and necessary in a democratic society in the interests of… protection of health or morals, protection of reputation and rights of others…'*. 'Others' includes consumers and competitors, and many of the claims with which the ASA deals involve health and morals. The courts have found that the CAP Code is prescribed by law (*ASA v. ex parte Matthias Rath BV*[16]). Commercial expression is protected by Article 10, but restrictions on commercial free speech are easier to justify than for political speech (widely defined). Animal Defenders International sought to obtain from the court a declaration that the prohibition on 'political advertising' in section 321 of the Communications Act 2003 was so widely drawn as to be incompatible with Article 10. The BACC had refused to clear ADI's inoffensive 'My Mate's a Primate' advertisement concerning the use of primates by humans, on the basis that ADI's objects were mainly political. The House of Lords upheld the ban on a number of grounds, including that the aim of the ban – preventing the distortion of the democratic process by high spenders – could not be achieved without a wide ban, and the potency of broadcasting justified its special treatment. However, the court left the door open for further challenge if a social advocacy group wanted to counter commercial advertising on a specific issue or influence public opinion on an issue of public controversy, or to broadcast an advertisement unrelated to its (political) objects.

The decisions of other bodies which control advertiser access to the media may also be challenged. In 2003, Ann Summers successfully challenged the decision by Jobcentre Plus, an executive agency of the Department of Work and Pensions, to refuse to handle advertisements for job vacancies associated with the sex or personal services industry. And in 2005, North Cyprus Tourism Centre successfully challenged a ban by Transport for London (based on its own, more restrictive code) on advertising for holidays in North Cyprus. But the courts will generally be reluctant to overturn the views of a long-established regulator acting within its field of expertise. Generally, the advertiser will be better off seeking to work with the regulator, rather than battling with it in the courts.

Rupert Earle, Bates Wells & Braithwaite

Notes

1   *Animal Defenders International v. Department for Culture, Media and Sport, 2008 UKHL15*
2   Charity Commission's Guidance on Campaigning and Political Activity by Charities (CC9, March 2008)
3   *Director General of Fair Trading v. Tobyward Ltd [1989] 2 All England Report 266*
4   Television Without Frontiers Directive (89/552/EEC)
5   Audiovisual Media Services Directive (2007/65/EC)
6   *Komm Austria v. ORF (2007)*
7   The Audiovisual Media Services Directive (2007/65/EC)
8   *O_2 Holdings Ltd & Anor v. Hutchison 3GUK Ltd Case C-533/06*
9   Business Protection from Misleading Marketing Regulations 2008 (implementing Directive 2006/114/EC)
10   *Gintec International v. Verband Sozialer Weltbewerb, 2007 ECJ*
11   *SmithKline Beecham v. ASA (2000)*
12   *Office of Fair Trading v. The Officers Club (2005)*
13   *R v. ASA ex parte Insurance Service plc (1989)*
14   *International Fund for Animal Welfare v. ASA (1997)*
15   *Stephen Buxton trading as The Jewellery Vault v. ASA (2002)*
16   *Advertising Standards Authority Ltd & Ano'r, ex parte Matthias Rath BV (2000)*

Celebrities in advertising

C elebrity endorsement of a product or service is undoubtedly effective and appealing. The IPA Effectiveness Awards have over many years demonstrated just how effective celebrity endorsements can be. The Jamie Oliver adver-tisements by Abbott Mead Vickers.BBDO for Sainsbury's increased its profits by an estimated £153m per year.

Similarly, celebrities can make substantial money from their merchandising careers. The endorsement market is worth several hundred millions of pounds in the UK alone and a decent six-month advertising campaign will net a celebrity face at least half a million. Endorsing products has become more lucrative than the day job. A successful pop band can make more from licensing, sponsorship and product endorsement than from records.

Thus this chapter is divided into two. The first part concentrates on the unauthor-ised use of celebrities and politicians and the various rights such individuals can utilise to protect their image. The second part considers the pitfalls and legal issues surrounding authorised celebrity endorsement.

UNAUTHORISED USE OF CELEBRITIES

English law, unlike many European countries and the USA, has striven to create a balance between freedom of commercial expression, creativity and humour while protecting the rights of individuals. This means that it is possible to refer to living indi-viduals without their consent in certain circumstances. It is worth noting that using images of dead individuals is almost always acceptable in English law. However, the unauthorised use of celebrities has become a big issue in marketing communication terms over the past few years, as living celebrities have increasingly sought to protect their image. Until recently celebrities have shied away from bringing expensive and risky litigation, unlike their American counterparts, but maybe times are changing.

THE MYTH OF 'IMAGE RIGHTS' IN ENGLISH LAW

Image rights do not exist as a right in English law. W R Cornish in his book *Intellectual Property*[1] writes that English law *'steadfastly refuses to adopt any embracing prin-ciple that a person has a right to his or her name, or for that matter, to identify a characteristic such as a voice or image.'*

Interestingly the issue of the validity in law of 'image rights' arose in the 1990s in a totally different context – the Inland Revenue sought to question the payment to English football clubs and players for use of their images. Lawyers for both parties admitted no such rights exist in English law. Players from Europe however were used to such additional payments. Image rights are recognised in many European countries. In Spain for example Article 18 of the Constitution entitles anybody to forbid the commercial use of his or her name, other than for purely information purposes.

The Inland Revenue considered that if no such rights existed in English law the payment of vast sums under agreements to use players' images was nothing other than a tax free means of topping up wages. A decision by the Special Commission in April 2000[2] decided image rights agreements were genuine commercial agreements but that 'image rights' did not adequately describe the full nature of these agreements. Thus the agreements were recognised while the issue of 'image rights' in English law was side stepped.

While there is no such concept as 'personality rights' in English law there has been an extension of the law of privacy with the introduction of the Human Rights Act and the Data Protection Act, and as a result of some high-profile High Court decisions in this area. The implications for advertisers and their agencies is that not only are individuals exploiting their celebrity to the maximum financial advantage, but they are also taking whatever steps are needed to protect their images from unauthorised use.

This chapter will not describe the law of copyright, trade mark, passing off, defamation and privacy, as these are covered in earlier chapters, but will cover how the law is being extended in these areas in relation specifically to those wishing to protect their names, voice and image, and in any media including the internet.

As a checklist for advertisers and agencies the issues one should consider are always:

- the law of passing off;
- copyright;
- trade mark registrations;
- defamation;
- privacy and the Human Rights Act and Data Protection Act;
- self-regulatory codes.

PASSING OFF

As described earlier the law of passing off protects goodwill. Until 2002 celebrities were unwilling to risk the costs and uncertainties of bringing legal action for use of their name and image in advertising, largely because of a 1947 case, *McCullough v. May*[3]. In that case children's radio presenter, 'Uncle Mac' brought an action against a cereal manufacturer for unauthorised reference to him. The court held because there was no common field of activity between Uncle Mac and the cereal company, Uncle Mac could not have suffered any financial loss.

The commercial reality today is very different. Celebrities have active and growing merchandising careers from which vast sums of money can be made. In 2002 Eddie Irvine brought the first successful claim in passing off in this arena for many years.

Previously there had been a long history of failed attempts by, or on behalf of, celebrities trying to protect their image rights. In the 1980s Adam Ant failed to establish that copyright subsisted in his distinctive facial make-up[4]; Elvis Presley Enterprises failed to restrain the unofficial merchandising activities of Sid Shaw trading as 'Elvisly Yours'[5] because Mr Justice Laddie held that the public would not necessarily believe that the claimant officially licensed Mr Shaw's products. Other well-known cases include a claim by Princess Diana's estate which attempted to register her likeness as a trade mark and restrict the merchandising of her image.

Eddie Irvine v. TalkSport Radio[6]

Eddie Irvine brought successful legal proceedings against TalkSport about the unauthorised use of his image. TalkSport had however blatantly used a photograph of Eddie Irvine speaking into a mobile phone. The telephone had been removed and superimposed with a TalkSport radio implying that Eddie Irvine was listening to TalkSport and thereby endorsing the product. Some commentators have called this case a watershed with the law finally recognising personality rights. However, the case has not changed the position as drastically as at first thought. The necessity of implied endorsement was of paramount importance in this case.

In addition, Eddie Irvine was initially only awarded £2000 damages and ended up paying legal costs of several hundred thousand. Somewhat of a pyrrhic victory, but on appeal this amount was increased to £25,000 plus his costs which greatly exceeded the award itself. Eddie Irvine stated in his evidence he would *'not get out of bed for less than £25,000'*. Thus for the first time the court accepted the commercial reality that celebrity endorsement was big business and that, in the circumstances of this specific case, Mr Irvine's rights had been infringed. Nevertheless it is notable that the amount of damages was still relatively small.

In order for a celebrity to bring a successful claim of 'passing off' three elements have to be established: loss of goodwill, misrepresentation and damage. In the Irvine case it is important to recall that Eddie Irvine was at the height of his career and also had an active career endorsing products such as sunglasses, clothes and footwear. He therefore had little difficulty in establishing goodwill and damage. The judge also held that 'doctoring' the mobile telephone was intentionally meant to misleadingly imply endorsement of the product by Irvine.

Some celebrities, especially those with no merchandising career, and certainly most politicians, will struggle to prove the necessary elements of goodwill and damage. If the celebrity is dead this element of damage cannot be achieved and hence passing off can never be used by the estate of a dead individual. Most importantly, if there is clearly no implication of endorsement by a living celebrity of the product advertised then a claim for passing off would not succeed, as the Spice Girls discovered some time ago.[7]

The Spice Girls applied for an injunction to restrain an unofficial sticker book using their image. Their application was rejected and the judge stated: '*The defendants in the case are doing no more than catering for the popular demand for effigies and quotes of today's idols*'. The judge was also very critical of the argument that the absence of words 'not authorised' on the book cover meant there was some form of implied endorsement.

These cases do not however completely prohibit the unauthorised use of living celebrities in advertising. There were rumours in August 2002 that Ian Botham was intending to sue the makers of Guinness for allegedly exploiting his image in a national advertising campaign. He complained that Diageo used images of him in the Ashes series in 1981 without his permission. The important point to note was that there was an allegation that the advertisement suggested Botham was endorsing the product. The case appears to have settled out of court, no doubt both parties wary of the costs and vagaries of the law as a remedy.

What the Irvine case does not establish, as claimed by many, is the extension of the law creating a new 'personality right'. Any celebrity without a merchandising career, or indeed a politician, will find it difficult to establish damage and goodwill in his/her image. Interestingly in his judgment Laddie J stated that he had not decided that passing off had developed sufficiently to cover false endorsement and that it may be necessary to consider whether the Human Rights Act would be a more effective remedy. The impact of this Act and rights to privacy are discussed on page 95.

Other cases

Zeta-Jones

The increasing awareness of image rights has been largely brought about by a spate of high-profile cases over recent times. Advertisers and agencies need to be careful of using images beyond the UK where image rights are more protected than under English law. Catherine Zeta-Jones has, for example, issued a suit against French cosmetics company Claudalie seeking $15m damages for spreading the idea she had been spotted purchasing the complete Claudalie range of skincare products and used the company's anti-ageing spa in Las Vegas, all denied by Zeta-Jones.

It is important also to appreciate such celebrities are subject to various obligations under existing merchandising contracts. Thus Zeta-Jones would undoubtedly be forced to defend her position because of her existing deal to promote Elizabeth Arden cosmetics.

118 118

Another high profile case is the 118 118 commercial by The Number featuring a moustachioed runner created by advertising agency WCRS. David Bedford, a 1970s athlete who broke the 10,000 metres world record in 1973, complained to the regulators that his image had been used without permission and claimed still to be seeking compensation for the alleged use of his image. WCRS claim the characters in the

commercial are loosely based on US athlete Steve Prefontaine and a mix of other 1970s athletes and that no image rights have been infringed.

The Content Board of Ofcom gave its first adjudication on 27 January 2004 on David Bedford's claim against The Number. It was without doubt a pyrrhic victory for Bedford.

In a nutshell, the Content Board held that Mr Bedford had been caricatured by The Number in specific breach of the old ITC Code, now adopted by Ofcom, clause 6.5 of which prohibits, amongst other things, caricatures of living individuals without obtaining the prior consent of such individual. It is worth noting this is much stricter than the CAP Code governing non-broadcast advertising. The ASA had already decided not to uphold Bedford's complaint in relation to the print advertisements.

Though Ofcom decided that The Number had caricatured David Bedford, it also held that he had suffered no financial damage and that it would be *'disproportionate to direct that the advertisements are not shown in future'*. Thus, The Number is free to continue use of the commercials.

Bedford subsequently claimed he would commence a separate court action against The Number to recover damages, even though Ofcom held he had not suffered damage. More importantly, Ofcom were applying the ITC Code in relation to his complaint not the law. No legal proceedings have been brought to date. Bedford would be foolish indeed to seek a legal remedy against The Number under the law of passing off. In order to succeed he would need first to prove he had been caricatured, but even more importantly that he had suffered damage. Since Bedford had no merchandising career prior to this episode it is very difficult for him to establish financial damage.

It is also worth noting that though Ofcom made a finding that Bedford had been caricatured, this finding is still disputed and Ofcom in its adjudication firmly states that *'there were a number of disputed issues of primary fact raised on the written evidence, and none of the witnesses gave oral evidence, but in the end we found it unnecessary to resolve any of these disputes.'*

While under present English law it would seem remarkable indeed if Bedford had grounds for a claim, the incident nevertheless demonstrates again how individuals have realised the potential value of their image and how costly it can be to dissuade such claimants that their rights have been infringed, or that such rights are not necessarily as valuable as might at first be believed.

easyJet and David Beckham

David Beckham is a sports star who has gone out of his way to protect his image, to the extent of registering his name as a trade mark. In 2003 budget airline easyJet used a picture of David Beckham without his consent three times in the space of a few weeks. Beckham objected. The response by easyJet was that there was no implicit or implied endorsement of the product by Beckham. The dispute was purportedly settled with easyJet agreeing to make a donation to the NSPCC with Beckham chipping in as well.

Again no court case was brought, but it is interesting to consider the various possible causes of action, as set out in the checklist on page 88:

- it is doubtful whether there is any claim for breach of copyright in the actual photographs, which were not owned by Beckham, but probably legitimately purchased from a photo library;

- it would be difficult to succeed on a claim in passing off, as the use clearly did not suggest endorsement by Beckham of the product;

- though 'David Beckham' is a registered trade mark it is not generally possible, nor should it be, to register a first name as a trade mark. Also, registration only offers Beckham limited protection in relation to certain goods and services. Though trade mark registrations can be an effective means of protecting a mark there are limitations to the protection such registrations offer. He was not named in the advertisement anyway;

- it is unlikely that suggesting Beckham flies a budget airline is defamatory, though arguably it may lower his reputation;

- no claim has ever been brought for the use of personal data under the Data Protection Act (see page 97);

- while there have been successful cases brought pursuant to the Human Rights Act, English law has still not accepted a freestanding right to privacy for which damages can be awarded;

- the CAP Code[8] urges advertisers to obtain prior consent before referring to individuals in advertising. The ASA cannot award damages, and even if the ASA held there had been a breach of the Code the only penalty would have been the removal of the offending advertisement.

Thus, the case demonstrates how it is feasible to use living celebrities in non-broadcast advertising without consent providing steps are taken to ensure there is no implied endorsement, there is no use of a registered trade mark, the use is not defamatory or denigratory, and licences are obtained to use actual photographs or illustrations.

The use of look-alikes and sound-alikes

As celebrities require greater remuneration for the use of their image and voices a short cut is often to use a look-alike. There are dangers though if the use is such that it might mislead the public into believing the celebrity is real, which may lead to a potential claim by the celebrity for passing off. Many humorous commercials and advertisements have been created using look-alikes, such as the award-winning advertisements by Mother for Schweppes featuring look-alikes for the Duchess of Cornwall (formerly Camilla Parker Bowles), Margaret Thatcher with Lord Archer, Tony and Cherie Blair and others. It would be disappointing to see such creativity being stifled, but care has to be taken to ensure the consumer is aware the real celebrity is not endorsing the product.

The Schweppes campaign was clever in many ways. The advertisements do not display the product and they use celebrities and politicians who either do not have merchandising careers or who are not in a position to complain. However, the printing of the real models' names in small print would not have assisted in defence against an action for passing off.

The UK royal family has also been reported to be concerned about the use of royal look-alikes in a TBWA advertisement for Eurostar. This campaign was published in Brussels and would not have been permissible in the UK as the Codes[9] forbid the use of royal images to endorse commercial products.

In one advertisement a Queen Elizabeth II look-alike has been superimposed on a Marilyn Monroe figure. In another a Prince Charles look-alike's head has been

superimposed on a running athlete clad in Lycra emblazoned with the Union Jack. As image rights are developed to a greater degree in Belgium it is not beyond the royal family to take their complaint further if the use continues.

As with one's image there is no copyright in a voice, but if a voice is used to mislead, in the same way as a celebrity image, then the most likely action will again be a claim of passing off.

There is no copyright in a person's image, voice or name. There may well be copyright protection for a photograph or illustration, or a recording of the celebrity's voice, but invariably the advertiser can obtain a licence for the use of photographs, film or recording, or indeed the advertiser may already own the copyright in the material being used.

However, one point to always bear in mind with film and sound recordings is that the actors' performances may well be copyright protected as dramatic works. Hence using film clips or recordings of celebrities may be an infringement of their performance rights in the film or recording and an estate could sue for compensation for use of a dead celebrity's performance. It is prudent, therefore, to be extra careful about use of dramatic works on radio or the internet for example, even if the celebrity is dead. As the BCAP Code (see page 98 on self-regulation) prevents the use of living celebrities without consent, this issue of whether the performance is protected by copyright or not does not arise, because clips featuring living celebrities in broadcast advertising will have to be cleared and consent obtained before use in any event.

TRADE MARKS AND CELEBRITIES

It is an increasing tendency for celebrities to register their names as trade marks. To date this has been particularly the case with well-known pop stars and sports stars, especially footballers. David Beckham, Alan Shearer, Eric Cantona, the Spice Girls, Charlie Dimmock, Jamie Oliver and Delia Smith to name a few.

There have also been applications to register dead artists such as Linda McCartney and Princess Diana. Victoria Beckham attempted to register the word 'Posh' but failed.

Advertisers and agencies should check the register of UK and European trade marks before referring to a celebrity in any commercial.

DEFAMATION

A claim in defamation is unusual in the context of marketing communications. Suffice to say the era of huge libel awards once seen in the courts is not now so common, but nevertheless care should be taken. (See Chapter 1.5.)

In 1998 Jilly Goolden of the BBC's *Food and Wine* programme was reported to have accepted substantial damages and costs after a Domestos print campaign inferred her kitchen was un-hygienic. The advertisement merely reproduced a photograph of Ms Goolden and her kitchen with the extract from an article from *Today* newspaper but omitted the section of the article that made it clear the kitchen was beyond reproach.

PRIVACY – HUMAN RIGHTS ACT AND DATA PROTECTION ACT

We are familiar therefore with the fact that there is a limited right to privacy in English law, unlike the USA and other European countries such as France and Germany. However, with the enactment of the Human Rights Act 1998 and Data Protection Act 1998 a few cases touching on the issue of invasion of privacy in commercial cases have arisen. Contrary to some reports a freestanding right of privacy entitling a claimant to seek damages does not exist.

In a case before the House of Lords in 2003 the Lords clearly stated the reform of privacy law *'can be achieved only by legislation rather than the broad brush of common law principle.'*[10] In June 2002 the Parliamentary Select Committee for Culture Media and Sport published its first report on Privacy and Media intrusion. The Report recommended a package of measures including a specific right of privacy law to clarify the protection of individuals from unwarranted intrusion into their private lives. The Government's response rejected the recommendation and supported self-regulation as the best possible form of regulation for the press.

The Government has indicated that the newly established Ofcom will need to consider a review of the code that sets out guidance on the principles to be observed by broadcasters in avoiding unwarranted infringements of privacy, and that the Press Complaints Commission implement some changes to existing practices. However, there appears no willingness to extend the right to privacy by the present Government at least.

While broadcasters and the press have additional defences against an allegation of invasion of privacy than do advertisers, namely fair comment and public interest defences, the reluctance to introduce stricter privacy laws stretches to marketing communications.

The case law utilising the Human Rights Act and Data Protection has been limited to a few high profile cases:

Zeta-Jones and Douglas v. *Hello!* magazine[11]

In April 2003 the English High Court held that *Hello!'s* publication of secretly obtained photographs of Catherine Zeta-Jones's wedding to Michael Douglas was wrongful. Damages were awarded in November 2003. These damages were broken down into:

- damages for personal distress;
- damages for breach of the Data Protection Act; and
- £1m for commercial damages for the loss by *OK!* magazine, which had obtained exclusive rights to publish the wedding photographs, as a result of the publication by *Hello!*.

The judge held that *OK!* should recover £1,033,156 loss of profit from *Hello!,* though this was overturned on appeal in 2005, only to be re-instated by the House of Lords in 2007! However the non-commercial damages amounted to a mere £14,500, awarded to Zeta-Jones and Douglas personally. They were awarded only £50 for breach of the Data Protection Act.

What is worth noting though is the cost of this action. On 23 January 2004 the Judge, Mr Justice Lindsay, gave judgment on which party should bear the substantial costs of the action. He ordered *Hello!* to pay over £1m towards the costs of the (first) trial. He placed emphasis on the fact that *Hello!* had been guilty of misconduct during the trial when it produced an '*untruthful and misleading*' letter. It is however estimated the whole case cost the parties £4m over a period of nearly seven years (2000–2007).

The case is important in so far as it confirms that celebrities are unlikely to be guaranteed vast awards for invasion of privacy if their images are used without their permission. The case also continued the established judicial line that the Human Rights Act has not established a right of privacy breach that entitles an individual to damages.

Advertisers should not take too much comfort however from these very unique cases, which unfortunately cannot fail to reflect the nature of the celebrities and the unique circumstances and context of their legal claims, and therefore turn very much on specific facts.

The Sara Cox case[12]

Sara Cox succeeded, where others have failed, in a claim for invasion of privacy pursuant to Article 8 of the European Convention on Human Rights as enacted into English law by the Human Rights Act 1998. However, rarely can there have been such a blatant case of intrusion into private and very new family life as in this case.

Sara Cox, the Radio 1 disc jockey, brought proceedings for damages against the *Sunday People* for invading her privacy by publishing naked pictures of her and her husband on their honeymoon on a private island. The Press Complaints Commission (PCC) negotiated an apology from the paper, but Cox decided that this was not enough. She took legal action and obtained £50,000 damages. Few cases are likely, however, to be as clear cut as this obvious invasion of privacy.

Hugh Grant, J.K. Rowling and others

In 2008 Hugh Grant, Liz Hurley and her husband Arun Nayar brought a successful action against Big Pictures UK and Eliot Press for invasion of privacy over photographs taken of them on holiday on a private island in the Maldives. Contributions to the damages awarded of £58,000 were made by Associated Newspapers and the News Group Newspapers who published articles and the images.

Also in 2008, J.K. Rowling succeeded in the case brought on behalf of her baby son, David, in the Court of Appeal, again against Big Pictures UK, for invasion of privacy over pictures taken and published of David in his buggy. These cases are limited to special circumstances but demonstrate a growing tendency for the English Courts to recognise a right to privacy, and this is a growing concern for advertisers using images in a commercial context.

Data Protection Act

It has been argued that the use of a photograph identifying an individual is the use of 'personal data' as defined by the Data Protection Act. Indeed, it was established in a case brought by Naomi Campbell against the *Daily Mirror* in 2004 that publishing a photograph was processing data as defined under the Act. However, this is not certain. Leaving aside the various decisions of the Court of Appeal and the House of Lords in this case, the *Mirror* sought to rely on the defence of public interest, a defence that is of little assistance in any event in the arena of marketing communications.

The Zeta-Jones decision reinforced what was decided by the Court of Appeal in the Naomi Campbell case.[13] The court declined to award substantial damages for breach of the Data Protection Act for misuse of personal data by way of publication of photographs of individuals without their consent. What appears plain from the case law to date is that unauthorised use of a photograph will not entitle the claimant to huge damages, even if there are grounds for any claim at all.

To date there has also been no case where an individual has successfully obtained an interim injunction to prevent the further processing of the data. So far, the courts have not investigated the issue of personal data in the advertising context, therefore the position is not clear. However, a very recent case against the Financial Services Authority[14] has further defined what is meant by the term 'personal data' and the term 'relevant filing systems'. In this case the Court of Appeal appears to have put paid to the argument that the use of visual or verbal references to individuals in advertising can in some way give rise to problems under the Act.

It now seems unlikely that the use in advertising of a photograph by an advertiser falls within the definition of personal data being held in a 'relevant filing system'. It is even less likely that the mere holding of an individual's name or photograph for the purpose of its use in advertisements can be regarded, without some other biographical reference in the advertising, as processing information that is 'biographical in a significant sense', and thus falling within the 'personal data' definition.

Thus unless an individual is prepared to become the first test case in the truly advertising sense, which is unlikely, advertisers must simply weigh up the risks when they use photographs or other information relating to living individuals, unless prior consent is obtained.

Crowd scenes

Under the CAP Code it is acknowledged that the use of crowd scenes or general public locations may be acceptable without prior permission. If an individual cannot be identified then clearly no problem arises in any event. Arguably if an individual is identifiable the Data Protection Act will apply but, as already explained above, the likelihood of any damages being awarded is indeed minimal.

If filming in a public area it is sensible to erect signs indicating filming is taking place so individuals have the option to avoid the cameras. The use of the man in the street is no longer the safe option it once was.

It is perhaps a loss rather than a gain for modern society that photographs, such as those of the great artist Henri Cartier-Bresson, may not be possible in the future because of over rigid attempts to protect privacy. England has taken a reasonable approach to date in ensuring a sensible compromise in protecting the legitimate rights of individuals with the freedom of artistic expression, including advertising.

SELF-REGULATION

The CAP Code that covers non-broadcast marketing communications and the BCAP Code, which deals with broadcast advertising, both refer to the use of living individuals in marketing communications. Unsurprisingly, the broadcast media is stricter than is the case with non-broadcast advertising and living celebrities cannot be referred to, portrayed or caricatured without consent in television.

The CAP Code does not require prior consent of living celebrities and politicians, but it does 'urge' advertisers to do so where reasonable. More importantly the Code clearly forbids the derogatory reference to individuals.

Neither Code prevents the use of dead individuals.

While neither Code has the ability to award damages or impose fines an advertiser may be required to remove an infringing commercial or advertisement. If an individual objects to the use of his/her image and merely wishes the withdrawal of the advertisement, a complaint to the ASA is a useful and cheap tool for achieving that aim. It is also a way a politician or celebrity without a merchandising career may prevent an advertisement from appearing where he or she would have no claim under the law of passing off. This was the route taken by David Bedford (see page 90).

A WORD OF CAUTION – THE POSITION ABROAD

The freedom to use living and dead celebrities in the UK is almost unique, bar a few old commonwealth countries that have similar laws to that of England. The position

is very different elsewhere in Europe and the USA. This also means care has to be taken when uploading advertising to the internet which may be safe to publish in the UK but not in other jurisdictions.

Nicolas Sarkozy – France

By way of example, Nicolas Sarkozy and his new wife Carla Bruni brought a claim in February 2008 in Paris against Ryanair for using an image of them in an advertisement for cheap flights with the tag line 'With Ryanair my whole family can attend the wedding.'

The Parisian court had little trouble in finding the advertisement infringed the 'image rights' of the couple. The court awarded Carla Bruni €60,000, but also ordered a further assessment of damages to take into account the 'buzz 'effect of the campaign for Ryanair.

Princess Caroline of Monaco – Germany

In 2004 the Princess won a landmark ruling from the European Court of Human Rights which confirmed that publishing paparazzi photographs of the Princess in a public place was a violation of her right to privacy. The ruling was the start of courts throughout Europe taking a stronger line over intrusion of privacy, and again a possible concern in the future. Advertisers should be careful where they source images and the types of images they use of the celebrities appearing in their advertisements.

AUTHORISED USE OF CELEBRITIES

The value and effectiveness of using celebrities to endorse a product or service is undisputed. Twenty per cent of all advertising employs celebrities. In his book *Celebrity Sells*[15] Hamish Pringle states *'...one of the fastest and most effective ways of giving a brand lift-off is to harness the power of an established star.'*

Difficulties are not necessarily overcome however by obtaining the authorised endorsement of your product by a celebrity. Leaving aside the cost of a well-known celebrity endorsing the goods or services advertised, there are many other issues that need to be addressed and these should be covered in a celebrity agreement.

The main points are covered by the IPA's draft agreement, but each contract should be tailored to cover all relevant issues in each individual case. The case of Roy Keane during the Football World Cup illustrates the dangers of celebrity endorsement and the importance of contractual terms.

7-Up chose Roy Keane to front their World Cup advertising campaign in the summer of 2002. Keane's fee was reported to be £500,000, but the cost of the advertisements and promotional cans of 7-Up would have been a great deal more. When Keane was banned from playing in the tournament for Ireland the campaign became a PR nightmare. Posters were defaced and pulled down in Dublin, but it was too late to recall the product.

There are other infamous mistakes in the world of celebrity endorsements. On occasions there is simply a change of circumstances which could not have been anticipated, worse though is when a celebrity shows contempt or outright dislike of the product he/she is paid to endorse. Britney Spears was repeatedly seen drinking Coco-Cola while endorsing its rival brand Pepsi. Ian Botham was allegedly quoted as saying of Dansk low-alcohol larger that he would never drink the *'gnats piss'* himself, and Helena Bonham Carter declared she never wore makeup despite agreeing to be the face of Yardley.

Celebrity contracts

A good celebrity contract should aim to protect the advertisers and agency from all eventualities, and while some incidents are simply unavoidable the fall out from such occurrences can be reduced. It is essential to:

- choose your celebrity with care in the first place;
- ensure there are clear contractual obligations between the celebrity and advertiser, in particular ensure you cover:
  - the term of the contract

- whether there is an element of exclusivity, for example a prohibition by the celebrity endorsing a similar product
- the fee and if possible tackle re-usage fees from the outset
- a licence to use the celebrity's intellectual property rights in all the relevant media and the territory in which the celebrity image may appear, including the internet if need be
- availability of the celebrity for shoots and promotional events
- the consequences of early termination of the contract;
- insure against the event of death and/or disgrace of the celebrity.

'Death and disgrace' insurance is available to cover the cost of production, pre-booked airtime, costs of withdrawing print and press campaigns, but like all insurance there are limitations. The advertiser will not be able to cover consequential loss of profits, and certain controversial celebrities will not be capable of insurance cover. For example Vinnie Jones, rightly or wrongly, has a reputation for violence. Indeed in December 2003 he pleaded guilty to air rage against another passenger and crew. Jones had a lucrative career endorsing Bacardi. In this case his hard man image was unlikely to damage the brand, but at a time when alcohol advertising to young people was, and still is, under considerable criticism it is not attractive or helpful to have your brand associated with such behaviour. Bacardi withdrew a Vinnie Jones pre-Christmas 2003 commercial following the air rage saga and Herefordshire Police revoked his firearms licence. The advertiser and agency used a different advertisement while they decided whether the actor and former footballer was suitable to remain the public face of the drink. Of course this sort of advertisement is not possible today under the new stricter code rules for alcohol advertising.

The main problem with death and disgrace insurance is defining what is meant by 'disgrace'. The Roy Keane case illustrates the difficulty. Is an argument by a football player with his manager resulting in his expulsion from the team a disgrace? Using the Vinnie Jones example, is his behaviour damaging to the advertiser? Arguably it merely endorses the image he and the advertiser wish to promote.

Agencies should:

- include obligations in the contract concerning the conduct of the celebrity in relation to the product.

  It will be necessary to consider the exact nature of each agreement and include such obligations on the celebrity as are sensible and relevant. Obtaining relevant warranties from a celebrity is important in order to ensure the advertisers' death/ disgrace insurance covers a breach. Thus, if the advertiser were an airline, taking the Vinnie Jones example of air rage referred to above, it would be disastrous not to have investigated his criminal record. It is not unknown for insurers to refuse to honour disgrace clauses in situations where an advertiser and its agency have failed to take reasonable steps to investigate the past conduct of a celebrity;

- include an absolute requirement for media training and education about the product for the celebrity;

- include the ability to claw back fees if the celebrity breaches warranties. While advertisers are unlikely to wish to enforce such clauses through the public arena of the judicial system the sanction should nevertheless be included as an option and penalty for inappropriate behaviour;

- beware of pan European and global advertisements. If the advertisement is appearing in the USA for example, the celebrity may demand an indemnity from the advertiser against any product liability claims.

CONCLUSION

Advertising agencies have used celebrities and politicians in creative, humorous and intelligent ways and it would be a loss to us all if this creativity were prevented. Humour and satire in advertising in the UK contributes to what makes advertising in the UK some of the best and most entertaining in the world. Thus while genuine rights should be protected, it appears the law has got the balance about right at present.

Marina Palomba, Institute of Practitioners in Advertising

Notes

1   W R Cornish *Intellectual Property* 4th Edition para. 16.34
2   *Sports Club, Evelyn and Jocelyn v. HM Inspector of Taxes SC 31s14-16/99*
3   *McCulloch v. Lewis A May (Produce Distributor) (1947) 5 RPC 58*
4   *Merchandising Corporation v. Harpbond [1983] FSR 32*
5   *Elvis Presley Trade Mark [1997] RPC 543*
6   *Eddie Irvine v. TalkSport Radio Limited [2002] IPLR 12, [2002] EWHC 367, Chancery Division*
7   *Halliwell & Ors v. Panini (1997)*
8   British Code of Advertising, Sales Promotion and Direct Marketing, (CAP Code Section 13.1). See also Chapter 2.
9   British Code of Advertising, Sales Promotion and Direct Marketing, (CAP Code Section 13.4). See also Chapter 2.
10 *Secretary of State for the Home Office Department v. Mary Jane Wainwright and Alan Joseph Wainwright HL 16.10.2003*
11 *Douglas/Zeta-Jones v. Hello! magazine November Times 11 April 2003*
12 *Sarah Cox v. Sunday People June 2003*
13 *Naomi Campbell v. Mirror Group Newspapers [2003] QB 633*
14 *Michael Durant v. FSA CA Dec 2003*
15 *Celebrity Sells* by Hamish Pringle, Director General of the IPA, 2004

Comparative advertising

WHAT IS COMPARATIVE ADVERTISING?

Comparative advertising is, legally speaking, one of the most complex areas of the law, and full of potential pitfalls. Commercially speaking, it is also one of the most important forms of marketing to get right. All companies look to grow market share through their advertising, which either directly or indirectly compares their goods/services with their competitors.

It is essential that the issues and risks associated with comparative advertising, and described further in this chapter, are carefully considered when compiling a claims and campaign strategy and before launching any new products or services off the back of strong claims and/or a comparative campaign.

A technical definition of comparative advertising is 'any advertising that explicitly or by implication identifies a competitor, or goods or services offered by a competitor'. Common examples are comparisons in terms of quality, price or performance. It is fairly obvious that direct comparisons with competitors are comparative advertising, but a claim to be the 'best', 'cheapest' or 'fastest' (or whatever the claim might be) is an indirect statement that your competitor is not, and is also therefore a comparison. Comparisons can be specific or generic, for example where advertising is used to criticise a competitor's service or brand generally, as opposed to the specific qualities of a particular product. It also includes the use of advertising to conduct a smear campaign against a competitor.

EXAMPLES OF COMPARATIVE ADVERTISING RULES – PAST AND PRESENT

Before 1994, the UK comparative advertising regime was strict, particularly in relation to the use of trade marks, and competitors *could not* refer to one another by names that were protected by trade mark registration. The 1938 Trade Marks Act meant that competitors in the UK wanting to run a comparative advertising campaign were restricted from using registered third-party marks and instead had to refer to the relative merits of their goods over 'Brand X'. The famous 'take the Pepsi challenge' directly compared the Pepsi brand with the Coke brand, and whilst this was permissible in the US (and very successful with consumers there) such advertising was not permissible in the UK.

The Trade Marks Act 1994 replaced the 1938 Act. In the interests of promoting competition, the new Act *allowed* competitors to refer to their rivals and their goods or services by using the registered trade mark, but only so long as they complied

with the new trade mark rules (very basically, being able to objectively show that the advertisement and mark use was 'honest'). Advertisers began to test the water and ran campaigns that directly compared each other's goods/services. The boundaries were far from clear as the rules were complex, so some advertisements looked to push them as far as possible (and in some eyes went much too far), such as the Ryanair campaign which compared their prices with British Airways under the slogan 'expensive ba****ds'.

There have been a number of cases on the use of trade marks in comparative advertising, and these will be looked at in further detail below.

WHAT REGULATES COMPARATIVE ADVERTISING?

There are a complex variety of advertising controls for comparative advertising ranging from statutory legislation to self-regulation, and from common law to industry best practice. Comparative advertising must, of course, comply with the general as well as specific controls. In particular, the European Comparative Advertising Directive[1] (CAD) regulated comparative advertising across Europe, and was implemented in the UK by the Control of Misleading Advertising Regulations.

In 2008, there was a major shake-up of the existing UK regime brought about by two new sets of rules which came into force on 26 May 2008.

The Consumer Protection from Unfair Trading Regulations 2008 (CPRs) implement the Unfair Commercial Practices Directive 2005[2] (UCPD) and repeal and replace many sections of the Trade Descriptions Act 1968, Consumer Protection Act 1987, Consumer Credit Act 1974 and the Control of Misleading Advertising Regulations

1988. The Business Protection from Misleading Marketing Regulations 2008 (BPRs) implement the Misleading and Comparative Advertising Directive 2006[3] (MCAD).

These developments, and some further laws and legislation that make up the complex web of rules for comparative advertising, are dealt with in more detail below.

These regulations are enforced by a number of regulatory bodies:

- *Advertising Standards Authority (ASA)* – the ASA is the first-stop-shop for any complaints about misleading, harmful or offensive advertising, sales promotions or direct marketing. The ASA reviews reported advertisements under the advertising standards codes (codes for TV, radio and all other types of advertisements). The ASA has no authority to enforce its decisions through the courts but can refer offenders to the OFT or Ofcom who do (e.g. in 2008 they did so in relation to Ryanair);

- *Trading Standards* – monitor claims on websites, shop window displays, and in-store advertising; and

- *Office of Fair Trading (OFT)* – enforces the CPRs and BPRs, although this will be done in conjunction with the ASA, who should remain the first port of call for a complaint.

APPLICABLE LAW AND REGULATION

As the above examples show, agencies must bear in mind a number of different laws and regulations when making comparative claims in advertisements, and all forms of comparative advertising need careful consideration. The rest of this chapter will consider each element in more detail in order to ensure that agencies avoid common pitfalls.

Trade mark infringement

Most comparative advertising will want to refer to a competitor's brand or specific product. Often this will involve the use of the competitor's registered trade mark which therefore could give the owner the option of suing for trade mark infringement if his trademark is used incorrectly.

Generally speaking it is not possible to use another entity's registered trade mark without permission. However, section 10(6) of the 1994 Act provides a defence to trade mark infringement by stating that nothing in the Act prevents *'the use of a registered trade mark by any person for the purpose of identifying goods or services as those of the proprietor or a licensee [but] any such use otherwise than in accordance with honest practices in industrial or commercial matters shall be treated as infringing the registered trade mark if the use without due cause takes unfair advantage of, or is detrimental to, the distinctive character or repute of the trade mark.'*

The majority of trade mark case law since 1994 addressed the meaning of *'honest use'*, *'taking unfair advantage of'*, *'use detrimental to repute'* and how far an advertisement could go in its comparisons between competitors' goods/services. A number of key cases looked at these very issues.

In *Barclays Bank v. RBS Advanta*[4], Barclays, as the proprietor of the trade marks 'BARCLAYCARD', and 'BARCLAY/BARCLAYS', sued RBS when they used those marks in promotional comparative material for a proposed new credit card. Mr Justice Laddie held that Barclays had a weak case in view of section 10(6) of the 1994 Act and that the balance of convenience lay in favour of allowing RBS to continue to refer to the trade marks in their literature. The onus was on Barclays to show that the mark was not being used in accordance with honest practices and '*it was most unlikely that any reasonable reader [of the advertisements] would take that view*'.

In *British Airways v. Ryanair*[5], British Airways brought an action under the 1994 Act for infringement of their trade mark 'BA', and for malicious falsehood, when Ryanair used two advertisements under the headlines 'EXPENSIVE BA....DS!' and 'EXPENSIVE BA'. Mr Justice Jacob (Jacob J) held that sections 10(6) and 11(2)(b) of the 1994 Act saved Ryanair as these sections permit comparative advertising when it is being used to describe goods in accordance with honest practices. Despite the fact the advertisements were actually incorrect in the fares quoted, showing the British Airways fares higher than they were, the court said that the average consumer would not find the price comparison misleading and would expect there to be some conditions to the comparison made. The judge said that in substance the advertisements were true (British Airways was still more expensive) and the comparisons were not significantly unfair. A number of commentators have differed in their views on this, particularly given the disparaging strapline and swear words used.

In *Cable & Wireless v. British Telecommunications*[6], BT made some price comparisons with Cable & Wireless using their trade mark in a brochure. Cable & Wireless were granted an interlocutory injunction. Jacob J held that the objective test to be applied was whether a reasonable trader could honestly have made the statements he made based upon the information that he had. On the facts, it was not established that no honest man would be prepared to put out these calculations as part of his advertising. Further, there was no reasonable likelihood of people being misled by the details in these tables to any significant degree. The judge lifted the interim injunction accordingly.

In summary, therefore, the guidance from the UK courts in relation to the use of a third party's trade marks was to consider whether the use is 'honest'. Would a consumer be likely to take the view, upon being given the full facts available upon reasonable enquiry, that the advertisement is not 'honest'? This honesty is tested against what the members of the public to whom the advertisement was addressed would reasonably expect of an advertisement for that product. Therefore, the test takes account of the fact that members of the public do expect a certain degree of 'puff'. However, how much 'puff' is allowed will depend on the product in question. There are still questions over the extent to which the use can be 'detrimental' or 'take unfair advantage' and advertisers would still be wise to take advice on any such use.

The O$_2$ 'Bubbles' case
The European Court of Justice (ECJ) judgment[7] in June 2008, in the UK trade mark infringement suit *O$_2$ v. H3G*, has clarified the law on trade mark infringement actions in relation to comparative advertisements.

The facts of the O_2 case are as follows. In 2004 Hutchison 3G ('H3G'), a mobile phone service provider, launched a comparative advertising campaign in which it compared its services to O_2's (a leading mobile phone service provider with a distinctive get-up featuring bubbles). H3G, in particular, ran a television commercial which used bubble imagery very similar to O_2's bubbles (O_2 had registered various bubble device marks). In the advertisement the bubbles changed from blue (the O_2 colour) to black as the sound-alike voiceover became quite ominous. O_2 sued for trade mark infringement under the 1994 Act.

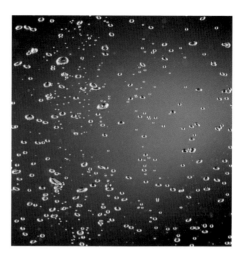

Although on one level the case seemed to some to be fairly pedantic, for O_2 a huge element of the business' value was tied up in its very distinctive brand. The business had been transformed, with the help of IPA member agency Vallance, Carruthers, Coleman and Priest (VCCP), from the old BT Cellnet business into the UK market leader, by creating a hugely successful and award-winning brand identity through high profile and distinctive marketing and appropriate sponsorships, such as Arsenal FC, the England Rugby team, *Big Brother* etc.). Anything which was seen to allow competitors to interfere with and possibly damage or erode that distinctive identity was a major threat, hence O_2's decision to sue. This point was acknowledged by the UK High Court judge, Mr Justice Lewison (Lewison J), who commented in his examination of O_2's case, '*Brands are big business. They can be worth many millions of pounds. The value of the Coca-Cola brand has been said to be worth sixty per cent of the market capitalisation of the Coca-Cola Corporation*'.

Lewison J initially found that there was *prima facie* infringement under section 10(2) on the basis the bubble use was confusingly similar, but that section 10(6) provided a defence for H3G and therefore ruled in their favour. He also rejected the claim of infringement under section 10(3) as the advertisement did not take unfair advantage of, nor denigrate, the O_2 marks.

O_2 appealed (as did H3G against the finding of section 10(2) infringement), but the Court of Appeal agreed with the High Court saying it thought that H3G had a defence. The Court of Appeal's view was also that the CAD was the 'exhaustive' legislation to deal with comparative advertising and not trade mark law. This would in effect have prevented companies suing under trade mark law in future in respect of use of their trade mark in comparative advertising.

Therefore, given the uncertainties over the relationship of the 1994 Act to the CAD and whether the CAD should be viewed as the 'exhaustive' set of rules, the court referred the question of priority between these two governing laws to the ECJ.

The ECJ decision largely agreed with this interpretation, but did leave the door slightly open for trade mark owners to sue in future. The ECJ ruled that:

1. Use of a mark identical or similar to a competitor's registered mark in a comparative advertisement *can* still be regarded as 'trade mark use'.

2. *However*, the provisions of the 1994 Act and those of the CAD are to be interpreted to the effect that a mark owner *cannot* use trade mark rights to stop a competitor using his mark (or a similar sign) in a comparative advertisement, *provided* the advertisement *satisfies* the CAD checklist. In effect, therefore, the CAD overrides the 1994 Act.

3. However, *if* there is likelihood of confusion, then one of the key CAD conditions will not have been satisfied, and therefore a claim under the 1994 Act is still possible.

H3G therefore won the case. Although they had used O$_2$'s registered trade mark bubbles, their use complied with the provisions of the CAD (which are dealt with in more detail below), and therefore they fell within the defence under section 10(6) of the 1994 Act.

Conclusion

This latest ECJ ruling and the BPRs implementation means that 2008 marks a watershed for the use of trade mark rights. The views of some lawyers that trade mark rights can always be relied upon as a tool to prohibit comparative advertising activity, and will take precedence over the misleading and comparative advertising rules have been shown to be completely wrong. The position is quite the opposite: strict compliance with the CAD by one advertiser will always provide a defence to any claim by a trade mark owner in respect of use of the registered trade mark in comparative advertising.

However, agencies should exercise caution. The CAD/BPRs checklist must be followed if you wish to engage in comparative advertising (see page 113). There is still a risk you could be sued for trade mark infringement if there is a likelihood of consumer confusion (because one of the rules would be broken). There is also, arguably, still a risk (although this point was not specifically covered by the ECJ in the O$_2$ case) of being sued under the 1994 Act if the context of the advertisement means that one of the other elements in the CAD checklist has not been met (denigration or discrediting or taking unfair advantage of the reputation of the competitor's mark).

Passing off

A claim in 'passing off' has also been used by companies to attack competitors who they feel have overstepped the mark through a comparative campaign. For a passing-off action to succeed, the claimant must show a number of elements:

- goodwill or reputation attached to the goods and services;
- a misrepresentation (express or implied) on the part of the defendant which leads to confusion or deception in the minds of the customers;
- damage (see also Chapter 1.4).

A good example of this is *McDonald's Hamburgers v. Burger King*[8]. Burger King advertised its 'Whopper' hamburger on cards saying *'It's Not Just Big, Mac'*, continuing

'Unlike some burgers, it's 100 per cent pure beef, flame grilled, never fried, with a unique choice of toppings.' McDonald's brought an action in passing off, trade libel and malicious falsehood. They argued that customers seeing the advertisement would think that they could get a Big Mac from a Burger King establishment, therefore McDonald's goodwill would be diluted. On passing off, McDonald's were able to convince the court that, despite clear Burger King branding, the advertising would confuse customers. As far-fetched as this argument may now seem, the court accepted the argument that customers would be likely to purchase a Whopper instead of a Big Mac. The court held that there would be a direct loss of revenue to McDonald's by virtue of lost sales resulting from the advertising and granted an injunction to restrain this.

Defamation and malicious falsehood

Defamation, and in particular the tort of malicious falsehood, has also been the basis of claims to prevent comparative advertising campaigns. Details of the components of these are set out in Chapter 1.5. The following cases illustrate how these claims have been used to attack inaccuracies in advertisements.

In *Compaq v. Dell*[9], Compaq claimed that Dell's advertising amounted to a malicious falsehood because the claim that Dell equipment was cheaper but just as fast and powerful as the equivalent Compaq machines was false. Compaq argued that Dell had not made it sufficiently clear that the comparison was not strictly like for like. The price quoted for the Dell equipment was a special promotional price as opposed to its usual price and was being compared with the full recommended retail price for the Compaq equipment. The judge in this case held that the balance of convenience lay in favour of Compaq and granted an injunction to restrain Dell's advertising.

In *Vodafone Group & Vodafone v. Orange*[10], Vodafone brought an action in response to an Orange advertising campaign, the basic slogan of which was *'On average, Orange users save £20 compared to Vodafone…equivalent tariffs.'* In this case, Jacob J held that Vodafone could not prove the elements of the tort of malicious falsehood, i.e. that the statement complained of was false; that it was made maliciously; that it was made either recklessly as to whether it is true or false or knowing it to be false; and that the making of the statement was calculated to cause Vodafone pecuniary damage. In fact, the judge found the statement to be true, describing the claim in malicious falsehood as 'hopeless'. Therefore Vodafone lost the action for malicious falsehood.

In *Jupiter Unit Trust v. Johnson Fry*[11], Jupiter took issue over Johnson's ISA advertisements claiming defamation and malicious falsehood. In the defamation claim Jupiter complained that the advertisements suggested that Jupiter were unable or unwilling to work as hard as, or as effectively, in the management of its funds as Johnson and therefore achieved a substantially lower return on them than Johnson, leading investors to the conclusion that it would be foolish to entrust their money with Jupiter. The judge in this case, however, held that no reasonable reader of the advertisement could come to the conclusion that it contained any meaning defamatory of Jupiter in relation to its trading reputation, and the defamation claim therefore failed.

In its malicious falsehood claim, Jupiter complained that Johnson had maliciously made false statements. The judge, following a number of leading cases including *Vodafone v. Orange*, said that Johnson had not, in 'puffing' its own products, overstepped the permissible limit of denigration or disparagement of Jupiter's products, so that a reasonable man would take the claim seriously. The judge said the advertisements were *'a clear example of comparative advertising with a degree of knocking.'*, and the malicious falsehood claim also failed.

In *DSG Retail (t/a Currys) v. Comet*[12], Currys sought an injunction against Comet when Comet used posters claiming their price was lower than a Curry's '10% off' and '£10 off' weekend promotion. The judge in this case held that the posters were directed at Currys, that their meaning was clear and that the claims were, on the evidence, false. Further, the judge considered that Comet must have known that the statements were false when they were made, and that the statements were intended and likely to be taken seriously and amounted to a denigration or disparagement of Currys goods. As such, there was a malicious falsehood and a likelihood of damage and the injunction was therefore allowed.

In *British Airways v. Ryanair*[5] (see page 108), Jacob J held that there was no difference in the measure of damages recoverable between a claim for trade mark infringement and one for malicious falsehood. However, the tort of malicious falsehood requires a higher standard of liability than trade mark infringement. The judge commented that, although in some cases it might be worthwhile obtaining a judgment for malicious falsehood for publicity reasons, that was not the case here and, notwithstanding that Ryanair had incorrectly illustrated the higher cost of British Airways fares (although the judge agreed that the fares were higher), held the claim for malicious falsehood did not even 'get off the ground'.

Copyright infringement

Companies looking to take issue with a competitor's marketing have also used the claim of copyright infringement to prevent use of trade marks. When conducting a comparative advertising campaign it is necessary to be extremely careful before reproducing any graphics, logos, photographs, music, straplines, and other 'works' used by a competitor and which may be protected by copyright. Logos are usually regarded as artistic work, and consequently protected by copyright. Agencies are therefore advised never to use a competitor's logo.

Regulation

As mentioned above, a series of EU Directives have sought to deal with the problem of comparative advertising which has been notoriously tricky, not just in the UK but across Europe which had a wide variety of different local laws. The Comparative Advertising Directive[1] (CAD) was implemented in order to try to give advertisers something of a 'level playing field'. This was implemented into UK law by way of the Control of Misleading Advertisements (Amendment) Regulations 2000. However, two new Directives in this area were implemented in 2008, repealing this previous legislation.

Business Protection from Misleading Marketing Regulations 2008 (BPRs)

The CAD has now been replaced by a new Misleading and Comparative Advertising Directive[3] (MCAD) which was implemented in the UK as of 26 May 2008 by the Business Protection from Misleading Marketing Regulations 2008 (BPRs). This is aimed primarily at business-to-business advertising.

Consumer Protection from Unfair Trading Regulations 2008 (CPRs)

The other European Directive, the Unfair Commercial Practices Directive[2] (UCPD), was aimed primarily at business-to-consumer advertising. It has been implemented in the UK by the Consumer Protection from Unfair Trading Regulations 2008 (CPRs), and also came into force on 26 May 2008.

The BPRs checklist for comparative advertising

The BPRs now permit comparative advertising *provided* it complies with ALL of the following key rules:

- it is not misleading (under either the BPRs or the CPRs – so this covers both misleading businesses and consumers);

- it compares products meeting the same needs or intended for the same purpose;
- it objectively compares one or more material, relevant, verifiable and representative features of those products, which may include price;
- it does not create confusion among traders (i) between the advertiser and a competitor or (ii) between the trade marks, trade names, other distinguishing marks or products of the advertiser and those of a competitor;
- it does not discredit or denigrate the trade marks, trade names, other distinguishing marks, products, activities, or circumstances of a competitor;
- for products with designation of origin, it relates in each case to products with the same designation;
- it does not take unfair advantage of the reputation of a trade mark, trade name or other distinguishing marks of a competitor or of the designation of origin of competing products;
- it does not present products as imitations or replicas of products bearing a protected trade mark or trade name.

'Product' in this context means 'any goods or services and includes immovable property, rights and obligations'.

The BPRs define 'advertising' as:

> *'any form of representation which is made in connection with a trade, business, craft or profession in order to promote the supply or transfer of a product and 'advertiser' shall be construed accordingly'.*

The BPRs further define 'comparative advertising' as:

> *'advertising which in any way, either explicitly or by implication, identifies a competitor or a product offered by a competitor'.*

In short, therefore, the BPRs set out an all-inclusive checklist which applies widely and whether or not a competitor is expressly identified in the advertising. Agencies should ensure that any comparative advertising complies with this checklist.

STATUTORY AND SELF-REGULATORY CODES AND BODIES

In addition to specific statutes, agencies seeking to make direct (or indirect) comparisons need to be aware of, and comply with, the regulatory advertising standards codes.

The Committee of Advertising Practice is the industry body responsible for the UK's advertising codes for broadcast and non-broadcast advertisements (the 'CAP Codes'). These are enforced by the Advertising Standards Authority – see Chapter 2.

The non-broadcast CAP Code also applies to website content for sales promotions and advertisements in paid-for space. It mirrors the EU Directive by requiring that:

- comparisons should be clear and fair;
- advertisers should not unfairly attack or discredit other businesses or their products;
- advertisers should not make unfair use of the goodwill attached to a trade mark;
- no advertisement should so closely resemble any other that it misleads or confuses; and
- claims should be capable of substantiation.

In practice, under the non-broadcast CAP Code agencies must seek to ensure that their comparisons with competitors are fairly selected and explained. It will not be enough, for example, to state that one car is 'better than' another simply because it has a higher top speed, particularly if the other car has, say, better fuel consumption or other superior qualities. On the other hand, in the same situation it may be acceptable to claim that the car is 'faster', provided that it is clear that the comparison is limited to speed.

The broadcast CAP Code (which comes in two parts: the Radio Advertising Standards Code (RASC) and the Television Advertising Standards Code (TASC)) also allows comparative advertising, but in the interests of competition:

- the customer must not be misled;
- the principles of fair competition must be complied with (although this is not in the TASC which instead states that the spirit of the law and not just the letter must be complied with);
- the basis of comparison must not be chosen so as to confer an unfair advantage;
- points of comparison must be capable of substantiation;
- there can be no superiority claims on the basis of selective comparisons (this is not in the TASC).

Both broadcast CAP Codes copy out the comparative advertising rules while the non-broadcast CAP Code implies that compliance is required.

PENALTIES/SANCTIONS

A breach of the applicable statutory provisions can be serious, given that in many cases a breach involves a criminal sanction by way of a fine (which can be unlimited) and a risk of liability for 'consenting' and 'conniving', or even just 'negligent', directors, managers, secretaries or other similar officers (e.g. marketing/sales directors, etc.) who may be prosecuted on a personal level and risk imprisonment.

Separately, if sued by a competitor by way of a civil action, a company might face a potential injunction, immediately preventing further use of the material (with the knock-on effect of the loss of any media that has already been paid for), a claim for damages, an order for delivery up or destruction of said material and, of course, costs.

Aside from fines and the civil remedies mentioned above, an infringing company may also face censure from one of the industry regulators, usually the ASA, in relation to breach of one of the regulatory Codes. In serious cases these regulators have the power to require an advertising campaign to be immediately pulled. Again, this can result in serious wasted expenditure, as well as significant brand damage and negative publicity.

The ASA can also impose a boycott of the relevant media, withdraw financial incentives or subject an advertiser to mandatory pre-vetting procedures, and can refer advertisers to the OFT. This happened in 2008 with the ASA referring the airline Ryanair to the OFT.

Both the BPRs and CPRs provide the OFT and Trading Standards with significantly enhanced powers to investigate complaints, request information, enter premises (without warrant), seize products and documents, break open containers to get access to goods and documents and issue directions. It is also an offence to 'obstruct' an officer of the OFT or Trading Standards.

The OFT also has the power to seek an injunction to prevent specific misleading advertising, and the activities of advertisers with a track record of producing misleading material. Generally, as mentioned above, the OFT requires complaints to come via one of the regulatory bodies such as the ASA and will, more often than not, act on a referral from one of the bodies, as in the Ryanair case. However, complaints from individuals without first going through one of the 'established channels' may, exceptionally, be entertained.

Advertisers should note that under the new regulations (the BPRs and the CPRs) a misleading advertisement could result in a two-year prison sentence or an unlimited fine, or both. However, this sanction is not applicable to an advertisement that infringes the comparative advertising rules (so long as it does not break the rules by being a misleading advertisement). Advertisers who break the comparative advertising rules ultimately face a court injunction (and costs) not to repeat the advertisement, and of course they may face a private suit with potential damages.

OPTIONS FOR THE AGGRIEVED

If a party who is the subject of a comparative advertising campaign feels aggrieved, there are a number of options available for remedy. When deciding which avenue to pursue, one of the principal questions should be: 'What solution would we like?' For example, if damages are sought, a civil remedy is the only option. Alternatively, if it is desired to prevent publication, depending on the media involved, several options are open. Another consideration is the speed and cost balance.

If some urgency is desired, it is as well to bear in mind that finding grounds to sue directly (e.g. for copyright infringement or passing off or trade libel) allows the advertiser to move at its own pace and control the process. However, it can be very expensive going the court route and there is the risk of further costs awards (from the competitor's side) if the advertiser loses.

Regulatory action (whether OFT, Trading Standards or ASA) is not guaranteed (although there is a duty to act) and the timing of investigations and adjudications can vary a great deal – although the ASA has put a lot of effort into speeding up its process.

One major benefit of the regulatory process is its relative low cost and the fact the administrative and cost burden is largely on the shoulders of the regulator; once the papers have been put together and filed with them, the advertiser can sit back to a large degree while the regulator goes to work and the competitor has to substantiate, answer queries, adduce evidence and so on. It can be a very cost-effective way to secure an 'injunction' and prevent the comparison from being made.

The aggrieved must also think carefully about pursuing dual remedies. Although in some cases, where available, more than one remedy can certainly be sought and would be the right thing to do, this is not always the case. For example, it is important to note the ASA will not investigate a complaint while another remedy is being pursued elsewhere. Furthermore, in *Cable & Wireless v. BT*[6] the judge criticised the claimant's claim for both trade mark infringement and malicious falsehood. He made similar comments in *British Airways v. Ryanair*[5]. Such criticisms often have costs implications.

CONCLUSION

As one can see from the above, comparative advertising is a highly complex area, made all the more so by the high degree of change brought about in 2008 by the CPRs and BPRs implementing the new EU Directives into UK law. This is the biggest shake up of UK/EU marketing, trading and consumer law for many years.

Much of the UK legislation that businesses were previously familiar with that governed marketing, pricing, trade descriptions, claims and so on, has been repealed or revoked and there are new criminal offences, definitions, tests, significantly increased enforcement powers and sanctions to get to grips with.

With the O_2 case, 2008 has also seen some very important ECJ guidance and clarification of the role of trade mark law in advertising and its relationship with the comparative advertising rules set out in the Comparative Advertising Directive (as just amended).

This all gives greater clarity to those seeking to engage in comparisons using the registered trade marks of a competitor; such comparisons using others' trade marks are permitted provided the CAD/MCAD rules are followed.

Certainly, some of the changes should, in theory, make it easier for the comparative advertiser, but the reality of the increased sanctions and number of hurdles to navigate means advice should certainly be sought to help put it into practice in the least risky way. Some basics remain. Consider well in advance whether any proposed statement is 100% true and capable of substantiation. Substantiation data robust enough to withstand rigorous examination is needed. Attempts to stretch the truth with claims almost always come unstuck and if they are also 'misleading' could, for example, allow the possibility of a trade mark claim. Like should be compared with like, with no misleading exaggerations or omissions.

In summary:

- comparisons, whether explicit or implied, are notoriously fraught;
- comparisons can expose advertisers to litigation from competitors and prosecutions from regulators;
- comparative claims need detailed, independently reviewed substantiation data to be robust;
- comply with the new Misleading and Comparative Advertising Directive rules/ checklist;
- ensure your comparison or claim is 'honest' and not 'unfair' (is it like for like?);
- note increased regulator powers to investigate and fine/prison risk for officers/ managers;
- seek specialist advice at any early stage – prevention is almost always better than the cure!

Rafi Azim-Khan, Pillsbury Winthrop Shaw Pittman LLP

Notes

1   Comparative Advertising Directive (CAD) 97/55/EC
2   Unfair Commercial Practices Directive 2005/29/EC
3   Misleading and Comparative Advertising Directive 2006/114/EC (MCAD).
4   *Barclays Bank plc v. RBS Advanta* ChD [1996] RPC 307.
5   *British Airways plc v. Ryanair Ltd* ChD [2000] FSR 541.
6   *Cable & Wireless plc & Anor v. British Telecommunications plc* CHD (1998) FSR 383.
7   ECJ judgments are binding in the UK.
8   *McDonald's Hamburgers Ltd v. Burger King* CA [1986] FSR 45.
9   *Compaq Computer Corporation v. Dell Computer Corporation Ltd* ChD [1992] FSR 93.
10 *Vodafone Group plc & Vodafone Ltd v. Orange Personal Communications Services Ltd* Chd [1997] FSR 34.
11 *Jupiter Unit Trust Managers v. Johnson Fry Asset Managers plc* [2000] EWHC QB 110
12 *DSG Retail Ltd (t/a Currys) v. Comet Group plc* QPD 2002 EWHC 116.

Contemporary art in advertising

INTRODUCTION

Ever since Andy Warhol transformed commercial graphics into lucrative prints, artists have borrowed from the world of advertising. So is it fair to criticise advertisers for 'borrowing' ideas from contemporary artists? Arguably, the relationship between advertisers and contemporary artists is a two-way street, although it is probably fair to say that traffic is heavier in the direction of advertisers. Does this mean that advertisers are free to imitate contemporary art as they please? Similarly, do contemporary artists have a monopoly in their ideas?

In this chapter, we shall consider the boundaries of permissible copying of contemporary art in advertising. We shall focus on the use of art in advertising, as opposed to the commissioning of art for advertising.

There is an ongoing effort to harmonise the law on copyright and related intellectual property rights in the European Union (EU). However, important differences remain amongst EU Member States. In this chapter, we shall focus on the position in the UK. It would be wrong to assume that the courts in other European countries would share the view of the English courts. In the USA, we find the same general principles of copyright and other intellectual property rights, but here again there are important differences in the way US courts apply them. When considering the issues raised in this chapter, we have assumed that English law applies.

USING ARTISTS' WORKS IN ADVERTISING

Art has been used in advertising since the 19th century. Artists such as Doré, Daumier and Matisse contributed to advertising images. In the 1880s, Pears' soaps were advertised using paintings bought at the Royal Academy.

Art has been used in advertising in several ways:

- advertisements have included existing works of art as a background image or as part of a logo. Well known images have been used by advertisers, for example *The Milkmaid* by Vermeer for French brand of yoghurts Chambourcy, and *le Moulin de la Galette* by Renoir for French beer Kronenbourg. These images are in the public domain;

- artistic styles have inspired advertisements, for example Impressionism or cubism. When the tails of its aircraft were painted with colourful designs, British Airways took inspiration from various artistic styles;

- the style or the creativity of a particular artist has inspired advertisements. Examples of advertisements 'in the manner of' include an Air France advertising campaign inspired by paintings of Dufy, and the Mondrian style of design on L'Oréal hair styling products.

Using art in advertising, or making references to art or a particular artist, can be beneficial to both the artist and the advertiser. There have been many instances of happy collaborations between artists and advertisers.

Conflicts have arisen where the artist is not consulted or heard, or where his contribution is not properly acknowledged. Conflicts may also arise because the artist is uninformed, believing for example that he has a monopoly in his creative ideas, no matter how those ideas have been expressed or implemented.

Conflicts between artists and advertisers are seldom tried in court, for several reasons. Artists can feel ill-equipped to engage in legal fights against powerful, global companies. They are often unable to afford the expenses of legal action. Companies themselves may prefer to settle where the amount at stake is comparatively small. As a result, legal precedents do not abound.

Before addressing how advertisers have used contemporary art, let us consider briefly the legal protection afforded to contemporary art in the UK.

CONTEMPORARY ART – BUT IS IT PROTECTED?

Contemporary art has broken traditional boundaries. The courts have attempted to apply existing legal principles to new forms of art such as video displays, installations, 'ready-made' art and appropriation art, with widely differing results, often dependent on the subjective appreciation of the courts. Accordingly, in a number of areas, the law is in a state of flux. This can discourage claimants from taking legal action because the outcome of a trial, and their potential liability for legal costs, are too uncertain. For advertisers, the state of flux has its advantages in that it allows more flexibility to settle disputes with artists when they arise. There is also the concern that case law might extend artists' rights in ways that might prejudice advertisers from taking inspiration or borrowing from artists' works.

Artists looking to protect their art from appropriation for commercial purposes have mainly three options. They can claim copyright infringement, passing off or breach of their moral rights. They may also, in certain cases, rely on breach of confidence where the artist has taken steps to keep his work confidential.

Copyright

Under the Copyright, Designs and Patents Act 1988 (CDPA), copyright protects the original works of living artists and of artists who died less than 70 years ago, subject to certain conditions.

Is it an artistic work?

Any claim of copyright infringement will require, first, that the artist show that the work is protected by copyright. The definition of 'artistic work' in section 4(1) of the CDPA by reference to its nature and support, e.g. a painting, a collage or a photograph, requires that the courts consider whether a particular work fits within the definition. Works outside the boundaries of traditional art forms may not be protected if they cannot be squeezed into one of the categories in section 4(1).

The wording of section 4 makes it clear that, except for works of 'artistic craftsmanship', 'artistic quality' is not a relevant factor. However, if a work cannot easily fit within a category, the courts may consider the intention of its creator and its status. If the author is known as an artist, the status of an ordinary object may be elevated to that of a work of art – like Marcel Duchamp's *Urinal*. Accordingly, an ordinary object in a certain context may attract copyright although it would not attract copyright by itself. The same issue can arise in relation to an object of design. In *Metix v. GH Maughan*[1], the court would not agree that plastic moulds used for making cartridges were sculptures protected by copyright under the CDPA. This was because those who designed the moulds did not consider themselves, or were not considered by others, as artists and they were not concerned with the shape or appearance of what they were making, but with their functional effect. This suggests that where the author is concerned with the shape or appearance of a functional object (e.g. a fashion designer), the object may attract copyright protection as an 'artistic work'. However, this is far from clear.

If a contemporary work does not fit within any of the categories in section 4(1)(a) (being graphic work, photograph, sculpture or collage), can the artist claim that his art is a 'work of artistic craftsmanship' (section 4(1)(c))? The courts seem to struggle with the definition of this category, and unfortunately for artists (and perhaps fortunately for advertisers), it cannot be seen as the category of last resort when the work in question has failed the test of the other categories listed in section 4(1). To qualify, the work must clearly be made by craftsmen. There seems to be a consensus that the utility of the work does not prevent it from attracting copyright protection (*George Hensher v. Restawile Upholstery*[2]). The intention of its author seems to be a consideration too, although it is not decisive. In that case, it was held that a drawing room furniture suite did not fall within the definition of 'work of artistic craftsmanship'. In a later case, a baby raincosy was similarly denied copyright protection (*Merlet v. Mothercare*[3]). A film set, on the other hand, was held as arguably qualifying as a work of artistic craftsmanship (*Shelley Films v. Rex Features*[4]). So was an Ossie Clark dress (*Radley Gowns v. Costas Syrou*[5]). It is difficult to find a thread amongst these cases. The subjective appreciation of the court seems to play a part, perhaps unsurprisingly since the wording of section 4(1)(c) requires them to make a judgement on whether there is craftsmanship and that craftsmanship has artistic appeal. Worryingly perhaps, judges have on occasion agreed that they are not called to make aesthetic judgements whilst basing their decision on such a judgement. The examples of the drawing room furniture suite and the baby raincosy are cases in point (see, for example, Lord Reid in *George Hensher v. Restawile Upholstery*[2]). The view expressed in *Merlet v. Mothercare*[3] that a work of artistic craftsmanship is protected if it is a work of art, appears to exclude from copyright protection many works of design (from furniture to household goods and fashion). In a case involving a dispute between two fashion designers, the court declined to consider fashion garments (a sweater, a cardigan and a shirt) as capable of attracting copyright protection as works of artistic craftsmanship. The court was willing, however, to recognise that the garments attracted unregistered design rights (although that decision was reversed on appeal) (*Guild v. Eskander*[6]). In conclusion on this point, the courts' interpretation of the phrase 'works of artistic craftsmanship' is far from settled.

A case involving the pop group Oasis illustrates the difficulty in matching a particular work with the definition of 'artistic work' in section 4(1). Photographs were taken of the members of the pop group in a scene consisting of a white Rolls-Royce car positioned in the swimming pool of a hotel, together with various other props. The intention was to use one of the photographs on the cover of the group's forthcoming album. A third party took photographs of the shoot and published them. It was accepted that one of the photographs taken by the third party was very similar to one of the photographs taken by the group's photographer. The group claimed copyright in the scene. This was rejected by the court on the basis that the scene was neither a sculpture, nor a collage, nor a work of artistic craftsmanship. Nor was it a dramatic performance because it was static. Accordingly, it did not warrant copyright protection (*Creation Records v. News Group Newspapers*[7]).

Is it an original work?

The next question is whether the work is 'original'. Only original works attract copyright protection. The standard required is traditionally low. The artist will need to show that some skills and labour have gone into making the work. Skills and labour may be trivial, provided that they are visually significant. Accordingly, the precise reproduction of an artwork, even if it required considerable skills and labour, will lack the necessary originality. On the other hand, the photograph of an object will generally qualify for copyright protection (separate from any copyright in the object itself) on the grounds that there is an element of skill and labour involved in making the photograph. Given the low standard required for the originality of a work, that test is likely to be met by almost any artistic work, unless the work is copied from another work and so cannot be said to originate from its author (*University of London Press v. University Tutorial Press*[8]).

Is the work sufficiently permanent?

Another question is whether the work is sufficiently permanent to attract copyright. In the case of literary, dramatic or musical works, copyright will subsist in the work only if it is recorded in writing or otherwise. There are no equivalent provisions for artistic works, although the traditional copyright distinction made between the idea and its expression suggests that the expression must at least be capable of being perceived and communicated. It was held that a work of 'kinetic art' (a picture made of sand, and in this case, other substances) was not sufficiently permanent to attract copyright protection (*Komesaroff v. Mickle*[9]). Similarly, the scene of assembled objects in a swimming pool with members of the pop group Oasis was deemed too ephemeral to attract copyright protection, lasting only a few hours (*Creation Records v. News Group Newspaper*[7]). However, the proposition that something that has a mere transient existence cannot qualify as a sculpture was rejected in *Metix v. G.H. Maughan*[1].

Passing off

Artists have relied on the law of passing off to protect their work. In order to succeed, an artist must show that firstly, he has acquired a reputation or good will for his artworks, secondly, that reputation or good will has been misrepresented, and thirdly, this misrepresentation has caused him damage.

Misrepresentation is a key element. The question will be whether a substantial number of viewers are being misled (or will be misled) about the authorship of the work which, the artist argues, passes off as his own work. This could be the case where an artist has developed a specific style to which viewers would generally associate that particular artist, e.g. colour-painted images of famous people by Andy Warhol, although even in that case, passing off may be difficult to prove in the case of a dead artist (e.g. an image of Britney Spears 'in the manner of Andy Warhol'). The English courts seem generally reluctant to accept that a claim for passing off can succeed where someone adopted or imitated the style of an artist (*Gordon Fraser Gallery v. Tatt*[10]).

Moral rights

Moral rights in the UK include the right to be identified as the author of an artwork, also called 'right of paternity', and the right to object to certain derogatory treatments of one's artwork, also called 'right of integrity'. Alongside those two moral rights, the CDPA added the right to object to false attribution and the right to privacy of certain photographs and films.

The right of paternity gives the artist the right to be identified as the author of the work whenever the work is published commercially, provided the artist has asserted his paternity right, for example by signing his work. Unless the artist has waived this moral right, the artist could claim infringement if his work is being used in an advertisement without an acknowledgment that it is his work. The right to object to derogatory treatment of a work arises where the treatment amounts to a distortion or mutilation of the work, or the treatment is otherwise prejudicial to the honour or reputation of the artist. If through digital manipulation the work is substantially altered, this may amount to derogatory treatment.

There are few reported cases dealing with moral rights in the UK. Moral rights were introduced only in August 1989 when the CDPA came into force. Moral rights are more likely to be invoked in order to stop someone from using an artist's work in a certain way rather than in a claim for compensation. Indeed, compensation awarded solely on the basis of a breach of moral rights is likely to be substantially lower than compensation awarded for breach of copyright.

WHAT HAVE I DONE TO DESERVE THIS (CLAIM)?

Style

The use in advertising of a particular style can be problematic. If a substantial part of a protected image is copied, for example by keeping the lines and changing the colours, it is arguable that there has been a breach of the artist's copyright. On the other hand, if the advertisement is inspired by a particular style practised by several artists, for example cubism or pointillism, this is unlikely to constitute a breach of anyone's copyright. This is a matter of degree. Several years ago, a whisky company produced an advertisement with a drooping chair, a drooping book and a drooping bottle. The advertisement was obviously inspired by Dali's drooping *Clock*. However, the advertisement was unlikely to have infringed Dali's copyright because Dali does not have a monopoly on drooping objects. At about the same time, a company ran an advertisement depicting men raining down from the sky on to a row of houses. The advertisement was clearly inspired by a painting by Magritte showing businessmen in bowler-hats falling out of the sky. This might have been an infringement of Magritte's copyright if it were found that the advertisement had 'borrowed' the theme, style and colours of the original painting, thereby copying a substantial part of it.

Name

Companies have relied on the fame and prestige of artists to market their products or services. Examples include the use by Citroën of the name Picasso to market a car, and the use by Iberia of the name Dali on one of its aircraft. By associating the name Picasso to its Citroën Xsara, the company estimates that it has saved about 30% in marketing the car.[11] However, members of the Picasso family have complained about

the use of the artist's name to market a car. In the UK, trade mark law would have protected the name 'Picasso' had it been successfully registered as a trade mark. Whether the name could have been registered as a trade mark in relation to cars is uncertain. Earlier cases have involved the names 'Elvis Presley' and 'Jane Austen', which were both sought as trade marks for toiletries. In both cases, it was ruled that the public would not view the names as a badge of origin of the products for which the trade mark was sought, and therefore they could not be registered as trade marks for those products (*Elvis Presley Trade Mark* and *Jane Austen Trade Mark*[12]). Factors the courts will consider in determining whether an artist's name can be sufficiently distinctive as to be taken as an indication of trade origin include the extent of the reputation of the artist, whether there is a trade in the artist's memorabilia, established rights in the name and the type of goods for which registration is sought. Paradoxically, the more famous the artist, the more difficult it will be to show distinctiveness. The courts will be reluctant to grant monopoly rights in a famous name especially, it would seem, if that name has been applied to a range of merchandise goods bearing the name or image of the artist.

Taking 'inspiration' from a protected work

At one end of the scale there is the blatant intellectual property theft, a carbon copy of a protected work. Although copying may involve technically complex methods, the issue is straightforward once the artist can show that an advertisement is a copy of the whole of his work. At the other end there is the open-ended exchange about ideas and styles that is one of the distinguishing marks of creation. Judging the much more common, and yet more subtle, issues of 'influence', 'inspiration' or 'borrowing' for commercial advantages is much more difficult.

There have been several recent instances of allegations of copyright infringement by artists against advertising agencies and their clients.

Gillian Wearing came to prominence as an artist in December 1992 with a series of photographs that appeared in *The Face* magazine. She asked random members of the public to write down what came into their minds on a sign, and she photographed them holding that sign. The series was called 'Signs'. The idea was simple but effective. It was taken up by an advertising agency in a campaign for Volkswagen.

Swiss artists Peter Fischli and David Weiss have argued that an advertisement for the Honda Accord car is based on their 1987 30-minute film which explores the impact of chain reactions on objects. They claimed that 'Cog', a slow-motion ballet of gears, levers and other parts of a Honda Accord that celebrates the automobile's precision engineering, was taken from their own work *Der Lauf der Dinge*.

In some cases, the acknowledgment of an artist's contribution as the inspiration of a campaign can help assuage the artist's concerns about appropriation. However, an acknowledgment does not always address the artist's concern about endorsement of a particular product. This can be an issue for the artist who through an advertising campaign may be perceived as having endorsed the advertised product.

Contemporary art is especially vulnerable where the artist's idea does not require artistic skills to implement. Simple ideas can be very effective, and advertisers have been tempted to borrow ideas from artists. The Volkswagen 'Sign' campaign is a case in point. However, copyright does not protect the idea, only the expression of the idea. In order to be copyright infringement, the expression of an idea must be copied, rather than the idea itself (*Designers Guild v. Russell Williams*[13]). Accordingly, unless the advertisement copies the physical expression of the idea, the artist will find it difficult to show copyright infringement. The artist may succeed in showing passing off, but as we have seen the tests are relatively stringent and the artists may struggle to show misrepresentation by the advertiser.

The three cases below give practical examples of the boundaries of acceptable copying by advertisers.

The case of the Guinness advertisement

Mehdi Norowzian, a film director, brought an action for breach of copyright against Guinness and Arks, an Irish advertising agency. Norowzian alleged that the television advertisement for Guinness, featuring a man performing a fitful dance whilst waiting for his pint to settle, was copied from a short film called *Joy* which Norowzian had produced and submitted to Arks a few years before.

In the Guinness advertisement, called 'Anticipation', there were two characters (a drinker and a barman) but an editing technique similar to the technique used by Norowzian in *Joy* was used showing the dancing man performing a series of jerky movements which could not have been performed in reality, giving the film a 'surreal' effect.

The court was asked whether 'Anticipation', by reproducing the essential feature of *Joy*, namely the 'jump-cutting' editing technique, had been a copy of *Joy* within the meaning of the CDPA. The argument put forward by Norowzian was that Guinness had infringed his copyright in *Joy* by copying a substantial part of the film. The court answered that there could not be infringement of copyright in a film unless the whole or a part of the film itself has been copied, for example by a photographic process or by copying it onto a disc or a video (*Norowzian v. Arks*[14]). Copying by imitating a substantial part of a film did not amount to an infringement of copyright in the film. As we shall see when considering copyright infringement of artistic works, subject to certain conditions, copying by imitating a substantial part of a protected artistic work is, by contrast, a breach of copyright in the artistic work.

The court of first instance then decided that the film 'Anticipation' itself could not be a dramatic work, only the recording of a dramatic work. The question was whether the performance recorded by the film *Joy* was a dramatic work capable of attracting copyright protection. The court answered in the negative because in this case, the work shown in the film was not capable of being physically performed in real life (*Norowzian v. Arks*[15]).

The Court of Appeal disagreed. It considered that the film itself was capable of qualifying for copyright protection as a dramatic work, irrespective of whether the underlying dance was or was not a dramatic work. The Court of Appeal then considered whether 'Anticipation' copied all or a substantial part of the film *Joy*. It decided that it did not. While it accepted that there was a 'striking similarity' between the filming and editing styles and techniques used by the respective directors of the two films, the court submitted that there was no copyright in mere style or technique.

Each film had its own subject matter and it could not be argued that one copied the other (*Norowzian v. Arks*[16]). Accordingly, Norowzian failed in his copyright infringement action against Guinness.

The case of the Swedish doll

Another interesting case arose at about the same time in Sweden in connection with an advertisement for a radio station, representing a reporter holding a microphone before the face of an inflatable doll, which clearly resembled the figure in Munch's famous painting, *The Scream*. Munch died in 1944, so *The Scream* is still protected by copyright in Sweden (and in the UK). The estate of Munch sued for breach of copyright. The Swedish Court of Appeal found that the representation of the doll was clearly copied from the figure in *The Scream*. The fact that the figure was represented on a different support was irrelevant. The doll was an adaptation of the figure in the painting and infringed the artist's copyright. The court rejected the argument that the doll was a parody, for the court did not agree that the doll made a ridiculous or amusing impression different from the impression given by the figure in the painting (*HEM v. Sveriges Radio Aktiebolag*[17]). So in this case, the advertiser lost against the copyright claimant.

This raises the issue of whether a parody is or is not copyright infringement. Parody may include an element of satire or ridicule, or it may use the work that is the object of the parody for another effect. Unlike plagiarism, where the intention is to conceal the appropriation of another work, in parody one relies on the fact that the viewers are well aware of the subject matter of the parody. In some European countries, including Sweden, parody is a defence against a claim of copyright infringement. Not so in the UK. In this country, the defence of parody is not available as a matter of law, and a parody may also infringe the artist's moral right protecting against the derogatory treatment of his work. However, in practice, if the emphasis of the work is clearly on parody rather than on copying, and there is an acknowledgment of the author of the original work, the risk of infringement is reduced.

The Copyright Directive 2001 provides that Member States may make 'caricature, parody or pastiche' a defence against a claim of copyright infringement.[18] The defence of parody is currently not available in the UK but its introduction is under review (Consultation on Proposed Changes to Copyright Exceptions, UK Intellectual Property Office, closed on 8 April 2008). However, parody is available as a defence in the USA under the doctrine of 'fair use'. In *Annie Leibovitz v. Paramount Pictures*[19] for example, a New York Federal district court held that a parody that appears in the form of an advertisement can constitute fair use of a copyright work.

The case of the Habitat advertisement

More recently, Andy Goldsworthy, a British artist, claimed copyright infringement and passing off against Habitat. The advertising agency Devarieuxvillaret ran an advertising campaign for Habitat which showed a pair of wooden chairs protruding from a melting snowball. This was reminiscent of the artist's earlier show during which he exhibited, on the streets of London, 14 snowballs which when melting revealed the

natural material of the sticks and stones trapped inside. The dispute was settled out of court so we do not know if the artist would have succeeded in his claim in the courts.

Had the case gone to court, there might have been some debate as to whether the snowballs qualified as original artistic works attracting copyright protection. It is not clear that there was a sufficient element of permanence given that the snowballs would melt. The decision in *Creation Records v. News Group Newspapers*[7] suggests that that element might have been lacking, although the proposition that something that has a mere transient existence cannot qualify as a sculpture was rejected in *Metix v. G.H. Maughan*[1]. In that decision, the court considered that a sculpture made from ice was a sculpture even though it would melt as the temperature rose. Had the artist successfully argued that his snowballs attracted copyright protection, there was a considerable risk that Habitat would have been found in breach of his copyright on the basis that the Habitat advertisement copied a substantial part of Goldworthy's work. Given his reputation as an artist, Goldworthy might have also succeeded in his claim of passing off, had he been able to convince the court that there was sufficient misrepresentation so that a person watching the advertisement would be confused into believing that the artist had contributed to the advertisement or otherwise endorsed the product being advertised.

WHEN IS A COPY AN INFRINGING COPY?

When considering artistic works, the principles are that:

- copying means reproducing the work in any material form (section 17(2) CDPA);
- copying includes the making of a copy in three dimensions of a two-dimensional work and the making of a copy in two dimensions of a three-dimensional work (section 17(3) CDPA); and
- copying a protected work will infringe copyright in that work if it is copying of the work 'as a whole or any substantial part of it' (section 16(3)(a) CDPA).

Where part of a copyright work is copied exactly, the question of whether it is a substantial part of the whole work will depend on whether the part alone would have attracted copyright had that part stood alone instead of being part of the whole (*Ladbroke (Football) v. William Hill*[20]). If the answer is affirmative, the part is likely to amount to a substantial part of the copyright work, and an exact copy of the part will thus amount to copyright infringement.

Where a copyright work has not been copied exactly, the position is more difficult. The courts will compare the copyright work with the work claimed to be a copy of that work, and decide if the degree of resemblance is too general to count as copy, or too close to be allowed as original work. If merely the general idea underlying the copyright work was copied, but the representation of the idea was different, the courts are unlikely to find copyright infringement. On the other hand, if the general idea and the main features of its expression are copied, the courts may find copyright infringement even where there are differences in the detail.

The question of what constitutes a 'substantial part' of a protected work was debated in a case involving wallpaper inspired by a painting. An English company claimed that a Dutch company sold wallpaper that was a copy of one of their wallpapers. It was accepted that the wallpaper of the English company was protected by copyright, and that the Dutch company had, to some extent, copied it. The question was whether the copying was substantial enough to amount to a breach of the English company's copyright.

The test of substantiality is one of quality and not of quantity. Just one feature of a painting may be regarded as a substantial part of the painting if that feature is the key feature of the painting. However, no clear consensus of opinion seems to have emerged in that case as to how you determine whether the part that is copied is substantial or not. The Court of Appeal considered each of the main features of the wallpaper in turn and decided that on balance the features that were copied were not substantial enough to warrant a finding of infringement (*Designers Guild v. Russell Williams*[13]). The House of Lords, on the other hand, suggested that the works should be looked at as whole to decide if one had borrowed a substantial part of the other (*Designers Guild v. Russell Williams*[21]). Helpfully for advertising agencies, the emphasis was placed on the protection of the expression of an idea, rather than on the idea itself. The principle that copyright was designed to protect the skill and labour of the author, rather than his ideas, was reiterated. There was also support for the principle that 'the more abstract and simple the copied idea, the less likely it is to constitute a substantial part'. This is because originality, in the sense of contribution of the author's skill and labour, tends to lie in the detail of how the idea is expressed.

This case confirms that copying a copyright work is not necessarily an infringement. The question will be whether the part that was copied is a substantial part. Unfortunately, it is difficult to give guidance on what constitutes a substantial part. There is no real consensus on the methodology and this, combined with the inherent subjective judgement involved in deciding whether two images look the same or not, suggests that at least for the time being, each case will depend on the personal appreciation of the individual judge(s).

ARE THERE ANY DEFENCES?

The CDPA lists various 'acts permitted in relation to copyright works' which can be invoked as defences against claims of copyright infringement (Chapter III, Part I, CDPA). These acts are limited in their scope and subject to various conditions. If a substantial part of a protected work is copied, there may be a defence of 'fair dealing' (sections 29–30). However, this exception is narrowly defined and unlikely to apply in advertising cases. There is a defence if a copyright work appears only 'incidentally', for instance purely accidentally in the background of an image or a commercial (section 31). Another exception applies where a sculpture or work of artistic craftsmanship permanently situated in a public place, or in premises open to the public, is represented by a graphic work, on a photograph or film. Such works can usually be reproduced in advertising, but a three-dimensional reproduction would amount to an infringement (section 62). All these exceptions are however unlikely to assist in cases where the advertisement is inspired by a work of contemporary art.

CONCLUSION

The boundaries between acceptable 'borrowing' from contemporary art and a violation of the artist's rights are ill-defined. When considering the few cases dealing with conflicts between contemporary artists and advertising agencies, it is often to predict how the court will apply existing principles to the facts of the case. Indeed, the court's often rather abstract pronouncements in cases of alleged infringements can be difficult to apply in practice.

The following guidelines may assist agencies when deciding if, and how, they might take inspiration from contemporary art:

- there is no copyright in ideas. An idea simply implemented or described, is unlikely to benefit from much copyright protection;
- imitating the style or technique of a period, school or group of artists is generally not a problem;
- the skill and labour involved in producing a work of art is key. There is, arguably, 'more copyright' in a video work by Bill Viola than in Carl Andre's brick sculpture;

- copying part of a protected work may not amount to a copyright infringement provided that the part is not substantial. Copying a small but key part of a work can amount to copying a substantial part of the work;
- copying part of an artist's work may, however, breach the artist's moral right to object to the derogatory treatment of his work;
- the incidental inclusion of a protected work in a photograph or a film is, in principle, not an infringement of that work.

Pierre Valentin, Withers LLP

Notes

1   *Metix (UK) Ltd v. G.H. Maughan (Plastics) Ltd* [1997] FSR 718
2   *George Hensher Ltd v. Restawile Upholstery (Lancs) Ltd* [1976] AC 64
3   *Merlet v. Mothercare plc* [1986] RPC 115
4   *Shelley Films Ltd v. Rex Features Ltd* [1994] EMLR 134
5   *Radley Gowns Ltd v. Costas Syrou* [1975] FSR 455
6   *Guild v. Eskander Ltd* [2001] FSR 38, [2003] FSR 3 (CA)
7   *Creation Records Ltd v. News Group Newspapers Ltd* [1997] EMLR 444
8   *University of London Press Ltd v. University Tutorial Press Ltd* [1916] 2 Ch 601
9   *Komesaroff v. Mickle* [1988] RPC 204
10 *Gordon Fraser Gallery Ltd v. Tatt* [1966] FSR 250
11 Anne Kieffer and Michèle Benattar, *Mettez de l'art dans votre com*, Editions d'Organisation, 2003
12 *Elvis Presley Trade Mark* [1999] RPC 567; *Jane Austen Trade Mark* [2000] RPC 879
13 *Designers Guild Ltd v. Russell Williams (Textiles) Ltd* [2000] FSR 121 (CA)
14 *Norowzian v. Arks Ltd* [1999] EMLR 57
15 *Norowzian v. Arks Ltd* [1999] EMLR 67
16 *Norowzian v. Arks Ltd* [2000] ECDR 205
17 *HEM v. Sveriges Radio Aktiebolag* [1998] EIPR 20(6) N98-99
18 Article 5.3(k) of Directive 2001/29/EC of the European Parliament and of the Council on the Harmonisation of certain aspects of copyright and related rights in the Information Society 1997/0359 (COD)
19 *Annie Leibovitz v. Paramount Pictures Corp* [1996] 948 F. Supp 1214
20 *Ladbroke (Football) Ltd v. William Hill Football Ltd* [1964] 1 WLR 273
21 *Designers Guild Ltd v. Russell Williams (Textiles) Ltd* [2000] WLR 2416

Consumer credit

onsumer credit advertising is a massive business; advertising expenditure in this category in 2003 was £806m;[1] the UK credit card industry's total advertising expenditure alone was £84m in 2004. Significant changes in the law on credit advertising have recently been introduced and these are described in this chapter.

INTRODUCTION

The rules and regulations relating to the advertising of consumer credit have undergone a period of considerable change over the last few years, with further changes expected in the future. One of the key areas highlighted for reform in the Government's White Paper 'Fair, Clear and Competitive, the Consumer Credit Market in the 21st Century'[2] was the system of advertising control, which ultimately led to the implementation of the Consumer Credit (Advertisements) Regulations 2004[3] ('2004 Regulations') on 31 October 2004 in order to achieve greater consistency and transparency in credit advertising. The advertising of consumer credit will also be significantly affected by the Consumer Protection from Unfair Trading Regulations 2008[4] ('the CPRs'), which came into force on 26 May 2008. The long awaited new EU Directive on Consumer Credit[5], which it is anticipated will be brought into UK law in 2010, is expected to make some further changes.

The underlying principle behind all of the legislation is that consumer credit advertisements should provide a fair and reasonably comprehensive indication of the nature and true cost of the credit terms being offered, covering both the content of an advertisement (i.e. the amount and type of information) and its form (i.e. the way in which the information is presented).

WHAT IS A CONSUMER CREDIT ADVERTISEMENT?

The Consumer Credit Act 1974 ('CCA') and the 2004 Regulations apply to any advertisements in which the advertiser indicates that he is willing to provide credit. In this context 'indicating' means the same as 'showing'. Stickers merely featuring a car price on the left and the trader's name and logo on the right do not, therefore, constitute credit advertisements.[6] The fact that it is well known that a particular advertiser provides credit does not mean that all its advertisements qualify as credit advertisements; they will only do so if the advertisement itself indicates such a willingness on the part of the advertiser.[7] Every type of advertising is caught, including direct mail packs, posters, television and radio advertisements, as well as material on internet sites, including website banners, and any other means by which consumers are informed that credit is available.

The rules are principally directed at business-to-consumer advertising. In particular, they apply to advertisers carrying on consumer credit or credit brokerage, including retail stores offering their own credit, and motor dealers arranging credit through third-party credit providers. Historically, there was an exemption for advertisements which indicated that the credit must always exceed £25,000 and is either unsecured or is not secured on land, but this no longer applies following the removal of the £25,000 financial limit under the CCA on 6 April 2008[8]. Advertisements for first-charge mortgage lending and certain other types of secured loan by authorised persons have been, from 31 October 2004, under the remit of the Financial Services Authority. The Financial Services and Markets Act 2000 and the CCA have been amended accordingly, to try to avoid dual regulation of these areas.

FALSE OR MISLEADING CREDIT ADVERTISEMENTS

The principle requirement for all consumer credit advertisements is that they must not be false or misleading in a material respect,[9] which it has been held means 'would not mislead an ordinary member of the public'. Information stating or implying an intention on the advertiser's part, such as an intention to loan money which he has not got, is false. An advertisement may be false or misleading even though it complies strictly with all the rules specified in the 2004 Regulations. The false or misleading information does not have to relate to the terms of credit. For example, quoting a price for a new car that excluded the cost of delivery, road fund tax and number plates was found to be misleading and in breach of the CCA.[10]

Examples of consumer credit advertisements which have fallen foul of this provision include the following.

APR

The annual percentage rate of charge for credit (APR) provides a yardstick for measuring the 'cost' of credit under different types of agreement, allowing consumers to compare the relative cost of credit from different sources, and must be included in many if not most consumer credit advertisements. Besides interest charges, the APR must reflect any other charges that have to be paid to obtain the credit, even if they do not arise directly under the credit agreement. For example, a car dealer's advertisement offering a new car on credit at '0% APR' was false as it did not state that the dealer would offer a smaller part-exchange allowance for a buyer's old car if he bought the new car on credit, rather than if he bought it for cash. The difference in the two part-exchange allowances represented a hidden charge which the advertisement failed to mention.[11]

'Interest free credit' and '0% finance'

These terms are frequently used in consumer credit advertisements, and have come under a great deal of scrutiny from the authorities. The Office of Fair Trading (OFT) has

taken action against various companies' advertisements which claimed '0% finance' or 'interest free credit', where interest was payable over the whole period of the loan if the amount borrowed was not paid off in full at the end of the interest-free period. Similarly, the phase 'nothing to pay for three months' was held to be misleading where payments only commenced after three months, but interest began to accrue immediately from the date of purchase.[12]

The OFT also succeeded in having a Barclaycard advertisement withdrawn because it gave a 'highly misleading impression' about the terms of a zero per cent interest rate offer on transferred balances. In particular, it contained the incorrect claim that the zero per cent APR was forever. The zero per cent rate was in fact only available on balance transfers and only if the consumer used the credit card to make purchases which attracted interest at the higher rate. In another case it was held to be unlawful, where cash purchasers received a percentage of the purchase price 'cashback', for an advertisement to claim 'interest free credit', as that term gives customers the impression that use of the credit facility would not be any more expensive than paying in cash.[13]

'Government licensed'

In the OFT's view, the expressions 'Government licensed' and 'Licensed by the Office of Fair Trading' can be misleading, as they can imply that the whole range of a trader's activity has been licensed or approved in some way. An expression that actually reflects the trader's status (for example 'Licensed under the Consumer Credit Act 1974' or 'Licensed credit broker') is acceptable however. The OFT's logo is Crown copyright, and must not be reproduced in any advertisement or other material.

THE CONSUMER CREDIT ADVERTISEMENTS REGULATIONS

Credit advertisements must also comply with the detailed requirements of the 2004 Regulations. The 2004 Regulations came into force on 31 October 2004 and replaced an earlier regime.[14] The intention is to ensure that consumers can compare financial products with confidence and make informed purchasing decisions.

The 2004 Regulations set out a number of rules which must be complied with.

General requirements

Every credit advertisement is required to use plain intelligible language, be easily legible and to include the name of the advertiser.[15] In this respect the advertiser is any person indicated in the advertisement as being willing to enter into transactions to which the advertisement relates. Information in an advertisement should be presented together as a whole, which means that it should be easy to assimilate.

The typical APR

The 2004 Regulations define the typical APR and set out a series of rules which determine when an advertisement must include one, and also set out the prominence which must be given to it.

The typical APR is an APR at or below which an advertiser reasonably expects, at the date on which an advertisement is published, that credit would be provided under at least 66% of the agreements he will enter into as a result of the advertisement. The test is therefore a forward-looking one, although information about previous business can be taken into account as evidence of agreements which are likely to be entered into in the future, following the publication of this advertisement. The advertiser should be able to demonstrate how the typical APR was determined and should keep records of this. The advertiser should also monitor what business is actually written and, if it transpires that their expectations were incorrect, should amend the typical APR on future advertising.[16]

APR 'triggers'

Not every advertisement need include a typical APR. The 2004 Regulations state that when one of a number of other items of information appears, then the advertisement must also contain a typical APR. These are commonly referred to as being APR 'triggers';[17] the main ones being where the advertisement:

- includes any other rate of charge. So, for example, if an advertiser wished to advertise a credit card balance transfer rate then he must also include a typical APR. Similarly, if a motor dealer wanted to advertise the various APRs at which he was prepared to offer credit facilities on a number of vehicles, then he would also need to show the typical APR for that advertisement;

- contains any of the information listed in items 5–7 of Schedule 2 of the 2004 Regulations. The items are the frequency, number and amount of repayments of credit, other payments or charges and the total payable by the debtor. It would follow therefore that, if an advertiser wanted to advertise that a loan could be repaid at £200 per month, then he would have to include a typical APR in that advertisement;

- indicates that credit is available to persons who might otherwise find their access to credit restricted (a 'non-status indicator'). An advertisement which stated that it did not matter whether the applicant had a previous poor credit history would fall into this category;

- indicates in any way that more favourable terms are available than may be found either from the advertiser themselves or elsewhere (a 'comparative indicator'). Advertising a rate as being 'our best ever' would be an example of this type of trigger;

- contains any incentive to apply for the credit on offer (an 'incentive'). It is often difficult to determine when a feature of a product amounts to an incentive. For example, a lender may be able to provide loans relatively quickly and, depending on how this information was presented, this could amount to an incentive to take the credit. Other features of advertisements are clearly incentives; if any advertiser offers a free satellite navigation system if the credit is taken out, then that would clearly be an incentive, so the advertisement would need to include a typical APR.

It is apparent from the comments above that one of the features of the 2004 Regulations is that there are some subjective elements to them, which can make ensuring compliance problematic.

Prominence and other requirements for the typical APR

The 2004 Regulations set out a further series of rules about the typical APR, including how it must be shown in an advertisement which requires one, and in particular the prominence which must be given to it. These include:

- the typical APR must be shown as, for example, 9.9% APR, and those elements must not be interspersed with other words or large spaces. It should be accompanied by the word 'typical' and, where appropriate, the word 'variable'. It should be shown to one decimal place only;

- when an advertisement includes any information which would be an APR trigger then the typical APR must be shown more prominently than that item of information. It is the rate itself, the percentage sign and the letters 'APR' to which the correct degree of prominence must be afforded. The logic of the 2004 Regulations is clear; if the advertiser wishes to entice the reader to take the credit product by making some offer, then the advertisement must also disclose the cost of the product by way of the typical APR.

Prominence is a subjective concept. Whether a typical APR is sufficiently prominent is not just a question of font size but can include its colour, location on the page and the number of times it is repeated;

- an advertisement can only contain one typical APR. It may contain other APRs and may include a range of APRs (subject to some specific rules about how the top and bottom of the range is determined), but there can only be one typical APR;

- the typical APR must be shown together with any information contained in the advertisement which is listed in Schedule 2 of the 2004 Regulation and must have greater prominence than this information. In advertisements in printed or electronic form the typical APR must be one-and-a-half times the size of the other information listed in the Schedule.

Schedule 2 items

The 2004 Regulations state that, where any one of a number of pieces of information linked to the cost of a credit product are displayed, a whole set of other information will have to be shown together with it, and with equal prominence. These items of information, which are listed in Schedule 2 to the 2004 Regulations, are:

1. amount of credit;
2. deposit of money in an account;
3. cash price;
4. advance payment;
5. frequency, number and amount of repayments of credit;
6. other payments and charges;
7. total amount payable by the debtor.

Whenever any advertisement includes an amount in respect of 5–7 above, the advertisement must also include all the other listed items and a postal address for the advertiser. The purpose of the provision is to ensure that the reader of the advertisement is not presented with one feature of a credit product, usually the amount of a monthly or weekly repayment, without also being presented with other important information about the product such as the number of repayments and the total he will have to repay. The requirement to show all of the information with equal prominence is designed to avoid advertisers 'cherry picking' items of information and including them very prominently in their advertisement in order to entice the reader to take the product.

Personal loan providers who wish to display loan repayment tables, and car manufacturers who want to advertise the monthly cost of buying their vehicles are particularly affected by this requirement.

The Spray Booth

TIME FOR A SWIFT EXIT?

THE SUZUKI SWIFT FROM £8,260

SUZUKI

Way of Life!

Model shown available at £9,515

Security

Where an advertisement is for credit for which security is required (such as a mortgage or loan secured on property) it must state that such security is required and specify the nature of the security. Where a mortgage or charge on the debtor's home is required one of a number of 'wealth' warnings will also need to appear.

Where the loan may be secured by a mortgage or charge against the borrower's home the following wealth warning must appear (in capital letters): 'YOUR HOME MAY BE REPOSSESSED IF YOU DO NOT KEEP UP REPAYMENTS ON A MORTGAGE OR ANY OTHER DEBT SECURED ON IT'. In cases where the advertisement indicates that credit is available for the payment of debts due to other creditors, the warning in the previous paragraph should be preceded by the warning 'THINK CAREFULLY BEFORE SECURING OTHER DEBTS AGAINST YOUR HOME'.

There are some other warnings which must be used in the case of certain equity release schemes and foreign currency mortgages or loans. There are rules regarding the prominence that must be afforded to any wealth warnings. Any such warnings must be given greater prominence than any other rate of charge (other than the typical APR), or any non-status indicator, comparative indicator or incentive, and no less prominently than any item of Schedule 2 information.

Current accounts

Where the credit takes the form of an overdraft on a current account the APR does not need to be shown. Instead, the annualised interest rate, expressed as a rate of interest, can be given, but the advertisement must also include a statement of the nature and amount of any other charges included in the total charge for credit. It appears that the dispensation is with respect to the disclosure of the APR only, so that the rest of the 2004 Regulations will continue to apply.

Restricted statements in credit advertisements

No credit advertisement may include any of the following:

- the word 'overdraft' or any similar expression describing any agreement for running account credit, except where the agreement allows the debtor to overdraw on a current account;
- expressions like 'interest free' indicating that customers are liable to pay no more than they would as cash buyers, except where the total amount payable does not exceed the cash price;
- the expression 'no deposit' or anything similar, except where no advance payments are to be made;
- the expression 'pre-approved' or 'loan guaranteed' or any similar expression, except where the agreement is free of any conditions regarding the credit status of the debtor;
- the expression 'present' or 'gift' or anything similar, except where there are no conditions which would require the debtor to return the credit or item offered;

- the expression 'weekly equivalent' or any similar expression, or any other periodical equivalent, unless such payments are provided for under the agreement.

THE CONSUMER PROTECTION FROM UNFAIR TRADING REGULATIONS 2008

The Consumer Protection Regulations (CPRs) came into force on 26 May 2008 and implement the Unfair Commercial Practices Directive into UK law. While the CPRs will have a wider impact than just upon advertising, it is clear that they will have a particular effect upon advertising and marketing, including credit products.

Historically, the basic requirement that advertisements must not contain information which is, in a material respect, false or misleading, was to be found in section 46 of the CCA. The CPRs have repealed this section so that the more general provisions of the regulations now apply and any enforcement action will probably be taken under these regulations.

The CPRs introduced three distinct areas of protection for consumers.

1. There is a list of 31 commercial practices which will always be considered to be unfair and are banned. No evidence will be needed of their effect upon the consumer in order to prove a breach of these prohibited practices. One of the banned practices which could have some effect upon advertisers is presenting rights given in law as a distinctive feature of the advertiser's product. If an advertiser were to indicate that the protections afforded to credit card customers under section 75 of the CCA were in some way peculiar to the advertiser's own credit card, then it appears that this would be an offence under the regulations.

2. The CPRs prohibit commercial practices which are misleading and which cause the average consumer to make a different decision, usually about whether to buy the product or not. In this respect an advertisement could be misleading either because of the information it contains or because of what it should contain, but fails to do so. An advertisement could be misleading under the regulations because of the way in which the information it contains is presented, even though the information may be factually correct.

   This prohibition will raise significant challenges for advertisers. It is not uncommon to find advertisements for consumer credit products which do comply with the strict technical requirements of the 2004 Regulations, but which do not really convey to the reader the fullest information they need about the product they are about to purchase, and particularly about the risks inherent in it. For example, many advertisements for debt consolidation loans contain prominent messages about the benefits of the loan (such as making significant reductions in monthly repayments and having extra cash to spend) without making it equally clear that the customer could pay far more in overall repayments under the consolidation loan than he would have done under his existing loan or credit arrangements. Similarly, some such advertisements fail to make clear that the consolidation loan is secured, as is often the case, so that his home is at risk of repossession if he defaults on the loan. Simply ensuring than such an advertisement contains a wealth warning may no longer suffice. Other advertisements proclaim very attractive typical APRs on car credit transactions without making it clear that the offer only applies to relatively low balances financed, or only apply to quite short finance periods, so that most readers who respond to the advertisement will not be able to benefit from the attractive rate. Such advertisements are likely to be misleading, as well as probably incorrectly stating the typical APR.

The CPRs define the 'average consumer' and, for most purposes, this will be the notional average consumer whom the advertisement reaches. Such a consumer should generally be assumed to be reasonably well informed and reasonably observant and circumspect, taking into account social, cultural and linguistic factors. Advertisers who target their advertising at specific sectors, or who target vulnerable sectors (such as sub-prime customers), will have to consider the likely effect of their advertisement on the average member of the targeted or vulnerable group, as appropriate.

3. There is a general duty not to trade unfairly, which is a provision that allows enforcers to take action against unfair commercial practices which do not fall into the group which are specifically banned or which are misleading. This is a catch-all provision that could affect advertising, although it is more likely that any action would arise as a result of an advertisement being misleading in some respect.

OTHER REGULATORY CODES AND CONTROLS

Non-broadcast advertising must comply with the Committee of Advertising Practice's British Code of Advertising, Sales Promotion and Direct Marketing ('the CAP Code') (see Chapter 2). All advertisements for consumer credit and other financial marketing communications are subject to the Code's general rules, such as avoiding serious or widespread offence, social responsibility and truthfulness of claims. The CAP Code requires that marketing communications should be clear, uncomplicated and easily understood by the likely audience. Advertisers should ensure that they do not take advantage of people's inexperience or credulity. Television and radio advertisements must comply with the Broadcast Committee of Advertising Practice's Television and Radio Advertising Standards Codes.

With effect from 31 October 2004 advertisements for first-charge mortgage lending became regulated by the Financial Services Authority (FSA). Any second-charge lending remains regulated under the CCA and the 2004 Regulations.

The Banking Code is produced by the British Bankers' Association, the Building Societies Association and the Association for Payment Clearing Services. It is a voluntary code which sets standards of good banking practice for financial institutions to follow when they are dealing with personal customers in the UK. The Code includes a short section on advertising and marketing, requiring advertising and promotional material to be clear, fair and not misleading, but is not directly concerned with regulating the content of advertisements. However, it does offer guidance about the sending of marketing materials to customers.

ENFORCEMENT AND SANCTIONS

It is both a civil and a criminal offence to contravene the requirements of the CCA or the 2004 Regulations relating to consumer credit advertising, punishable by a fine or imprisonment. The offence can be committed by the advertiser or by anyone who devised or published the offending advertisement or procured its publication,[18] and therefore includes advertising agencies. Following the implementation of the CPRs, actions could be taken for breaches of them which could lead to a fine not exceeding £5,000 or, on conviction on indictment in the Crown Court, a fine or imprisonment not exceeding two years, or both.

It is a defence for the publisher of the advertisement to prove that he did not know and had no reason to suspect that its publication would be an offence. It is also a defence for an accused to show that the act or omission resulting in the offence was due to a mistake, or to reliance on information supplied to the advertiser, or to an act or omission by another person, or to an accident or some other cause beyond his control, and that the advertiser took all reasonable precautions and exercised all due diligence to avoid such act or omission by himself or any other person under this control. This defence is, however, narrowly construed.[19]

The CCA and the 2004 Regulations are enforced by the OFT and by the Trading Standards Service, who often first seek to try and resolve complaints directly with the advertiser. Many advertisers build good relationships with their Home Authority Trading Standards Office, which can assist in resolving any complaints which are made without serious consequences arising.

Many complaints, particularly by private individuals, are made to the Advertising Standards Authority (ASA) which will investigate them and publish their findings. Where issues of compliance with the 2004 Regulations arise the ASA will frequently seek comment from the OFT to confirm whether there have been any breaches. The ASA does have the power to refer advertisers to the OFT if there are cases of persistent or various serious breaches. At the time of writing the ASA had recently investigated a number of claims that advertisements by lenders breached the CAP Code because they were irresponsible in encouraging people to take out loans for the wrong reasons, or because they misleadingly trivialised the nature of the service offered, which was commonly a secured personal loan and scarcely to be treated lightly.[20] Lenders should be aware that irresponsible lending is one of the factors which can give rise to an unfair credit relationship[21] under the CCA (as amended by the Consumer Credit Act 2006), which could lead to a claim for recompense against the lender and a possible right of referral to the Financial Ombudsman Service.

The OFT has published comprehensive guidance on the Advertisements Regulations,[22] that includes a series of examples which advertisers and agencies may refer to when preparing their own material. It is up to the courts to actually decide what the law does say, but in practice the guidance is treated as being a firm view of the law by Trading Standards Officers who have day-to-day responsibility for much enforcement.

The OFT does monitor published advertisements and will take action against individual advertisers. Various loan companies have given undertakings to the OFT following action. A common feature of the advertisements complained about is that they failed to afford the typical APR the required degree of prominence. However, action by the OFT does remain sporadic and a very significant proportion of advertisements still fail to comply. Following an exercise by the OFT in 2005 they reported that over 60% of advertisements in regional newspapers and 68% in popular car magazines failed to fully comply with the Advertisements Regulations.[23]

The OFT has the power to impose requirements on consumer credit licensees when they are dissatisfied with any matter in connection with a business being carried on by the licensee, which would extend to the content of their advertisements. Based on the approach the OFT adopted to enforcement when exercising their powers under the Enterprise Act 2002, it seems likely that they would seek a requirement to the effect that the offending advertiser would, henceforth, at the least fully comply with all the requirements of the Advertisements Regulations. Given the subjectivity inherent in the Advertisements Regulations, this could be an onerous responsibility. If the advertiser complained of were to fail to comply with a requirement then the OFT has the power to impose a fine of up to £50,000.

Jeff Vernon, DLA Piper

Images provided with kind permission of Suzuki (UK) and Nexus H.

Notes

1   Nielson Media Research 2004. 4th Quarter 2003 – Digest of UK Advertising Expenditure
2   December 2003 Cm 6040
3   SI 2004/1484
4   SI 2008/1277
5   Directive 2008/48/EC
6   *Paul Christopher Jenkins v. Lombard North Central plc [1984] 1 WLR 307*
7   *Jenkins v. Lombard North Central plc [1999] GCCR 623; Maurice Binks (Turf Accountants) Ltd v. Huss [1971] 1 All ER 104*
8   The Consumer Credit Act 2006 s2(3)
9   Formerly under s46 of the Consumer Credit Act 1974; from 26 May 2008 effectively under the Consumer Protection from Unfair Trading Regulations 2008
10 *Roller Group Ltd & Roller Finance Ltd v. Sumner [1995] CCLR1*
11 *Metsoja v. Norman Pitt & Co Ltd (1989) 1LR 31.1.89*
12 *Currys Ltd v. Jessop [1999] GCCR 3407*
13 *Holman v. Cooperative Wholesale Society Ltd (no. 1) [2000] 164 JP 699*
14 Consumer Credit (Advertisements) Regulations 1989 sI 1989/1125
15 SI 2004/1484 s3
16 OFT 746 3.6
17 SI 2004/1484 s8
18 Consumer Credit Act 1974 s47
19 *Coventry City Council v. Lazarus [1994] 160 JP 188*
20 ASA adjudications of 07/05/08 (Everyday Loans Ltd) and 14/05/08 (Loans.co.uk Ltd)
21 Consumer Credit Act 1974 s140A
22 Frequently asked questions OFT 746
23 OFT press release 181/05

DLA Piper DLA Piper DLA Piper DLA Piper DLA Piper DLA Piper DLA P
DLA Piper DLA Piper DLA Piper DLA Piper DLA Piper DLA Piper DLA P
DLA Piper DLA Piper DLA Piper DLA Piper DLA Piper DLA Piper DLA P

3.5

Financial promotions

A dvertising for investment products and other financial services is a complex area, on which specialist advice should be taken. Investment products include financial investments (equities, funds and derivatives), mortgages, bank accounts and insurance. This section provides a brief overview of the main issues that arise in this heavily regulated and scrutinised sector.

The body responsible for regulating the whole of the financial services sector, including its advertising and marketing, is the Financial Services Authority (FSA) which enforces the rules laid down in the Financial Services and Markets Act 2000 (FSMA). The FSA's statutory objectives include consumer protection and the promotion of public understanding of financial services and products.

The key rule is that all financial promotions must be communicated or approved for communication by an authorised person (meaning an entity regulated by the FSA), unless they fall into an exemption. It is a criminal offence for a non-FSA authorised person to publish or be involved in the publication of an unapproved financial promotion that does not fall within an exemption. Agencies must therefore ensure that any advertising created for a financial promotion is authorised by the client's compliance officer. Agencies must also ensure that any advertising carried out in respect of a financial promotion is authorised by the client's compliance officer.

In order for an authorised firm to communicate a financial promotion in compliance with FSA rules, the promotion must be clear, fair and not misleading. A fair and balanced picture must be given of the nature of the investment, the commitment and the risks involved. This is fundamentally important and agencies should avoid making any exaggerated claims. Financial advertising must also comply with the provisions of the various regulatory codes governing non-broadcast, television and radio advertising.

FINANCIAL PROMOTIONS: THE S.21 PROHIBITION

The basic, straightforward prohibition on financial promotions is contained in section 21 of the FSMA. This states that a person must not, in the course of business, communicate an invitation or inducement to engage in investment activity (such as investing in shares, unit trusts, ISAs, pensions or life policies, opening a bank account or engaging a firm for investment advice, portfolio management or stock broking) unless:

- the communicator is an authorised person; or
- the content of the communication is approved by an authorised person.

Guidance on the interpretation of the various elements that go to make up the section 21 prohibition is contained in the FSMA itself, as well as information published by the FSA,[1] as summarised below.

'Authorised person'

An 'authorised person' means someone permitted under the FSMA to carry on regulated activities such as dealing with, or advising on, investments. Authorised firms communicating or approving financial promotions are obliged to confirm that they are compliant with FSA rules. Agencies should always check with their client who is their 'authorised person'.

'Invitation or inducement'

The expressions 'invitation' and 'inducement' clearly suggest a promotional element to the communication. Such communications should be distinguished from those that seek merely to inform or educate the consumer about the mechanics or risks of generic types of investment.

The FSA will apply an objective test to decide whether a communication is an invitation or inducement. It will consider whether a reasonable observer, taking account of all the circumstances at the time the communication was made, would consider that the advertiser intended the communication to persuade individuals to engage in investment activity or that this was the purpose of the communication.

The FSA recognises that in many cases a preliminary communication may simply be an inducement to contact the advertiser to find out what he has to offer. For example, an advertisement which merely holds out a person as having expertise in providing services about investment management will not, without more information, be an inducement to engage in investment activity. In the FSA's view, the inclusion of contact details (for example of an investment company) should not in itself be determinative of whether the communication in which they appear is an inducement, but it is a factor which should be taken into account.

In its guidance, the FSA considers a number of particular types of promotional communication in giving guidance on what amounts to an invitation or inducement.

Directory entries

Ordinary telephone directory entries listing names and contact details will not generally be inducements, but specialist directories may be, depending on the level of detail included. Parts of a directory might seek to persuade persons to contact a firm listed in the directory in order to make an investment. That part of the directory will be an inducement to engage in investment activity. That does not mean, however, that the individual entries, or any other part of the directory, will be part of the inducement.

Tombstone advertisements

These are announcements of a firm's past achievements. They may be inducements depending on the extent to which their contents seek to persuade or incite persons to contact the advertiser for details of the firm's services, or to do business with it. Merely stating past achievements with no contact details would not be an inducement. Only if the advertisement contains other promotional material would it be capable of being an inducement.

Websites

Links that are activated merely by clicking on a name or logo will not be inducements. The links may be accompanied by or included within a narrative, or otherwise referred to elsewhere on the site. The links will only be inducements to engage in investment activity if they, or the narratives or reference in which they are included, specifically seek to persuade or incite persons to use the link for that purpose. Where this is the case but the inducement does not identify any particular person as a provider of a controlled investment, or as someone who carries on a controlled activity, it may be exempted as a generic promotion.[2]

Banner ads on websites are likely to be inducements. Whether they are inducements to engage in an investment activity would depend upon their contents, as with any other form of advertising.

Image advertising

Activities that are purely profile raising and which do not identify and promote particular investments or investment services, may not amount to either an invitation or inducement of any kind, for example sponsoring sporting events or putting a name or logo on the side of a bus. Company contact details may be included, which may involve an inducement to contact the advertiser, but this is too far removed from any possible investment activity to be considered to be an inducement.

Personal illustrations

A personal illustration (for example of the cost of, and benefits under, a particular investment) may amount to an invitation or inducement. This depends on the extent to which it seeks to persuade or incite the person to invest as opposed to merely providing them with information.

'Communicate'

The reference to 'communicate' includes 'causing a communication to be made'.[3] The FSA considers that a person is communicating where he gives materials to the recipient or where, in certain circumstances, he is responsible for transmitting the material on behalf of another person. In the FSA's view the following persons will *not* be 'communicating':

- advertising agencies and others when they are designing advertising material for their clients;
- persons who print or produce material for others to use in advertisements;
- persons who are responsible for securing the placing of an advertisement, provided they are not responsible for its contents (for example media agencies).

Neither the creative agency nor the media agency need therefore be authorised by the FSA in order to undertake work for a financial company. The advertiser, of course, does need to be authorised.

In addition, there is a 'mere conduit' exemption.[4] Where persons would normally be unaware of the fact that they may be distributing financial promotions, they will not be regarded as communicating them. This would include telecommunication service providers, broadcast service providers and newsagents or bookshops that sell newspapers and journals containing financial promotions.

Subject to the above, primary responsibility for a communication will rest with its originator, i.e. the person responsible for its overall content, usually the compliance officer.

'Engage in investment activity'

Engaging in investment activity means:

- entering or offering to enter into an agreement, the making or performance of which by either party is a 'controlled activity'. Controlled activities include accepting deposits of sums of money (i.e. banking) and managing, dealing in or advising on investments; or

- exercising any rights to acquire, dispose of, underwrite or convert a 'controlled investment'. Controlled investments include a deposit of a sum of money, rights under a contract of insurance, shares, options and futures and mortgages.

DIFFERENT WAYS TO COMMUNICATE FINANCIAL PROMOTIONS

Although the section 21 prohibition applies to all forms of financial promotion, it is necessary to distinguish between particular types of financial promotion as these are treated differently under the regulations, which recognises two particular types of financial promotions. These are 'real-time' (for example personal visits, telephone conversations or other interactive dialogue) and 'non-real-time' financial promotions (for example emails, letters, mailshots, newspapers, magazines, websites, television and radio commercials).

Real-time financial promotions are then divided into 'solicited' or 'unsolicited' communications. A real-time communication is 'solicited' where it is made in the course of the personal visit, telephone conversation or other interactive dialogue that was initiated by, or takes place in response to, an express request from the customer. An 'unsolicited' real-time communication (or 'cold call') is a communication which is made otherwise than where it was initiated by the customer, or takes place in response to an express request from the customer. A person will not have expressly requested a call, visit or dialogue simply because the person has not expressly indicated they do not wish to receive such communication, for example by failing to tick an 'opt-out' box. Agencies are unlikely to be involved in 'real-time' financial promotions, but should be aware of the terminology.

CONTENT OF FINANCIAL PROMOTIONS

The Financial Promotion Order 2005 sets out about 70 specific exemptions to the financial promotion restriction. Financial promotions that are not exempt must comply with the following rules which are set out in section 4 of the FSA Conduct of Business Sourcebook (COBS) which came into force on 1 November 2007.

The rules in COBS 4 apply to advertisers:

- communicating with a customer or potential customer in relation to its designated investment business; and
- communicating, or approving the content of financial promotions,

where this activity is carried on from an establishment maintained by the advertiser in the UK. The COBS rules apply to promotions concerning securities, derivatives, life policies and deposits. Parallel requirements are imposed under different FSA sourcebooks for mortgages and general insurance (MCOB relates to mortgages and ICOB relates to general insurance).

It is necessary to understand the meaning of the term 'MiFID business' as the application of the COBS 4 rules varies depending on whether the communication relates to Markets in Financial Instruments Directive business or not – this comprises investment services and activities and ancillary services carried on by a MiFID investment firm. There are therefore two key elements which must be satisfied before a firm will be carrying on MiFID business:

- it must be a *MiFID investment firm* (the FSA has designated all firms as MiFID or non-MiFID firms depending on the firm's permissions profile); and
- it must be providing an *investment service or performing an investment activity or an ancillary service*, as set out in MiFID. These include dealing on one's own account, executing client orders, investment advice, investment research, custody services and portfolio management.

Agencies therefore need to establish with their client whether the client is a MiFID investment firm performing an investment activity.

COBS requires that all financial promotions comply with the requirements outlined below.

Fair, clear and not misleading

The over-arching principle of COBS 4 is that all communications must be fair, clear and not misleading. This is made explicit under COBS 4.2 and is interpreted widely. This rule applies in relation to all communications to retail and professional clients in relation to investment services and non-exempted financial promotions.

Clearly identifiable as a financial promotion

COBS 4.3 requires financial promotions to retail clients to be clearly identifiable as such.

Compensation information

If any reference to an investor compensation scheme established under the Investor Compensation Directive is made in an advertisement to any client, under COBS 4.4 it must be limited to a factual reference only. There are no exemptions to this rule.

Provision of information to retail clients

COBS 4.5.2 lists the general information requirements, for example a requirement that the information is accurate and sufficient for the average member of the recipient group.

COBS 4.5.6 details the restrictions applicable when a firm provides information comparing relevant business or investments. Broadly speaking, a firm has a duty to ensure that any comparison is meaningful and presented fairly. When MiFID business is concerned, there is an additional duty to ensure that the sources of information are specified and that the key facts and assumptions used to make the comparison are included.

Past, simulated past and future performance

Many firms seek to place too much emphasis on past-performance information, or present it in a selective or misleading manner. COBS 4.6 contains restrictions on the use of such information.

Any information provided which gives an indication of past performance of relevant business, a relevant instrument or a financial index, must satisfy certain conditions, as listed in COBS 4.6.2. The indication must not be the most prominent feature of the communication and there must be a clear warning that the figures relate to past performance and should not be relied on as an indicator of future results.

This section applies in relation to information provided in relation to MiFID services and in relation to the promotion of investment products to retail clients, if the promotion relates to MiFID business.

Direct offer financial promotions

When a direct offer financial promotion (one which indicates the manner in which the recipient can partake in the investment activity by response) is intended for, or likely to be received by, a customer, an advertiser must ensure that prescriptive product information is provided to the recipient.

ENFORCEMENT AND SANCTIONS

Under section 25 of the FSMA a person commits a criminal offence if he carries on activities in breach of the section 21 prohibition. A person who commits this offence is subject to a maximum of two years imprisonment and an unlimited fine. However, it is a defence for a person to show that he took all reasonable precautions and used all due diligence to avoid committing the offence. A further consequence of a breach of section 21 is that certain financial agreements could be unenforceable.[5] This applies to agreements entered into by a person as a customer as a consequence of a communication made in breach of section 21.

The FSA specifically monitors financial promotions through a specialist financial promotions team. It may, in novel and complex cases, provide advice to advertisers prior to publication of a promotion, but this is very rare. The monitoring team will act on feedback from consumers and others as well as on key areas of concern.

Where serious or persistent rule breaches are found, advertisers may be referred to the FSA's Enforcement Division to be pursued under the disciplinary procedures. The criteria for determining whether disciplinary action is appropriate include whether a breach was deliberate or reckless, its duration and frequency, the risk of loss to consumers and/or the previous regulatory record of the firm. The FSA's enforcement policy also takes account of the conduct of the firm after the breach. Particular attention is paid to the remedial steps taken by the firm since the breach was identified. Where necessary, the FSA will take strong action. The FSA has taken enforcement action against 13 firms from 2005 to 2008, with total fines exceeding £1.5m.

REGULATORY CODES

British Code of Advertising, Sales Promotion and Direct Marketing (CAP Code)

This Code, which applies to non-broadcast advertising, applies to non-financial aspects of all financial advertisements and includes rules on substantiation, serious or widespread offence, social responsibility, fear and distress etc. The financial products rules in the Code apply to any financial advertisements that are not regulated by the FSA or the OFT. The Code basically says that marketing communications should be clear, uncomplicated and easily understood by the likely audience. Marketers should ensure that they do not take advantage of people's inexperience or credulity.

The Banking Code and Code of Conduct for the advertising of interest-bearing accounts

The Banking Code is produced by the British Bankers' Association (BBA), the Building Societies Association (BSA) and the Association for Payment Clearing Services. It is a voluntary code which sets standards of good banking practice for financial institutions to follow when they are dealing with personal customers in the United Kingdom. The Code includes a short section on advertising and marketing, requiring advertising and promotional material to be clear, fair and not misleading. The Code is not concerned with regulating the content of advertisements. However, it does offer guidance about the sending of marketing materials to customers.

The BBA and BSA also operate a Code of Conduct for the advertising of interest-bearing accounts run by UK banks and building societies. The Code contains detailed rules on content to be included in product-specific advertisements and descriptions of how interest rates must be shown. It also sets out rules relating to how terms such as 'instant access' may be used. This Code is enforced by the Banking Code Standards Board (BCSB) which can use its disciplinary sanctions if a subscriber breaches the Code. Sanctions available to the Board include public censure, the issue of directions as to future conduct, the issue of a reprimand and cancellation or suspension of a subscriber's registration.

CONCLUSION

The advertising of financial services, including investments, mortgages and insurance, is a complex and difficult area. Primarily, though, it is the client who has to take responsibility for the advertising, and agencies must ensure that there is a client compliance officer in place who will ensure that the advertising complies with the FSA rules. Agencies should also check that their client/agency contract does not try to make the agency responsible for this role: it is the client who by law must take it on.

David Blair, DLA Piper

Notes

1   FSA Perimeter Guidance Sourcebook, Chapter 8
2   Article 17 of the Financial Promotion Order (Generic Promotions)
3   Section 21 (13) FSMA
4   Article 18 of the Financial Promotion Order
5   Section 30 FSMA

n Advertising Institute of Practitioners in Advertising Institute of Vivac
n Advertising Institute of Practitioners in Advertising Institute of Practit
n Advertising Institute of Practitioners in Advertising Institute of Practit

3.6

Gambling

INTRODUCTION

Gambling advertising in Great Britain is governed by the Gambling Act 2005 (the Act). It was introduced in order to attempt to rationalise the laws on gambling, which dated back to the 1960s and were spread across four different pieces of legislation, and also reflected society's changed perception of gambling as a social activity: with the advent of the internet and interactive television, gaming and betting have increasingly become leisure activities. The gambling industry is worth billions. It is predicted, for example, that interactive television alone will account for half of an estimated £140bn online betting industry by 2015, and gambling services are the internet's fifth biggest advertising category.

In the face of significant lobbying from religious bodies and so-called consumer groups, the Government made efforts in the Act to ensure that children and the vulnerable were protected. The main safeguards in the new Act are:

- that gambling should be crime-free, honest and conducted in accordance with the new regulations;
- that players should know what to expect when gambling and be confident that those expectations are met;
- that there is adequate protection for children and other vulnerable sections of society.

LEGISLATION

The provisions of the Act came into force on 1 September 2007. The Act defines 'gambling' as including 'gaming, betting and participating in a lottery'. Lotteries are dealt with in the next chapter.

'Gaming' is defined as the *'playing of a game of chance for a prize'*, and represents what is traditionally viewed as gambling, i.e. the games played at casinos such as poker, roulette, blackjack etc.

'Betting' is defined as '*making or accepting a bet on:*

a) *the outcome of a race, competition or other event or process,*

b) *the likelihood of anything occurring or not occurring, or*

c) *whether anything is or is not true'*.

The Act introduces a new Gambling Commission whose remit includes the regulation of all advertising of gambling, as well as acting as licensor of casino and betting premises. All casino and betting operators are required to obtain a licence from the Gambling Commission before operating in the UK.

The new Gambling Commission is also primarily responsible for setting and enforcing the rules relating to the manner and content of advertising gambling, and a condition of retaining a casino or betting licence will be the adherence by the operator to these rules. The Secretary of State will retain the right to make further regulations in relation to the advertising of gambling if he deems it necessary.

However, the Gambling Commission agreed to hand over responsibility for drafting the content rules and for enforcing them to the current regulator, the Advertising Standards Authority (ASA), leaving itself as a backstop regulator. The new content rules are dealt with below.

The great advantage of the Act for casino and betting operators is that it greatly liberalises the previous restrictions on advertising of casinos and betting. It allows UK licensed casino operators to advertise on television for the first time, and also allows licensed casino and betting operators to advertise much more freely in non-broadcast media than ever before. Previously, UK casinos could only advertise through classified advertisements in the UK, whilst offshore online providers could advertise more freely in traditional non-broadcast media.

WHO CAN ADVERTISE?

The new law allows UK gambling operators who are licensed by the Gambling Commission to advertise in Great Britain. Advertisers and agencies should note that the Act does not apply in Northern Ireland, where the advertising of gambling is subject to separate laws (see page 161).

Licensed gambling operators from countries within the European Economic Area (EEA) and other 'white-listed' jurisdictions, will also be permitted to advertise in Great Britain. Some examples of jurisdictions which have already been white-listed include Gibraltar, Alderney, the Isle of Man and Tasmania.

Offshore gambling operators will only be allowed to advertise in Great Britain if they have received permission to do so from the Secretary of State, through the Gambling Commission. The Secretary of State has already decided that Antigua and the Canadian reservation of Kahnawáke will not be 'white-listed' for the time being, suggesting that the regulation of gambling in these areas does not meet the standards expected by the UK Government. Many offshore providers of gambling services cannot now therefore advertise in the UK, whereas they were able to do so prior to the introduction of the Act.

REGULATION

Gambling advertising will be subject to new rules incorporated into the CAP and BCAP Codes, and these rules cover all advertising for gaming and betting, including all promotions, market branding, direct marketing, both broadcast and non-broadcast media, the internet and other electronic communications such as SMS.

The new content rules were first published on 13 March 2007 and are similar to those developed for alcohol advertising in 2005. They are primarily designed, at the request of Government, to ensure that children and other vulnerable groups are adequately protected.

The rules are stringent and comprehensive and they emphasise the importance of social responsibility in gambling advertising, particularly with regard to protecting the more vulnerable members of society, children and young people. This chapter will not deal with all the new rules in detail but, in summary, the main rules state that the content of advertisements for gambling should not:

- portray, condone or encourage gambling behaviour that is socially irresponsible or which could lead to financial, social or emotional harm;
- link gambling to seduction, sexual success or enhanced attractiveness;
- exploit the susceptibilities, aspirations, credulity, inexperience or lack of knowledge of children, young persons or other vulnerable persons;
- suggest that gambling can enhance personal qualities, for example, that it can improve self-image or self-esteem, or is a way to gain control, superiority, recognition or admiration;
- suggest that gambling can provide an escape from personal, professional or educational problems such as loneliness or depression;
- be likely to be of particular appeal to children or young persons, especially by reflecting or being associated with youth culture; or
- include a child or young person in the advertisement. No-one who is, or seems to be, under 25 years old may be featured gambling or playing a significant role, and no-one may behave in an adolescent, juvenile or loutish way.

Furthermore, the new rules prohibit advertisements for gambling from being directed at children and young people in any media. These content rules state that gambling advertisements on television may not be advertised in or next to children's programmes or programmes likely to appeal particularly to children.

The full set of the content rules can be obtained at www.cap.org.uk.[1]

THE INDUSTRY'S OWN CODE

A few weeks before the Act came into force in September 2007, Gordon Brown replaced Tony Blair as Prime Minister. He was far less positive about this liberalisation of the gambling laws than his predecessor, and immediately stopped the development of the 'super-casino' in Manchester. He also put strong pressure on the gambling industry, which quickly agreed its own complementary set of rules to the CAP and BCAP content rules in order to avoid the entire Act being abolished.

This 'Gambling Industry Code for Socially Responsible Advertising' sets out additional rules for advertising. The three main additional elements are as follows:

1. It is a requirement for all gambling advertising (except radio) to carry the website address 'www.gambleaware.co.uk'. Ideally, advertisers should preface the website with the phrase 'For more information and advice, please visit…'.

    Where the advertising of gambling is not the sole or main part of the advertising, then the website need not be included. Radio advertisements are encouraged to use educational messaging instead of the website (see 2 below).

2. Gambling operators are encouraged to include some additional educational messaging, such as 'Don't let the game play you', 'Know your limit and play within it' or 'Please play responsibly'.

3. No gambling advertising (excluding bingo advertising) may be carried on television before the 9pm watershed, but there is an exemption for the advertising of sports betting around televised sporting events (which does not include sports-themed entertainment programmes). The guidance note fails to provide any clarity as to the extent of this limitation period – it is assumed that advertisements are permitted only until 6am.

WHO ENFORCES THE RULES?

The Advertising Standards Authority (ASA), not the Gambling Commission, will now be responsible for administering the new advertising content code and will respond to public concerns about gambling advertisements. Any advertisements found in breach of the new codes will have to be amended or withdrawn. If serious or repeated breaches of the advertising codes occur then the ASA may refer advertisers to the Gambling Commission, and broadcasters to Ofcom, to consider further sanctions against the advertiser. The Gambling Commission has the right to withdraw the licence from the operator if it is deemed necessary.

SPONSORSHIP OF TELEVISION PROGRAMMES

Although Section 5.3 of the Ofcom Code of Programme Sponsorship states that those categories which are unacceptable for advertising are also unacceptable for the sponsoring of programmes, it has allowed the sponsorship of certain programmes by gambling advertisers. This allowance presaged the Act, and has now been confirmed in it. Gambling is now an acceptable category for advertising and therefore also for sponsorship of television programmes, but advertisers and agencies need to be aware of the Industry's own code which includes certain scheduling and content restrictions.

RECENT ADJUDICATIONS

Clearly many UK gambling advertisers have taken advantage of the liberalisation of the rules and started advertising. The first significant complaint to the ASA was in relation to an advertisement for Ladbrokes featuring well-known football pundits, including Ian Wright and Ally McCoist, dressed up as builders. Viewers complained that the commercial suggested gambling was a way to gain recognition and linked gambling to toughness, and also that the featured football pundits appealed to children and young people. The ASA did not uphold any of these complaints and stated that the football pundits were unlikely to appeal to children.

In April 2008, the ASA investigated two gambling advertisers, Paddy Power and Intercasino. Paddy Power ran a national press advertisement, in *The Times*, showing a short man in the back of a stretch limousine holding a glass of champagne and a cigar and flanked by two glamorous-looking women. The body copy stated 'Who says you can't make money being short? Financial Spread Betting lets you bet on falling (going short) as well as rising share prices (going long), allowing you to make the most out of volatile markets'. The ASA decided that this advertisement breached the new codes by linking gambling to seduction, sexual success and enhanced attractiveness, and by implying that gambling could improve self-image or self-esteem and was a way to gain control, superiority, recognition or admiration.

In the second investigation, the ASA investigation team monitored Intercasino television commercials which used a Japanese-game-show style. The ASA Council decided that these commercials also infringed the new codes because they believed the Japanese-game-show style of the commercial was of particular appeal to children and young persons, especially by reflecting or being associated with youth culture, and because the commercials featured characters behaving in an adolescent, juvenile or loutish way.

NORTHERN IRELAND

The relaxation of the gambling advertising restrictions in the Gambling Act 2005 does not apply in Northern Ireland, which has its own gambling law. The gambling law in Northern Ireland is contained within the 1985 statutory instrument, the Betting, Gaming, Lotteries and Amusements (Northern Ireland) Order 1985, as amended by the Betting and Gaming (Northern Ireland) Order 2004.

Under the 1985 Order the advertising of gaming (as opposed to betting) is subject to certain restrictions. Article 130(1)(c) of the 1985 Order (the Article) prohibits an advertiser from:

> 'inviting the public to subscribe any money or money's worth to be used in gaming whether in Northern Ireland or elsewhere, or to apply for information about facilities for subscribing any money or money's worth to be so used.'

The advertising of gaming is therefore legal, but subject to this limitation. Any form of advertising which invites the public in Northern Ireland to pay money for use in gaming is prohibited. This includes the advertising of both remote and non-remote gaming and wherever that gaming is based or licensed. The Article does not say that an advertisement may not invite the public to *participate* in commercial gaming overseas, it merely states that they must not be invited to *subscribe money* to be used in gaming.

To contravene the Article, an advertisement would either have to expressly seek a financial contribution from a member of the public in Northern Ireland to be used in offshore gambling, or expressly invite applications for information about facilities for subscribing money, or send such a strong indirect message to the reader as to be tantamount to an express solicitation or invitation.

All gambling advertisements to be published in Northern Ireland will need to be carefully screened to ensure compliance with this restriction. Advertisements stating that operators offer gaming services and describing what games are on offer will be allowed, but not those which invite consumers to play for money, and certainly not those which encourage or incentivise playing.

The following wording in advertisements in Northern Ireland, for example, would not be acceptable:

- £20 free chips on registration;
- Buy $ ... get $ ... free;
- We will match your first deposit;
- Join today and get a bonus;
- Referral bonus for every friend you introduce to the party;
- £150 free for all new players;
- Win big cash prizes;
- Win a trip for two to Las Vegas;
- Free million-pound poker tournament;
- Daily jackpots.

Agencies should also avoid referring to 'free entry' or 'play for free' in relation to gaming, as this could also amount to an indirect invitation to subscribe for money (in particular, for example, in situations where the player goes to the play-for-free website and there are direct exhortations to play for real money).

The inclusion of a disclaimer in an advertisement to the effect that the advertisement does not apply to Northern Ireland, or to Northern Irish residents, is not a sufficient measure to ensure compliance with the legislation.

The restrictions in Northern Ireland apply to commercial radio stations and national newspapers and magazines as well as television, but do not apply to the advertising of betting.

The advertising of betting (as opposed to gaming) is therefore permitted in Northern Ireland, but will be subject to the CAP and BCAP Codes and also the Industry's own code.

CONCLUSION

The Gambling Act is certainly good news for legitimate casino and betting advertisers and for advertising agencies. There is far greater scope to advertise now than previously, even with the self-imposed scheduling restrictions implemented by the industry's own code. The Government has signalled that it intends to keep a close eye on the advertising of these services to ensure strict compliance with the codes. It is hoped that casino advertisers and their agencies will therefore adhere closely to the new content rules in order to ensure that this freedom to advertise is not short-lived.

Christopher Hackford, Institute of Practitioners in Advertising

Note

1   www.cap.org.uk/cap/codes/cap_code/ShowCode.htm?clause_id=2187

Turton Swan Turton Swan Turton Swan Turton Swan Turton Swan Turton Swan Turton Swan Turton Swan Turton Swan Turton Swan Turton Swan Turton Swan Turton Swan Turton Swan Turton Swan Turton Swan Turton Swan Turto

3.7

Lotteries and prize promotions

INTRODUCTION

There are a number of different methods an advertiser can use to achieve increased sales. One of the most common is to provide an inducement to consumers to buy its goods. A very popular inducement is to offer consumers the chance to win a prize, either by entering a competition or a prize draw.

There are many types of prize promotions. Some have one large prize for only one winner; some have a number of smaller prizes for a larger number of entrants. Some promotions can be entered simply by handing in coupons or filling in questionnaires; some will require a degree of skill in order to win. The size and scale of both the promotion and the prizes are entirely at the discretion of the advertiser.

An advertiser and its agency must take care when running a promotion to ensure that it complies with all legal and regulatory requirements. This chapter will examine the pitfalls involved in running a prize promotion or competition, and sets out in detail the regulatory requirements under the advertising codes which need to be adhered to in order to ensure that the promotion is administered properly and the consumer is treated fairly.

Since the Gambling Act 2005 ('the Act') came fully into force in 2007, there are important differences between the law in Great Britain relating to lotteries and competitions and the law in Northern Ireland. This chapter will focus on the British law as set out in the Act, with key differences between British and Northern Irish law highlighted on page 180. The corresponding laws in the Republic of Ireland are not covered in this chapter.

In order to stay on the right side of the law in this area, when running either a prize draw or a competition, an advertiser needs to avoid promoting any activity which is classified legally as gambling. The Act defines gambling as:

'a) gaming,

b) betting, or

c) participating in a lottery.'[1]

Gambling, gaming and betting are considered in Chapter 3.6. This chapter deals with lotteries and prize promotions.

LOTTERIES AND PRIZE DRAWS

Lotteries are illegal unless they are organised within statutory provisions regarding, for example, the National Lottery and lotteries at local fetes. Running a lottery is a criminal offence, and great care should therefore be taken to ensure that any prize promotion which an advertiser wishes to run complies with the provisions of the Act.

It is also illegal under section 2 of the Act to advertise a lottery, subject to certain exceptions. The main exception is the advertising of the National Lottery, and the Office of the National Lottery has issued guidelines regulating the advertising and

promotion of the National Lottery. Advertising agencies should always be fully aware of this important prohibition.

What is a lottery?

The courts under previous legislation had defined a lottery as 'an arrangement involving the distribution of prizes by chance, and payment to enter'. The Act now provides for the first time a statutory definition involving two types of lottery, a *simple lottery* and a *complex lottery*. An arrangement is a lottery if it falls within these definitions, irrespective of how it is described.[2]

A simple lottery is one where:

- persons are required to pay in order to participate in the arrangement;
- in the course of the arrangement one or more prizes are allocated to one or more members of a class; and
- the prizes are allocated by a process which relies wholly on chance.[3]

A complex lottery is one where:

- persons are required to pay in order to participate in the arrangement;
- in the course of the arrangement one or more prizes are allocated to one or more members of a class;
- the prizes are allocated by a series of processes; and
- the first of those processes relies wholly on chance.[4]

An example of a simple lottery is a normal raffle. You pay for a number and the winning number is picked out of a hat. An example of a complex lottery would be a quiz on a television show where participants dial a premium rate telephone line and callers are randomly selected to answer the question.

An arrangement is *not* a lottery if the first stage involves skill and the second stage relies wholly on chance. It is therefore now lawful to pick the winner of a paid-for crossword competition out of a hat. The first stage of the competition, completing the crossword, relies on skill, so the arrangement is not a lottery.

The prize in a lottery may include any money, articles or services, whether or not described as a prize. If the prize is provided by participants rather than the organiser, the arrangement will still be a lottery.[5]

Some competitions are so easy that in reality they are lotteries. Before the Act came into force competition organisers were setting questions that were so simple that few people could fail to get the right answer. For example: 'The capital of England is (a) London (b) Paris (c) Timbuktu?' The Act has introduced a statutory test for the skill level in such competitions, which is considered in the section on prize competitions and lotteries on page 172.

Prize draws and payment to enter

One of the essential elements of a lottery is payment to enter. The most important change introduced by the Act was to allow product promotions where prize draws are linked to the purchase of goods or services. Previously these were considered as involving payment to enter and promoters were therefore obliged to provide a free entry route in such circumstances. This remains the law in Northern Ireland, but it is now legal in Great Britain to offer entry into a prize draw as an inducement to buy a product.

The term 'payment' includes both paying money and 'transferring money's worth'.[6] Prize draws are often used as an incentive to encourage people to provide data, for example in customer satisfaction surveys. The Gambling Commission has issued guidance on this subject. The Commission does not, as a general rule, think that the provision of data by individuals amounts to payment and will not seek to argue that 'proportionate requests for data' involve transferring money's worth. However, the Commission considers that the position might be different where large quantities of data are requested, particularly where data is obtained in circumstances where it is intended to be sold to third parties.

It makes no difference whether a payment is made to the promoter of the prize draw or to someone else, or who receives the benefit from a payment.[7] Hence, if a prize draw organiser makes no charge for entry but a telephone company does, that will involve payment (but see below on the subject of stamps, telephone calls etc.). It is also irrelevant whether participants know when they make a payment that they are thereby participating in a draw.[8]

As stated above, paying for goods or services at their normal price is no longer considered as payment to enter. However, there will be payment for the purposes of the Act if participants in a product promotion are required to pay for goods or services 'at a price or rate which reflects the opportunity to participate in an arrangement',[9] i.e. where the advertiser increases the price for the duration of the promotion.

In most cases this is unlikely to cause difficulty, but there will be issues in some cases. The Commission has issued the following guidance on this subject:

> 'As a general rule ... a [product] linked to a promotion which is charged
> at a price which bears little relation either to its cost of production or
> to comparable products may mean the promotion will be challenged as
> an illegal lottery. On the other hand, an increase in price just before or
> coincident with the introduction of a promotion need not necessarily give
> rise to difficulty if it can be shown that the price rise is unrelated to the
> promotion itself, for instance because of higher costs of such things as raw
> materials or transport ... The Commission acknowledges that ultimately the
> costs of any product promotions must be recovered through the revenues
> obtained from sales. However, the test is whether an identifiable element
> within the price of the product during the promotion can be said to be a
> participation fee.'

Most prize draws can only be entered by post, telephone, text or internet. Participants generally pay for these services, but do they amount to payment to enter? The Act now provides statutory rules in this area. The following do not amount to payment to enter:

- sending a letter by ordinary post;
- making a telephone call; or
- using any other method of communication,

provided any expense incurred is at the 'normal rate' for that method of communication.[10] Ordinary post means 'ordinary first-class or second-class post (without special arrangements for delivery)'.[11]

Text-to-win promotions are only acceptable if the text message is charged at the standard rate. Premium rate text entry would be regarded as payment.

Internet entry is not regarded as payment to enter, despite there being a general charge to use broadband (or analogue) connections by the service provider.

The Commission has issued the following guidance on 'normal rates':

> *'The test for whether a charge is at the 'normal rate' is whether or not it reflects the opportunity to enter ... This is a question of fact in each case. However, it is irrelevant to this test whether different methods of communication cost different amounts. For instance, different mobile phone operators have different tariffs. The fact that, as a result, some participants pay more than others for their call to enter ... does not affect the question of whether or not that method involves 'payment to enter'. The test is rather whether the costs of the call includes an element which involves a payment to enter ... if the call is charged at a tariff which includes an element of paying for a service, that involves, in the Commission's view, a payment, for the opportunity to enter, again regardless of who benefits from that element of the payment. Here there is some additional payment over that which relates to the provision of the telecommunications facilities.'*

The following are also treated as payments to enter:

- a payment in order to discover whether a prize has been won;[12] and
- a payment in order to take possession of a prize which has or may have been allocated.[13]

The Gambling Commission has stated that this second example does not cover instances where the prize is, for example, a digital camera, and the winner is required to send a cheque to cover postage and packaging, as long as the postage and packaging is charged at cost. It would also not include a situation where the prize is tickets to see Robbie Williams in concert at Knebworth, for example, when the winner would have to pay to get to the venue. On the other hand, a requirement to phone a premium rate number for entrants to find out if they have won would not be acceptable.

Free-entry routes

Under the previous legislation it was generally accepted that if you included a genuine method for entering a prize draw which did not involve either buying the product or making any other payment, then you would avoid the draw being an illegal lottery. This principle was never clearly defined and led to difficulties and abuse.

You no longer need a free entry route if entry into a prize draw involves buying a product at its normal price, as this is not treated as payment to enter. In other cases where there is payment to enter, you will still need to provide a genuine free entry route, and the Act now defines what this means. There is no payment to enter if:

- each individual who is eligible to participate has a choice whether to participate by paying or by sending a communication;
- the communication ... may be:
  - a letter sent by ordinary post,[14] or
  - another method of communication which is neither more expensive nor less convenient than entering the lottery by paying;
- the choice is publicised in such a way as to be likely to come to the attention of each individual who proposes to participate; and
- the system for allocating prizes does not differentiate between those who participate by paying and those who participate by sending a communication.[15]

If an alternative route involves payment, but that payment costs the same as ordinary first- or second-class post, that alternative route will still not qualify as 'free'.

The Commission has issued the following guidance on the issues involved in free entry routes:

'... to qualify as a method which does not involve payment, it is not sufficient that the alternative route costs nothing for those who use it. It also has to be such that, for instance, individuals wishing to participate have a choice whether to use the alternative route and it is no less convenient than the paid route. As an example, many people do not have ready access to the World Wide Web at home. Although, for many of those that do, use of it costs nothing in the sense that they pay a single amount for access and nothing for subsequent use, [but] others cannot access it, at least [not] quickly. A competition which offers an alternative 'free' entry route via the web may not offer substantial proportions of those who wish to enter a genuine choice, or at the very least, that alternative may not be as convenient for them as the paid route. This is particularly the case where the need for immediate responses is emphasised to enable the participants to win the prizes on offer, or the competitions are run only for relatively short periods. Reflecting all this, the Commission has developed the following principles, which we intend to use as a guide when considering whether web entry is a sufficient alternative route for those who seek to use it:

- *Potential participants who do not have home web access need sufficient time to gain web access elsewhere. The Commission considers three working days around the date of the particular draw as a reasonable length of time to obtain such access.*

- *Participation by web access should be available at all times while the scheme is being actively promoted. Therefore, a quiz taking place during a television programme should permit web entries while the programme is being aired.*

- *The availability of free entry via the web should be made widely known, for example as the general policy for schemes organised by the operator concerned.*

- *Where any doubts exist as to whether the web entry arrangements in any particular case fully satisfy the Act's requirements, other routes, for example by post that has been specifically sanctioned by Parliament, should be offered in addition.'*

Summary

The main change introduced by the Act has been to allow product-purchase-linked prize draws without requiring a free entry route, providing that the price of the product is not increased for the promotion. This is of great significance to agencies running prize draw promotions, and makes the administration of such draws a lot more convenient. Agencies should note however that, when running pay-to-enter prize draws, the requirements for the free entry route are stricter than before.

PRIZE COMPETITIONS

Prize competitions, like free draws, are not regulated under the Act and are therefore lawful. A free draw is essentially a lottery which doesn't involve payment to enter. Prize competitions are defined negatively in the Act. They are not gambling unless they are gaming, participating in a lottery or betting.[16]

Prize competitions and gaming

Gaming means 'playing a game of chance for a prize'[17], including games that involve pure chance, such as roulette, or an element of chance and an element of skill, such as backgammon.[18] A game that involves an element of chance that can be eliminated by superlative skill is still gaming.[19] A game that is 'presented as involving an element of chance' is still gaming,[20] but a sport is not gaming[21].

Computer games can amount to gaming, which may involve only one participant in a game, and may involve computer generated images or data representing the actions of others in the game.[22] Care is therefore needed if agencies intend to run online tournaments.

It is irrelevant whether or not a player risks losing anything at a game. The essential element is acquiring a chance to win a prize by playing the game.[23] Prize means 'money or money's worth' and includes both a prize provided by the organiser of the game and winnings of money staked.[24]

Gaming is generally of little relevance in the context of prize competitions. Of more relevance are the other two types of gambling, lotteries and betting.

Prize competitions and lotteries

When running a prize competition it is important to include a sufficient element of skill to avoid the promotion being considered a lottery. A lottery is defined as involving the allocation of prizes by a process which relies 'wholly on chance'. However, the Act defines certain low levels of skill which are ignored for these purposes. The wording of the section is difficult and is likely to give rise to test cases in which the courts will have to explain what it means in more detail:

> 'A process which requires persons to exercise skill or judgment or to display knowledge shall be treated for the purposes of this section as relying wholly on chance if:
>
> (a) the requirement cannot reasonably be expected to prevent a significant proportion of persons who participate in the arrangement of which the process forms part from receiving a prize; and
>
> (b) the requirement cannot reasonably be expected to prevent a significant proportion of persons who wish to participate in that arrangement from doing so.'[25]

In simpler terms, a game involving a low level of skill may nevertheless be treated as a lottery if the skill element does not (1) prevent a significant number of players from receiving a prize and (2) deter a significant number of players from entering in the first place. If either one of these barriers to success or entry is present, the competition will not be a lottery.

The Commission has issued detailed guidance on this issue, including the following:

- a crossword puzzle, where entrants have to solve a large number of clues and where only fully completed entries are submitted, would obviously be a genuine prize competition. So, too, would other types of word and number puzzles such as those that feature in competition magazines, even if those who successfully complete the puzzle are subsequently entered into a draw to pick the winner;

- at the opposite end of the spectrum are the many competitions that ask just one simple question, the answer to which is widely and commonly known, or is blatantly obvious from the material accompanying the competition. These will be treated as lotteries;

- the more questions or clues which have to be solved, the more likely it is that the competition is not a lottery;

- a particular question or clue will not fail to qualify as involving skill or knowledge just because the answer can be discovered by basic research, whether on the internet or elsewhere;

- in practical terms, there are two elements to the statutory skill test set out above. Did the skill, judgement or knowledge requirement in fact eliminate a significant proportion of entrants and, if it did not, on what basis did the organisers conclude it was reasonable to expect that it would have done so?

- the phrase 'significant proportion' should take its ordinary, natural meaning. What proportion is significant will not be a specific figure, but is likely to depend on the context and facts of the case;

- the Commission takes the view that the onus lies on the organisers of competitions in the first instance to satisfy themselves that their competitions are compliant with the law. It therefore does not think it is unreasonable to ask those organisers how they have come to that view in cases where it has concerns about the legality of schemes. The Commission acknowledges that it is open to organisers to refuse to respond, preferring instead to reserve their defence for any possible prosecution. But the Commission thinks that an approach on the

lines it suggests will help avoid pursuing cases to prosecution and allow the two sides to resolve differences of opinion without resorting to costly litigation;

- the Commission should be willing to accept that, where steps have genuinely been taken by competition organisers to establish the way the competition will operate, a misjudgement may be made on the first occasion that a particular type of competition is organised such that it transpires that only an insignificant proportion of participants, actual or prospective, are eliminated by the skill, judgement or knowledge element. But further promotion of competitions of the same or similar types, in the face of evidence to suggest that the particular skill etc. element does not deter or eliminate a significant proportion of potential or actual participants, will be much harder to defend.

The Commission has issued a set of ground rules which it proposes to take as indicating that the skill, judgement or knowledge element is sufficient for the Commission not to need to pursue further.

Where a competition uses a multiple answer or other type of format, the Commission will not generally take action where:

- there are sufficient plausible alternative answers;
- the question is relevant to the context in which the competition is offered;
- the correct answer is not obviously given close to the question; and
- 'joke' answers are avoided.

Although the Gambling Commission is the statutory regulator, ultimately it is for the courts to decide whether any given promotion amounts to a lottery or other type of gambling. The guidance issued by the Commission is just that, guidance. However, most advertisers will be anxious to avoid having to defend their arrangements in court, even if they believe the Commission's interpretation of the law is incorrect. For this reason it is important to be aware of the guidance issued by the Commission, which as well as providing useful assistance on the interpretation of the Act also gives an indication of when advertisers can expect to be challenged by the Commission.

Prize competitions and betting

It is important when organising a prize competition not only to include a sufficient skill requirement to avoid a lottery, but also to avoid setting questions the answers to which require participants to guess certain matters which turn the arrangement into another form of gambling, i.e. betting.

A prize competition will amount to betting if:

1. participants are required to guess any of the following:

   (a) the outcome of a race, competition or other event or process;[26]

   (b) the likelihood of anything occurring or not occurring;[27] or

   (c) whether anything is or is not true;

2. participants are required to pay to participate; and

3. if the guess is accurate, or more accurate than other guesses, participants are to:

    (a) win a prize; or

    (b) enter a class among whom one or more prizes are to be allocated (whether or not wholly by chance).[28]

The term 'guessing' includes *predicting using skill or judgement.*[29]

These provisions are designed to ensure that prediction competitions such as fantasy football games are regulated as betting products and can therefore only be offered under a relevant betting licence. Agencies must therefore ensure that their client has a betting licence if they wish to run prediction-based league table competitions.

The provisions on payments to enter, including free entry routes, correspond to those for lotteries (see 1(a) and (b) above).

THE REGULATION OF PRIZE PROMOTIONS

The British Code of Advertising, Sales Promotion and Direct Marketing (the Code) governs sales and prize promotions.[30] The rules set out in the Code are designed primarily to protect the public and to ensure that consumers are not misled in any way.

The Code states that all promotions, including skill-based competitions and free prize draws, should be conducted equitably, promptly and efficiently and should be seen to deal fairly and honourably with consumers.[31] It also states that promoters are responsible for all aspects and all stages of promotions.[32]

The rules also apply to trade promotions and incentives as well as to consumer promotions.

Rules applicable to all sales promotions

The Code sets out the regulatory requirements for all promotions.[33] It states that promotions 'should specify clearly before any purchase (or before or at the time of entry/application, if no purchase is required)' the information below:

How to participate

The promotional material (or the terms and conditions of the promotion) should state clearly how the promotion works, and should also include any significant conditions and costs and any other major factors reasonably likely to influence the consumers' decisions or understanding about the promotion.

Start date

Although this is rare, if the promotion is yet to begin, then the start date should be clearly shown.

Closing date

All promotions should include a prominent closing date either for the purchases or for the submission of entries or claims.

There are some promotions where a closing date is not necessary, although this is very rare for prize promotions. Promotions that are running a special offer may not need a closing date, so long as they are stated to be 'subject to availability'. Some prize promotions based on skill may run on indefinitely until the required number of entrants have shown the required level of skill. In such cases a closing date may not be relevant. It may be sensible nonetheless to include a cut-off date in order to prevent the competition running on indefinitely.

Promoters should state if the deadline for responding to promotional material will be calculated from the date the material was received by consumers.

Finally, it is generally preferable that closing dates should not be changed unless circumstances outside the reasonable control of the promoter make it unavoidable. If they are changed for any reason, the promoter must take all reasonable steps to ensure that consumers who participated within the original terms are not disadvantaged. In the highly unlikely event that a closing date is brought forward, all efforts must be made to communicate as widely as possible. It will be very rare for such an occurrence to be permitted.

Proof of purchase
The promoters should state clearly whether any proof of purchase is required.

Prizes
The minimum number and nature of all the prizes should be given.

If the promoter wishes to use an image of the prize, it is important that this image accords to the actual prize. Caveats (such as 'The prize may not be the colour shown') may help to protect the promoter in the event that the prize is not exactly the same as the image. However, it would be regarded as a misleading advertisement if the differences between the image and the prize were significant and the consumer was led to believe that the prize was the image shown in the promotional material when this was not the case.

Agencies should take particular care when describing holiday, travel or car prizes. Full details of exactly what is and what is not included should be set out in the terms and conditions. A 'holiday' prize for two will be assumed to be fully inclusive of all food and drink, transfers and insurance, unless otherwise stated. Similarly, if there is a prize of a car, then it will be assumed to be fully roadworthy. It is also important to clearly state what the requirements are for visas, passports, travel or car insurance and driving licences.

Restrictions
The promotional material should include any restrictions on the entrants to the competition. These restrictions may be geographical ('UK residents only'), personal ('open only to those aged 18 or over) or technological ('this promotion is for internet users only').

Promoters should also state any need for an entrant to obtain permission to enter from an adult or employer as appropriate.

Availability of promotional packs
Where it is not obvious if there is likely to be a limitation on the availability of promotional packs during the campaign, then the phrase 'subject to availability' should be included on the promotional material and the terms and conditions.

Promoter's name and address

The promoter's full name and business address must always be shown prominently. This should be included in the terms and conditions, unless it is obvious from the context.

All entrants in the promotion should be able to retain the above information or have easy access to it throughout the promotion. It is important to remember that all promotional material, including any advertisements for the promotion, should specify all the significant conditions referred to above that apply.

Additional requirements

When running a sales promotion there are a number of additional factors to bear in mind.

All promoters should ensure that their promotions, including product samples, do not cause any harm to consumers or their property, and no promotion or promotional item should cause serious or widespread offence to the audience addressed.[34] Where necessary, safety warnings should be given on the promotional material and with any prize.

Promoters should make every effort to ensure that unsuitable or inappropriate material does not reach consumers.[35] This is particularly apposite in the case of food and drink manufacturers who should not run promotions, particularly when aimed at children, which would encourage children to over-indulge in food or drinks which are unhealthy when taken in excess.

Promotions aimed at children under 16 require special care. It is particularly important that alcoholic drinks do not feature in promotions directed at those under 18. Special care should be taken when products intended for adults may fall into the hands of children.[36] Parental consent should be actively sought in promotions aimed at children. Prize promotions addressed to or targeted at children always need a closing date.

It is a requirement under the Code that promoters can demonstrate that they made a reasonable estimate of the likely response to their promotion, and that they had sufficient prizes to meet that response.[37] It is not acceptable, for example, to run a promotion promising a valuable gift to all entrants and only having a small number available. Even if the phrase 'subject to availability' is used, it will still be a breach of the Code if the promoter cannot prove any correlation between the number of prizes or gifts on offer and the anticipated response to the promotion. In the event that there is a much higher response than was reasonably anticipated, the promoter is expected to offer refunds, substitute prizes or cash alternatives.

All promotions should be conducted under proper supervision and adequate time should be allowed for each phase of a promotion.[38] Promoters of prize draws should ensure that prizes are awarded in accordance with the laws of chance and under the supervision of an independent observer.

A survey by the Committee of Advertising Practice (CAP), in conjunction with the Advertising Standards Authority (ASA), checking the compliance rate of on-pack promotions over a six-month period, found that almost 95% of the promotions complied with the regulations. Significant failings were found, however, in the administration of the promotion rather than on the labelling and promotional material.

For example, in a quarter of the promotions, the promoter was unable to show that the draws were conducted under the supervision of an independent observer. Proper administration of the promotions is essential to ensure that consumers trust the integrity of the promotions and the promoters.

Rules specific to prize promotions

Whereas the preceding requirements relate to all promotions, the Code includes a number of important additional general requirements specifically for prize promotions.[39] It is important that promoters follow these, as it will prevent any prize draw or competition being regarded as misleading or unfair.

In the case of instant win promotions, for instance, winners should get their winnings at once (or should know immediately what they have won and how to claim without delay, unreasonable costs or administrative barriers). All instant-win tickets, tokens or numbers should be awarded on a fair and random basis. Verification should take the form of an independently audited statement that all prizes have been distributed, or made available for distribution, in that manner.

The Code also includes a list of points relating to the administration of a prize promotion which, if relevant, should be specified 'before or at the time of entry'.[40]

The terms and conditions should therefore state:

- whether there is any restriction on the number of entries (e.g. 'only one entry per household'). It is usually sensible to restrict numbers of entries per person or per household to reduce the amount of administration involved in judging competitions, and to prevent any one person or household receiving more than one prize or having a significantly greater chance of winning a prize;

- whether or not a cash alternative can be substituted for any prize. There is no requirement to substitute a cash alternative if the winner does not want the actual prize. Some promoters might however be prepared to allow for this;

- when the prize winners will receive their prizes. There is no need to include this if the prize will be delivered within six weeks of the closing date of the promotion. It would still be helpful, however, if some period were referred to informing a winner when to expect to receive the prize;

- how and when winners will be notified of results (e.g. 'winners will be notified in writing by [date]'). The method of notification can vary but should be appropriate to the type of promotion. An online promotion ought to notify the winners by email, for example. Winners should be notified as soon as possible after the judging of the competition or the prize draw is made;

- how and when winners and results will be announced. For the sake of fairness and to prevent promoters running false promotions in order to entice consumers to buy their products, it is a requirement under the Code for details of the winners to be made available. Promoters should therefore either publish, or make available on request, the name and county of prize winners and, if applicable, their winning entries. It is usual for promoters to ask consumers to send in a self-addressed envelope in order to receive the details requested, or a dedicated phone number could be provided. Promoters of online promotions should publish the details on their website. Promoters should ensure that *only* the name and county of residency of the winners is published. Release of more details than this, such as a full address, would be a breach of data protection rules;

- in a competition where prizes will be awarded on the basis of skill or judgement, the criteria for judging the entries should be established clearly in the terms and conditions. The criteria may be included in the description of how to participate in the competition. If a tiebreaker question is being used (e.g. 'Complete the following sentence in no more than x words: I enjoy ABC product because …'), then the criteria on which the winning entry is decided should be set out, whether it is humour, aptness, relevance or originality;

- where the selection of winning entries is open to subjective interpretation, it is vital that all promotions include an independent judge. A panel can be appointed to judge entries (e.g. of a photographic competition) and this panel must include at least one member who is independent of the competition's promoters and agents. All judges appointed should be competent to judge the competition; it would be inappropriate, for instance, to use as judge in a photographic competition someone who was not knowledgeable about photography;

- where judges are involved in deciding the winners, the full names of the judges should be made available on request;

- in any competition which involves the entrants creating original pieces of art, literary, musical or other copyright works, then it is important to state if the promoter is to have the copyright in the winning work (or any other of the entrants' work) after the competition. Terms and conditions could state, for example, 'By entering this competition, you agree to assign all copyright in the entry to the promoter';

- in a competition where original creations are sent in for judging, the promoter should explain how the entries will be returned. There is no obligation on the promoter to return any entries, but if this is the case, the terms and conditions should say so (usually with an apology as a matter of courtesy);

- if the promoter wishes to use the winner or winners in any post-event publicity. Promoters are required to obtain the permission of the winners before referring to or portraying them in publicity material. It is usually sensible therefore to include a term stating 'By entering the competition, the winner agrees that his or her name and image can be used by the promoter in post-event publicity'.

It is important in all prize promotions and competitions that the entrants can retain the terms and conditions, or have easy access to them (e.g. on a website) throughout the duration of the promotion and, if necessary, for a short time afterwards. This will enable them to keep a check on when any draw is to be held and when they are likely to be notified if they have won, and to check the names of the winners or judges.

The prizes described in advertisements and other marketing communications must be awarded, or reasonable equivalents.[41] Marketers must not claim or imply that the consumer has already won, will win, or will on doing a particular act win a prize (or other equivalent benefit), if the consumer must incur a cost to claim the prize (or other equivalent benefit) or if the prize (or other equivalent benefit) does not exist.[42]

Many companies will incorporate prize promotions onto their packaging. This is not a problem but, if coupons are used, companies should ensure that the terms and conditions for the competition or draw can still be retained by the consumer.

NORTHERN IRELAND

The sales promotion provisions of the CAP Code apply throughout the United Kingdom, including in Northern Ireland. The Gambling Act 2005, however, only applies in Great Britain. The law in Northern Ireland regarding lotteries and competitions is set out in the Betting, Gaming, Lotteries and Amusements (Northern Ireland) Order 1985 and, so far as the areas covered by this chapter are concerned, is the same as the law which until the Gambling Act 2005 applied throughout the United Kingdom. The key differences between Northern Irish and British law are as follows:

Stormont Castle, Northern Ireland

1. There is no statutory definition of a lottery in Northern Ireland. Nor is there any statutory definition of what the Gambling Act now refers to as 'payment to enter', or of what amounts to a valid free-entry route. The principles of lottery law are largely similar, the main difference being that you cannot in Northern Ireland link entry into a prize draw with the purchase of goods or services. This is why, where you have a prize draw advertised on the packaging of products sold throughout the United Kingdom, you will now find a free-entry route applicable only to Northern Ireland purchasers of the product (see sections on the lottery, prize draws & free-entry routes on pages 166–171).

2. Article 168 of the Order repeats section 14 of the now repealed Lotteries and Amusements Act 1976. As a result, the Gambling Act provisions referred to in the section on prize competitions and betting (see page 174). which define as betting certain types of prediction competitions, do not apply in Northern Ireland. Instead, the Order makes unlawful:

   (a) *any competition in which prizes are offered for forecasts of the result either:*

      (i) *of a future event; or*

      (ii) *of a past event the result of which is not yet ascertained, or not yet generally known;*

   (b) *any other competition in which success does not depend to a substantial degree on the exercise of skill.*

CONCLUSION

The Gambling Act has opened up a more flexible regime for prize promotions by allowing entry into prize draws to be linked to the purchase of products, without the threat of it being an illegal lottery. However, the Gambling Commission can be expected to prosecute advertisers in cases where the provisions of the Act are breached, although they may not always prosecute the first time an advertiser commits what they regard as an offence. Care should therefore be taken to comply with the Act's provisions, and cautious advertisers anxious to avoid a test case would be well advised to steer clear of the grey areas where the wording of the Act is open to interpretation.

Charles Swan, Swan Turton

Notes

1   Gambling Act 2005, section 3
2   Gambling Act 2005, section 14(1)
3   Gambling Act 2005, section 14(2)
4   Gambling Act 2005, section 14(3)
5   Gambling Act 2005, section 14(4)
6   Gambling Act 2005, Schedule 2 paragraph 2(b)
7   Gambling Act 2005, Schedule 2 paragraph 3
8   Gambling Act 2005, Schedule 2 paragraph 4
9   Gambling Act 2005, Schedule 2 paragraph 2(c)
10 Gambling Act 2005, Schedule 2 paragraph 5(1)
11 Gambling Act 2005, Schedule 2 paragraph 5(2)(b)
12 Gambling Act 2005, Schedule 2 paragraph 6
13 Gambling Act 2005, Schedule 2 paragraph 7
14 'Ordinary post' means 'ordinary first-class or second-class post (without special arrangements for delivery)'.
15 Gambling Act 2005, Schedule 2 paragraph 8
16 Gambling Act 2005, section 339
17 Gambling Act 2005, section 6(1)
18 Gambling Act 2005, section 6(2)(a)(i)
19 Gambling Act 2005, section 6(2)(a)(ii)
20 Gambling Act 2005, section 6(2)(a)(iii)
21 Gambling Act 2005, section 6(2)(b)
22 Gambling Act 2005, section 6(3)
23 Gambling Act 2005, section 6(4)
24 Gambling Act 2005, section 6(5)
25 Gambling Act 2005, section 14(5)
26 It may still amount to betting even if the race, competition, event or process has already occurred or been completed, and even if one party to the transaction knows the outcome. Gambling Act 2005, section 9(2)
27 It may still amount to betting even if the event has already occurred or failed to occur, and one party to the transaction knows that the event has already occurred or failed to occur. Gambling Act 2005, section 9(3)
28 Gambling Act 2005, sections 9(1) and 11(1)
29 Gambling Act 2005, section 11(2)
30 The British Code of Advertising, Sales Promotion and Direct Marketing (the CAP Code): paragraph 1.1 (g)
31 The CAP Code: paragraph 27.4
32 The CAP Code: paragraph 27.3
33 The CAP Code: paragraph 34.1
34 The CAP Code: paragraphs 28.1 and 28.3
35 The CAP Code: paragraph 28.2
36 The CAP Code: paragraph 29
37 The CAP Code: paragraph 30
38 The CAP Code: paragraph 31
39 The CAP Code: paragraph 35
40 The CAP Code. paragraph 35.9
41 The CAP Code, paragraph 35.10
42 The CAP Code, paragraph 35.11

ng Collins Long Collins Long Collins Long Collins Long Collins Long Col
ng Collins Long Collins Long Collins Long Collins Long Collins Long Col
Collins Long Collins Long Collins Long Collins Long Collins Long Co

3.8

Music in advertising

INTRODUCTION

What it is

'Talking about music is like dancing about architecture.'

Steve Martin, *The Independent*

Music can be easily heard for what it is, but not so easily seen for what it is, for the purpose of 'clearance' for use in advertising. Below the surface of notes, beats and rhythms and the heartbeat of performing artists, there lies an underworld of intellectual property rights and ancillary rights. This underworld will be a murky and difficult place to navigate without a grasp of the lay of the land and some real understanding of the composition of these rights. Intellectual property

rights form the business foundation of the structure of the music industry. Every advertising agency therefore needs some basic knowledge of these rights in order to go about its daily business of including the magic ingredient, which is the music, in its advertisements.

Music comprises two primary copyrights:

- copyright in the sound recording; and
- copyright in the underlying music composition, which itself may comprise two distinct key elements – the music itself (i.e. the instrumental element) and the lyrics (i.e. the words).

Copyright is a proprietary right of an exclusive nature, that is, it relates to the ownership of the intellectual property, and the laws of copyright look to protect such ownership in much the same way as land law looks to protect real property ownership. Copyright itself is governed nationally under domestic statutes (in the UK principally under the Copyright, Designs and Patents Act 1988 as amended) and is internationally reciprocally recognised by international conventions between signatory states.

Under UK law the period of copyright for new sound recordings and musical compositions which fall under current legislation is:

- *Sound recordings* – 50 years from the end of the calendar year in which it was made, or 50 years from the end of the calendar year in which it was released, provided it was released within that first period. (Note, 'released' includes playing it in public or broadcasting it on radio/television.)
- *Musical compositions* – for the life of the composer plus 70 years from the end of the calendar year in which the composer died.

As a consequence of different laws introduced, and effective at different times and in different countries, governing the applicable duration of copyright in different circumstances, there will be instances where certain recordings and/or certain songs will be wholly or partially out of copyright in some parts of the world but not in the UK, or vice versa, and specialist advice needs to be sought to ascertain the exact worldwide copyright position. Suffice to say that the effect of both the recording *and* the song being 'out of copyright' worldwide is that it falls into the 'public domain' and as such can be used without consent or payment (at least as a matter of copyright law). For a more detailed account of the laws of copyright see Chapter 1.1.

For the purposes of working through this chapter we are going to assume that both the sound recording and the musical composition are both 'in copyright'.

How it works

> 'If a literary man puts together two words about music, one of them will be wrong.'
>
> Aaron Copland, in Frank Muir book *Music*

In order to get permission to use the copyright in both the sound recording and the musical composition in an advertisement the right has to be granted by the person(s) or party(ies) which 'own' or 'control' the applicable copyrights.

So, by way of a typical example, the song 'Tomorrow' is written by John Lemon and Paul Mint and recorded by their band The Fab Five and the advertising agency XYZ wishes to use 30 seconds of it to promote a new product for a worldwide television campaign. The proprietary rights (i.e. the copyrights) in 'Tomorrow' are owned by the following parties:

- the copyright in the sound recording is owned by the record company IME for the whole world (as the recording artist The Fab Five assigned all their copyright in the recording to their record company under the terms of their exclusive recording agreement); and

- the copyright in the musical composition is 50% owned by TVA Music for the whole world (as this is John Lemon's 50% copyright interest in the song which he has co-written with Paul Mint and which he has assigned to his publishing company worldwide) and the remaining 50% ownership of the musical composition is vested in AVT Music (as this is Paul Mint's 50% copyright interest in the song which he has co-written with John Lemon and which he has assigned to his publishing company worldwide).

XYZ, the advertising agency, has to therefore get the advertising usage right for the worldwide television campaign from IME for the usage of the sound recording of 'Tomorrow', and from both TVA Music and AVT Music for the usage of the musical composition 'Tomorrow'.

Owners of copyright can grant rights to third parties principally in one of two ways:

- by way of an *assignment* of rights – which is an actual transference of property rights from the owner to a third party. This is an unlikely scenario relating to advertising usage except where music may be specially commissioned by the advertising agency; and

- by way of *licence* of rights – which is a licence of certain stated rights of usage by the owner to a third party. This is the most usual grant of rights to an advertising agency for music usage.

The licences required by XYZ for its worldwide television campaign will have to include the right to 'synchronise' the recording and the music to the visual element of the advertisement, and in order to do so the following specific licences will be required from the respective owners of the constituent copyright elements of the track 'Tomorrow':

- a 'Master Use Licence' from IME Records in order to licence the necessary rights in the sound recording of 'Tomorrow'; and

- a 'Synchronisation Licence' from both TVA Music (50% copyright owner) and AVT Music (50% copyright owner) in order to licence 100% of the necessary rights in the musical composition of 'Tomorrow'.

The terms of both the master use licence and the synchronisation licence must include all the creative, commercial, financial, legal and practical points governing the conditions upon which the advertising agency is allowed to use the music in the advertisement.

We will therefore review all the key terms, from both a *legal* and *practical* point of view, which most typically should be contained in these types of licences. We will also consider the issues that should be considered by the advertising agency in its dealings and in making sure it has got the necessary rights, and in determining what its ongoing obligations may be during the campaign, both financial and legal.

In doing so we will:

- consider the terms of the general licence for usage as applying to both the master use licence and the synchronisation licence, which run in parallel and for the most part will reflect similar terms. (Where there are material differences we will point out these differences);

- refer to both the 'musical composition' and the 'sound recording' as 'the work' below, making distinctions where necessary;

- refer a little later to usage of library music or specially commissioned music which will introduce some variation to the terms of the more typical licence considered below. That said, there are of course instances where the music for an advertisement starts with an existing or known piece of music, which is then worked on further by the original artist (or indeed another artist or producer or remixer) at the request of the agency, in the process creating a different version or a number of different versions, in the event of which the typical licensing terms should be varied to accommodate this.

THE LICENCE – THE AGREEMENT GOVERNING THE RIGHT TO USE MUSIC IN AN ADVERTISEMENT

'It aint no sin to crack a few laws now and then, just so long as you don't break any'.

Mae West in *Every Day's a Holiday*

The Licensor – the person/party who is granting the rights

Legal

The party granting the rights in the work has to be the owner or controller of the copyright in order to make the grant of rights under the licence agreement for the agreed usage. Because with music there is often split ownership or co-ownership of the copyright in the work, it is not uncommon to need the consent of multiple parties.

It is more usually the case that a single party 'owns' or 'controls' the rights to the sound recording, but it is often the case that there are a number of publishers that co-own and co-publish a musical composition which has in turn been granted certain rights by a writer who has co-written a musical composition with one or more other writers (who have in turn assigned their rights to another publisher).

There may however be a number of other additional reasons, e.g. ownership by the UK owner of the sound recording only extends to the UK or to certain other countries, and other third-party record labels control such rights in their respective territories; the sound recording and the musical composition incorporate a 'sample' which in turn requires the consent of the original sample owner(s) in the sampled sound recording and the musical composition.

Practical

The rights to the works of established artists and writers are usually vested in their respective recording and publishing companies.

Where productions for advertisements originate in the UK, the rights owners will most usually be in a position to grant rights directly for the world (and will deal directly with their overseas licensees), certainly in the case of the so-called major labels who by and large licence to their own companies overseas. Try in any event to put the onus on the record and publishing companies wherever possible to clear these worldwide rights.

The Licensee – the party to whom the rights in the work are granted

Legal

The party who is directly granted the rights may be either the agency as principal, or the agency expressly acting as agent for its client, or the client directly – the first scenario being the most common in the current market. The party who is directly liable for compliance with all its terms and conditions and ongoing obligations to the Licensor will be the party stated to be 'the Licensee'. The identity of the Licensee will also determine the extent to which the Licensee itself will need the right to 'sub-licence' certain rights to third parties to put the licence into effect. (See section on right to assign and/or licence, page 200.)

Practical

It is current industry practice for an agency to be the direct Licensee as principal contracting party under the terms of the licence agreement, and to directly negotiate and execute the Licence in its own name. You should ensure therefore that the contracting party name and details are absolutely correct so that the right legal entity is contracting.

The product and the production – what's being advertised and what's the advertisement?

Legal

This should comprise a brief description of the product and/or service which is being advertised and the nature of the production (i.e. is there one version of one particular film being made or will there be numerous versions dependent upon the media used), since each such version needs to be expressly covered by the grant of rights under the licence agreement.

Practical
It is important that the agency ensures that the rights granted expressly cover different versions of a production which might be substantially the same, but have material differences, since otherwise the argument can be raised that a particular version should attract additional fees or form an unauthorised use under the terms of the agreement.

What version and what duration?

Legal
The relevant agreement must expressly describe the accurate title of the sound recording and the featured artist in the case of a master use licence, and the accurate title of the musical composition and the accurate names of the relevant composers/ songwriters in the case of a synchronisation licence, and their interest(s). (It may of course be the case that the song is an established song, say, 'Yesterday', but that the sound recording is a cover version performed by an artist other than The Beatles.)

The duration of the music used should be expressly specified, and if the intention is to use the work in different versions of different durations then all of the various different durations should be expressly stated.

Practical
If it is intended that an edit of music be used from music that is not a continuous excerpt from the original work (i.e. it is altered other than by 'topping and tailing') then it is vital that it be made clear from the outset, as this constitutes a material change to the original work of a substantial nature and will require the express consent from the relevant music publishing and record company owner, and in most cases the additional consent of the recording artist and songwriter. This will also raise potential 'moral rights' issues, so make absolutely sure that this right is expressly inscribed in the agreement and expressly authorised by the Licensor.

Territory – in what countries the advertisement can be exploited

Legal
The agreement must state the country, or countries, where it is intended that the campaign will take place. (See also 'Primary rights granted', page 189). Any leakage of the advertising campaign beyond the stated geographic boundaries for the licensed music usage will constitute a potential infringement of copyright of the work and a material breach of the terms of the licence agreement.

Practical
It is often the case that a campaign is launched in a particular country, or countries, but with the intention that 'if it goes well' the campaign will extend to additional territories. The way to deal with this contingency is by way of an option, or a series of options, providing the licensee with the right to extend the country or countries licensed at a later stage during the currency of the term of the licence, for an additional set of fees. (See 'option rights', page 195.)

Term – how long can the campaign run for?

Legal
The agreement must state the full period for which the grant of rights will run (i.e. the length of the advertising campaign). Any advertisement usage which occurs after the Term has ended will constitute unlicensed usage, and may well also constitute (dependent on the words of the specific licence) an infringement of copyright, with the consequent right on the part of the Licensor to claim damages – the extent and scale of such claim being determined by the circumstance, the manner of the usage, and so forth.

Practical
It is not always known at the time the licence is applied for what period of time the client may be looking to run the campaign, and this may well be dependent upon a number of factors as the campaign rolls – the response, budgetary issues and so on. As in the case of determining the geographical extent of the campaign at the outset, the best way to deal with such uncertainty is to agree an Initial Period to cover the known campaign committed to at that time, and then to build in an option, or a series of options (as the case may be) to be exercised during the Initial Period of the Term to extend the Initial Period as and when required.

Primary rights granted – in what media and in what formats can the advertisement be run, and what other underlying rights are needed?

Legal
The rights expressly granted under the licence by the Licensor to the Licensee are the only rights which the Licensee can rely on for the advertising campaign, so the shopping list of relevant rights must be fully listed.

The media and activities required for a specific campaign will determine what should and what should not need to go onto this shopping list. Prior to the internet and mobile applications, this list was of a simpler nature. Now, however, both traditional and all aspects of new media need to be considered, which will include what (if any) interactive media rights may be required, including the ability of the consumer/customer to in any way alter, edit or amend the work in any way.

Some of the more usual items on the list are as follows:

- *Theatrical and non-theatrical usages* – cinema usage and usage in public venues (i.e. shopping malls, clubs and so on). There may be additional 'trailer' rights and/or 'out of context' rights required, but these rights are more usually associated with films than they are with advertisements. This may apply to bigger advertisements and advertising campaigns where, for example, an advertisement is shown within a film and the licensee needs the right to make use of that particular clip in a 'making of' the advertisement and/or the film or even as a preview of the advertisement. These rights are ancillary but additional to the primary rights and will need to be listed and paid for under the terms of the licence.

- *Television* – consider what forms and formats may be required (i.e. terrestrial, satellite, broadcast, narrowcast, cable etc.). (Note: ancillary radio advertisements will require a 'dubbing' licence – that is the right to dub the sound recording to the radio advertisement itself.)

- *Online* – consider if linear or non-linear; webcasts, downloads, streaming, blogs; banner advertising etc. (Part of a campaign, certainly in the future, may well be music/advertising revenue arrangements [i.e. where the advertisement is downloaded as part of the music file which the customer receives for no payment, but where the owner of the work is paid a consideration based upon a pre-agreed value by the brand owner of the advertisement]. This arrangement may of course be quite separate to this licence arrangement or agreed at the same time.)

- *Mobile applications* – similar considerations as for online, and in addition consider rights to tie-ins with handset owners and mobile operators and all forms of mobile exploitation – downloads, streaming, subscription services and so on.

- *Video/DVD* – the Licensee may wish to include the advertisement on DVDs prior to a feature film or a television programme, which may or may not be streamed and/or downloadable, dependent upon the rights granted.

- *Use on agency and clients websites.*

- *Versions and durations of the work* – as may apply to any or all of the permitted uses (see also page 188).

Practical

It is essential that the agency ensures that all the rights required for the campaign are granted to the Licensee to cover all intended media and campaign activities. It may be the case, as mentioned in respect of the Term and the Territory, that it is not known at the outset what rights may be required, and again the best way forward is to build in a series of Options during the Term to extend the rights as may be required. Certainly better to be granted one or two rights that may not be required than too few!

Ancillary rights granted – and what other underlying rights are needed

There are some additional ancillary rights which relate to the work, and the exploitation of the work, which the agency should have a basic understanding of and should be dealt with under the terms of the licence, either expressly or as a grant of rights 'catch all' provision under the terms of the licence.

The performance/performing right in the work

Legal

- With respect to the sound recording, this separate right in almost all cases is vested in the UK in Phonographic Performance Limited (PPL) which administers the public performance and broadcasting rights of both record company members and recording artists. So far as advertisements in the UK are concerned, this right is to be directly granted by the owner or controller of the sound recording under its licence with the Licensee, with the caveat that in any and all countries where monies may be payable under industry agreement then these be paid by the 'broadcasters' of the work (i.e. the television companies).

It is worth noting that the concept of an 'exclusive right of communication to the public' was introduced in the United Kingdom in 2003, which covers two aspects. The first relates to the 'broadcasting' of recordings, which covers wire or wireless transmissions effectively where it is not 'on demand' by the customer (i.e. streaming). The second relates to 'making available' where on demand by the customer (i.e. downloading). The artist's performing right continues in respect of the 'broadcast' element, but in addition he/she now has the new 'making available' right which is almost invariably assigned to the record company under their recording agreement. If downloading is an element of the advertising campaign ensure that this right is expressly covered under the terms of the licence.

- With respect to the music copyright, the separate right of performance of the music is vested, in almost all cases in the UK, in the Mechanical Copyright Protection Society/Performing Right Society (MCPS/PRS)[1] by both the songwriter/composer and the music publishers for their respective interest, and the right of performance is granted by the society directly to the relevant television broadcaster and/or webcaster etc., and such licence is granted subject to payment being made by the relevant broadcaster to the MCPS/PRS relating to such usage.

Practical

It is imperative to make sure firstly, that the rights for such performance/broadcast of the work are granted, or are acknowledged as having been granted, by the Licensor to the applicable society, and secondly, that there is no liability on the agency to make these payments directly itself. It may have to undertake to only license the advertisement for usage to bodies licensed by MCPS/PRS or equivalent, and also to provide the licensor with transmission schedules, ident/clock numbers etc. to enable the Licensor to claim for performance monies with the relevant societies.

The right of the featured artist and/or the session musicians to residual fees in respect of their performing rights arising from the exploitation of the work

Legal

In the vast majority of cases, the Licensor(s) of rights to established and published works will be the relevant record company(ies) and publishing company(ies) which own or control such rights to license for use in advertisements – in many cases subject to the approval of the applicable featured artist(s) and songwriter(s). Where the Licensor of the recording is a record company it is vital that it be made clear under the terms of the licence if there is a responsibility for the payment of residual fees arising from the exhibition of the advertisement (i.e. from the performance or broadcast of the sound recording incorporated in the advertisement), and which party will bear the responsibility to make such payments. These payments can be substantial and in a worldwide campaign can arise in many countries around the world. In respect of an existing established work the position will be broadly as follows:

- featured musicians under their exclusive recording contracts with record companies will, in most instances, have granted their consent for the exploitation of the sound recording against specific payments governed by the terms of their recording agreements, without the right to further residual payments;

- session musicians and other artists who appear on a sound recording, but who are not signed as recording artists to the particular record company (i.e. guest vocalists) may or may not have given their consent without the obligation of payment of such residuals.

In the event that residuals so arise, the scale of the fees will be governed by the applicable union body to whom the performer is allied, which in the UK will either be the Musicians Union[2] or Equity[3] (which may be the case, for example, with a vocalist). The rates applicable for each body are different, and far higher in the case of Equity members.

If the Licensor cannot warrant that either no such residuals will arise or that the Licensor will remain liable for such payments under the agreement, then the onus will rest with the Licensee, who will need to compute such costs into the campaign budget.

Alternatively, there is scope under the terms of the IPA/MU Recorded Advertising Music Agreement[4] (a voluntary agreement made between the Institute of Practitioners in Advertising and the Musicians Union effective from 1 September 2007), for advertising agencies to look to apply the agreed rates tariffs set out under the terms of this agreement, not only in respect of specially commissioned music for advertising purposes, but also, subject to complying with the procedure set out in the agreement, to existing sound recordings intended to be licensed for advertising usage. (For more details of the terms and rates set out under the agreement refer to the agreement itself.)

Practical

If the Licensee cannot obtain a warranty from the Licensor that the Licensee will not be liable for the payment of residual fees to performers, then the Licensee should look to rely on the provisions of the IPA/MU Recorded Advertising Music Agreement, and in particular the buy-out provisions which are contained in clause 3 of that agreement ('Branded Communications'). It may be the case that for a particular recording one form of clearance has to be met under the MU principles for some of the musicians, and that in addition a guest vocalist as an Equity member will give rise to the payment of considerable residual fees. Ensure that the terms of the agreement are crystal clear as to both what the position is in respect of the performers on the sound recording and precisely where the parties' responsibilities and liabilities fall.

Moral rights

Legal

The 'author' of a work has an additional right (a moral right) to that work which is in a sense additional but ancillary to both the laws of copyright and to whatever contractual terms the author can rely upon in his/her dealing with that work. This right originated outside of statute or common law from 'droits moraux' and governs three basic rights:

- *Right of Paternity in the work* – the right to be known as the creator of the work.
- *Right of Integrity in the work* – the right to not have the work changed in any way without the author's approval.
- *Right to Prevent False Attribution* – the right not to have a work falsely attributed to them (and vice versa).

Under UK law (Copyright, Designs and Patents Act 1988) it is possible to obtain a waiver from the author to his/her moral rights. It is most commonly the case in the UK that record companies obtain such a waiver, or at the least get an agreement that such right will not be asserted against the Licensor or against third parties authorised by the Licensor for such music usage.

Practical

It is essential that the Licensor warrants that such moral rights will not be asserted by the respective 'authors' of the work, as it can give rise to a number of possible actions which are ancillary to the terms of the Licence which the Licensee is otherwise relying upon for the usage of the work in the advertisement. For instance, in the USA a number of actions have been brought by artists based on 'sound-alike' voices being used where the original recording artist does not want to be associated with the advert in question (Tom Waits was awarded $2.6m in compensatory damages in respect of such an advertisement advertising 'Doritos'). Reliance upon moral rights in the UK might well give the artist a similar right of action in the UK in similar circumstances.

Publicity rights

Legal

It is the case that rights of publicity and privacy vary from country to country, and indeed many overseas laws are more stringent and restrictive than in the UK. In any event, it may well be the case that the identity or image of an artist is integral to a particular campaign, in which case the Licensor must expressly grant such identity and image rights to the Licensee in order for these to be used.

Practical

Direct usage of the artist and/or the image and/or the artist's logo would be more usually the case where there is an express tie-in or endorsement with the product or service being advertised, in which case the artist must be directly and expressly contracted in any event. It should never be implied that a songwriter or an artist is in any way endorsing a product or service being advertised unless under a direct agreement to this effect. It is not the case at the current time (although the industry may well be moving towards it) that a record or publishing company has any 'branding' or general 'image' rights of the artist or songwriter, nor can such companies provide their services in this regard.

General comment on rights

'The first thing we do, let's kill all the lawyers.'

William Shakespeare

With the speed at which both the music and media industries are changing, and with it the use of all media by industry and consumer alike, it is little wonder that advertising agencies and their clients will need to keep their 'options' very much open when it comes to determining which rights may be required for any particular campaigns in the future. The natural business tension will be that the music 'owners' will seek to obtain as much recompense as possible for the rainbow of rights that they are now being asked to grant; whilst the brand owners and agencies will be looking to ensure that they can cover as much of the fragmented market as possible by being granted a widespread net of media opportunities. The scale of fees and the concomitant options are therefore very much interlinked.

Licence fees

Legal

The fee that is being paid by the Licensee is 'in consideration' of the rights being granted by the Licensor to the Licensee. In the case of advertisements 100% of the fee is most usually paid upfront, that is, prior to the commencement date of the campaign and most advisably, upon the date of execution of the licence agreement. In many cases the Licensor will stipulate under the terms of the licence that the licence itself is not effective unless and until such payment is made. If the agency commences a campaign without such fee being paid and for any reason the licence is subsequently not agreed or withheld (i.e. deal terms not reached), any usage of the work may well be an infringement of copyright under law and will give rise to a substantial claim in damages by the Licensor, not only against the agency but also against all parties which have used the work unlawfully, each of which will have a claim in turn against the agency. A position to be avoided at all costs!

Where the rights granted by the Licensor are divided up into certain rights being made available at the beginning of the Term of the Licence, with subsequent options becoming exercisable by the Licensee to extend the rights, the fees will be split up along the following lines (by way of example):

- *basic rights* – United Kingdom/12-month period/media (all forms of television) £x;

- *option rights* (available to the Licensee during the Term) –

Option media	Option media fee
Cinema	£y.
In-store promotions	£z
Webcasting	£w

The option(s) will be exercisable by the Licensee giving written notice to the Licensor at any time during the Initial Term, together with the payment of the applicable Option Media Fee. There may also be additional territorial options which will be exercisable during the Initial Term, or at such other time or times as may be agreed by notice and payment of an Option Territory Fee. The Initial Term may itself be subject to an option, or a series of options, to extend the period against payment of an additional fee, or automatically as part of the exercise of another option, say to extend all the media.

The fees agreed in this way therefore remain in line with the potential growth of the campaign and the rights that are being granted to the Licensee.

One final aspect of the fee structure well worth mentioning is the reliance by copyright owners in the music industry on the 'Most Favoured Nations' clause when it comes to agreeing the size and scale of the fees. The intent of the clause for the copyright owners is to ensure that another party, or parties, which have an interest in the work will not be paid more than the Licensor is paid as owner of its interest in the work (and also in effect that the Licensor will get no less!). The width of these provisions can work in a number of ways; remember that we are always dealing with two principal distinct copyrights in the work, one relating to the sound recording and the other to the musical composition itself (comprising both the music and the lyric):

- Most Favoured Nations with all the owners of the copyright in the work pro rata to their respective interests (i.e. third-party co-owners of the master [if more than one] and third-party co-owners of the music copyright [if more than one]); or

- Most Favoured Nations between the third-party co-owners of the masters only; or

- Most Favoured Nations between the third-party co-owners of the music copyright only.

If such Favoured Nations provisions apply, then ensure that you are aware of this when agreeing a deal with any one party. Whilst this provision often applies between the respective record company(ies) and the publishing company(ies), which jointly own all the copyright interest in the work, be wary of agreeing this provision where the song itself may be a very successful 'hit', but the recorded version being licensed is a cover version by an unknown artist, as in such an instance a 'Favoured Nations provision' may be wholly inappropriate.

Practical
As a general comment average fees have been falling for two reasons: on the agency side because of smaller production budgets; on the music side because – against

a backdrop of failing and falling record sales – there is a general hunger for such usage in the music industry, an area which historically both the industry and the artists themselves were previously shy to embrace. The tie-up of music and brands is now becoming far more the rule than the exception, and consequently there is no longer any struggle on the part of the agencies to go underground mining for any and all genres of music. As to what a 'typical rate' may be for music, it is difficult, if not impossible to say. Average sums give no clue to individual deals.

On the music side, key factors that will undoubtedly influence price include:

- the rights being granted – as to the term; the territory; the media;
- the stature of the music/the track being used;
- the stature of the artist (Madonna is the highest-earning female musician[5]);
- any element of exclusivity.

On the advertising side, key factors that will undoubtedly influence price include:

- the production budget for the advertisement/advertising campaign;
- how integral a particular song or track is to the advertisement itself.

A typical 30-second advertisement for specific music usage might be anything from £20,000 to £60,000 for each of the 100% interest of the two principal separate rights owners for Europe for a 12-month period, but the truth is the range can be as much as £5,000 to £150,000, depending on the precise circumstances.

The nature and scope of these fees assume that the licence is for an existing work owned by third-party record labels and music publishers. The position is quite different if the music is specially commissioned for the advertisement, or the advertisement uses 'library music', that is, music which is readily made and available (both the master and the music composition) against either an agreed rate card or much lower available negotiated rates. This type of licensing and usage relates to unknown pieces of music which have been specifically created for relatively cheap and easy usage, e.g. for elevators, hotel lobbies or company promotions.

GENERAL TERMS AND CONDITIONS FOR THE LICENSING OF MUSIC – OTHER POINTS THAT ARE IMPORTANT TO LOOK OUT FOR

No rights granted to Licensee

Legal

The Licensee will have no rights to make any changes to the work, that is the recording itself or the music or lyric to the composition, unless the Licensor expressly grants that right. Any unauthorised changes will constitute a breach of the terms of the licence agreement and an infringement of copyright, and in addition may well be in breach of the songwriters and/or artists moral rights.

Also, the right under the licence will be granted for the work to be used for a specific period of time, and anything used in excess of that time will also constitute both a breach of contract and an infringement of copyright.

It is worth mentioning here that the general position is that provided the Licensee has the appropriate licence from the music publisher/owner for a cover of a particular musical composition, the making of a 'cover version' does not require under the laws of contract the further consent of the owner of the original recording of that particular song. The Licensee may wish to make a new cover either to create a different version for artistic and/or commercial reasons or by reason of budgetary constraints. In principle this is fine, with the one caveat which was mentioned earlier in this chapter, where the use of such a cover recording may give rise to other legal issues – potential claims for 'sound-alikes' and/or passing off and/or under a possible moral rights claim. Bear in mind the law may differ in this regard from country to country so that what might, say, be accceptable in the UK may give rise to a potential action in the USA. The only way to protect yourself is to take specific legal advice to cover the legal position in the applicable territories of the intended campaign. For example, in the UK it has been held that in certain circumstances in a sound-alike type case (i.e. an advertisement featuring a cover sounding like the original recording artist) there may indeed be a danger of a 'passing off' action being brought (that is, an action for passing off the recording as that featuring the original artist).

Practical

Make sure that the rights you intend to rely upon are clearly covered by the licence agreement. Bear in mind that the rights you are being granted by each of the rights owners are independent of each other and that there are instances where the agency may have to take separate legal advice to establish whether an activity may or may not be legal in particular circumstances – use of 'cover versions' may be just one example of this.

Additional Licensee responsibilities

Legal

There is usually an obligation to provide the Licensor with an agreed form of the finished advertisement either as a file or on DVD.

There will be an obligation as between the Licensor and the Licensee that it is for the Licensee to make sure that the parties down the line which use and/or exhibit the advertisements are responsible for all licences, clearances and consents as may be required to so use and exploit the work, over and above the specific rights granted by the Licensor under the licence agreement, which include the following:

- *Musicians/artists residual fees* – whilst the record label should be made liable and responsible under the licence agreement to have obtained all necessary consents from the performers in the sound recording, in circumstances where residual fees are payable upon usage (see the section on licence fees, page 194) this obligation may be passed on to the Licensee under the terms of the licence agreement.

- *Dubbing fees/broadcasting fees* – these fees are payable by production companies and/or television companies for the copying and broadcasting of the work. These fees are paid in the UK to PPL on behalf of the recording rights owners and to the MCPS/PRS on behalf of the music copyright owners, and are paid in many cases under industry agreements (e.g. ITV/Sky). [Note that in the UK the exhibition of the advertisement on television gives rise to the payment of PRS fees, but that there is no additional broadcast fee attributable to such exhibition, so that the right to such broadcast has to be included in the licence agreement with the master owner and included in the licence fee.]

- *Additional residual royalties* – if the advertisement is to be incorporated in a DVD (i.e. an advertisement is to appear before a feature film being released on DVD) then the licences will have to provide whether or not any further residual royalties will arise on sale of such DVDs (i.e. mechanical copyright royalties to the publisher), or whether the licence fee constitutes a 'buy-out' in lieu of any such residual amounts.

Practical

As the buck may well stop with the Licensee (as between the Licensee and the Licensor) for any and all hidden or residual monies that may be payable arising from this music usage, it is essential that the Licensee is absolutely clear as to what liabilities might arise, that the agreement is absolutely clear on this, and that these potential liabilities are covered down the line with the chain of advertisement/music users (i.e. that the exhibitors are held liable to the Licensee for payment of broadcast fees, and so on).

Licensee indemnity

Legal

An indemnity is most usually required by the Licensor from the Licensee in the event that any claim may arise against the Licensor as a result of any breach by the Licensee of the terms of the agreement. The consequence is that the Licensee will be held liable for any and all damages or costs that the Licensor may suffer from a third-party claim. An example of this would be that an agency has used the work in an unauthorised way and that as a result the artist or the songwriter is suing the Licensor (the Licensor would in such circumstances 'third party' the Licensee into the action, relying upon this indemnity) which might well include all the other parties' legal costs as well.

Practical

If you can, try and limit the Licensor's automatic entitlement to the indemnity either to where the claim has been reduced to a judgment against the Licensor, or where the Licensee has agreed to settle it. In addition, look for a reciprocal indemnity from the Licensor as to its rights to the work and the Licensee's rights of usage.

Breach and cure

Legal

There are two basic potential remedies available to the Licensor in the event that the Licensee, or in turn third parties authorised by the Licensee, is for any reason in breach of the terms of the licence agreement. Both these remedies will be affected by two factors, the terms of the agreement and the nature and circumstances of the breach.

- *Remedy in damages* – the Licensor may have the right to seek damages against the Licensee for a material breach of the terms of the agreement. For example, use of the work exceeding the duration permitted under the licence, or for a use that has not been authorised at all. The quantum of damages (that is, 'how much') will be governed by several factors relating to the nature and extent of the breach: whether it was innocent or wilful, how quickly the breach was terminated, and so on. The terms of the agreement may expressly state that unauthorised use will automatically constitute an 'infringement of copyright', the result of which may be that the damages claim will be greater than it would otherwise be if only constituting a breach of contract.

- *Remedy by seeking an injunction* – in equity the Licensor may have the right to 'injunct' the usage by the Licensee where the scale and nature of the breach is such that damages alone would not be deemed to be a sufficient remedy, for example, a flagrant breach of copyright by reason of unauthorised and inappropriate usage which could bring disrepute to the songwriter and/or the artist.

It is important for the Licensee to ensure under the terms of the licence that the Licensee is given prior written notice of any alleged breach, giving the Licensee the opportunity for a reasonable period of time to 'cure' the alleged breach. In the vast majority of cases the event giving rise to the breach will be in error or default, and this will give the Licensee the opportunity to rectify the situation.

Practical

It is advantageous, if possible, for the Licensee under the terms of the licence to restrict the Licensor's remedies for breach to an action for damages only, and to proscribe any injunctive relief, but this is a matter for negotiation and is more usually agreed in the case of feature films. Certainly, it is more difficult to proscribe this remedy where the artist/track has significant profile in the market place.

The practical advice is, of course, to ensure that the licence agreement adequately covers the uses which the Licensee intends for the advertisement and the music. Bear in mind that behind the scenes lie both the recording artist and the songwriter, and the Licensor may well be put under enormous pressure by them to take action should any unauthorised uses be made (which they would not have approved with the record or publishing company). It is therefore vital not to take a 'commercial view' of the terms of the licence in the hope or expectation that any problem can be solved on a business-to-business basis. Artists and songwriters can be extremely sensitive to what they may or may not want their music used for, or be tied in with. Comply with all the terms of the licence to avoid legal problems – a common sense approach!

Licensee right to assign and/or licence to third parties

Legal

The licence agreement is a contract between two parties, the owner or controller of the rights (in the guise of the Licensor) granting rights to a third party, most commonly the agency. These rights relate to certain rights to use a specific work in a particular advertisement. In order for the agency to give full effect to the rights granted to it in law two things have to be considered:

- the right for the Licensee to grant third parties the right to exercise rights to give effect to the terms of the licence, e.g. the right to 'make' the advertisement; the right to transmit and/or broadcast the advertisement, and so on;

- the right for the Licensee to assign the licence to its client and for its client to directly authorise third parties to give effect to the terms of the licence at some time in the future.

Practical

The legal effect of the Licensee granting third parties the right to exercise certain rights under the licence agreement, is that the Licensee must make sure that the terms covering the use of the rights by third parties mirror the obligations of the Licensee under its licence with the Licensor, much like the terms of a sub-lease and a head lease in a property transaction, as it is the Licensee that remains liable for any and all activities (including those by the authorised third parties) under the terms of its licence with the Licensor.

On the other hand, if at any time in the future, the Licensee is going to be out of the picture and its client is going to continue to rely upon the licence, then the Licensee needs the right to assign the licence itself to the client. In so doing, it should ensure that under the express terms of the licence agreement, the Licensee can get the assignee to enter into a direct covenant with the Licensor to take over all the obligations under the licence and thus relieve the Licensee from ongoing obligations.

A FEW FINAL IMPORTANT LEGAL POINTS UNDER THE LICENCE AGREEMENT

Notice provision for each party

It is important that there is a clear procedure and a time stipulated for each party to give the other written notice, and a deemed date that such notice is given. For example, if the Licensee is seeking to rely upon a notice from the Licensor to cure an alleged breach, the agreement might state that the written notice has to be sent by prepaid registered post, or delivered and signed for, and that it be deemed received two days after posting, or if delivered, when signed for by the recipient party.

Contracts (rights of third parties) Act 1999

It is important to state that only parties to the licence agreement can rely upon it and enforce the terms of the licence – otherwise the artist and/or the songwriter might have the additional right as a claimed 'beneficiary' of the agreement to directly sue the Licensee for any potential claim.

Law and jurisdiction

The agreement should state, certainly where the transaction is UK-based between UK companies, that it is governed by English law. The agreement may state that English courts shall have exclusive or non-exclusive jurisdiction (this will affect which source territories a claim might be brought), but it is a matter which will almost always be determined by the Licensor.

CONCLUSION

What will be....

> 'We are the music-makers,
> And we are the dreamers of dreams ...'

Arthur O'Shaughnessy

It is not only sometimes difficult to see what music is, but what it may become and how it may be used in conjunction with advertising in the future. Digital technology, both online and mobile, is rapidly introducing and inventing new ways to marry music with brands and services, and changing consumers' patterns of behaviour in the process. For example, companies like We7, Spiral Frog and Qtrax are at this moment

in time pioneering advertising-funded music (both with streaming and downloading models), looking to provide 'free' music to the public which is effectively paid for by the product or brand being advertised. Whether it will be a new type of widget or online gadget or device, or mobile application, the one thing that remains the same is the song, and whilst technology will continue to change and with it the bundle of rights necessary for advertising usage, the combined beat of music and advertising will only get stronger and stronger.

John Benedict, Consultant Collins Long Solicitors
Co-Managing Director, Just Music and Just Publishing

Notes

1   www.mcps-prs-alliance.co.uk
2   www.musiciansunion.org.uk
3   www.equity.org.uk
4   www.unionmusic.com
5   Madonna named by *Forbes* magazine as the highest-earning female artist 2007

iper DLA Piper DLA Piper DLA Piper DLA Piper DLA Piper DLA Piper DL
iper DLA Piper DLA Piper DLA Piper DLA Piper DLA Piper DLA Piper DL
iper DLA Piper DLA Piper DLA Piper DLA Piper DLA Piper DLA Piper DL

3.9

Price indications

INTRODUCTION

Advertisers must take great care to ensure that any price given or referred to in any advertisement is accurate and not misleading. Any mistakes in this area may give rise to complaints under the advertising regulatory codes and, more seriously, may result in criminal liability. The Consumer Protection Regulations 2008 ('CPRs') have recently made substantial changes to the law in this area which include the repeal of a number of pieces of legislation which formerly governed it, including large parts of the Trade Descriptions Act 1968 and Part III of the Consumer Protection Act 1987. The Code of Practice for Traders on Price Indications ('Code of Practice') is also now obsolete.

The Code of Practice has been replaced to a certain extent by the 'Guidance for traders on good practice in giving information about prices' ('Guidance'). This document was published in June 2008 by the Department for Business Enterprise and Regulatory Reform (BERR) and considers the legal obligations of traders in relation to price indications. However, the Guidance has no mandatory force and traders are under no legal obligation to follow the practices recommended.

The OFT and BERR have also jointly published interim 'Guidance on the UK implementation of the Unfair Commercial Practices Directive' ('Interim Guidance'). This again provides information to traders which may be of assistance when seeking to comply with the CPRs and this will be discussed in greater detail below.

MISLEADING PRICES

Historically, the main offences relating to misleading price indications were to be found in sections 20(1) and 20(2) of the Consumer Protection Act 1987. Under section 20(1) it was unlawful in the course of business to give by any means to any consumers an indication which was misleading as to the price of any goods or services. Under section 20(2) it was an offence to give an indication to consumers which, after it had been given, became misleading and where the trader failed to rectify it.

The implementation of the CPRs, have replaced these rules with a new set of requirements which are intended to prohibit traders from engaging in unfair commercial practices that are harmful to consumers' economic interests. Now traders will be guilty of an offence if they engage in:

- any one of a list of 31 practices (prohibited in any circumstances);
- a practice which is misleading (either by action or omission);

- a practice which is aggressive;
- actions which breach the general duty to trade fairly.

At the time of publication, the CPRs had only very recently come into force, and it is too early to say definitively what impact they will have, or how they will be interpreted by the courts. The CPRs will be reviewed by the courts on a case by case basis, and previous case law may not be helpful due to the introduction of many new concepts by the CPRs. It will inevitably take time for a level of certainty to be reached in relation to the implementation and operation of the legislation.

The recommended practices provided in the BERR Guidance and Interim Guidance described above are expected to be compatible with the CPRs and provide useful examples of potential breaches. The Guidance predicts that the CPRs will operate with flexibility to identify unfair practices, and while it is difficult to predict the path the courts will take in implementing this legislation, the Interim Guidance makes it quite clear that if businesses are treating consumers fairly, then they are likely to be considered to be complying with the legislation.

The Interim Guidance also attempts to illustrate how the CPRs will apply in practice, and will provide useful assistance to traders and enforcers alike in identifying and/or avoiding breaches in the short term.

Offences under the Consumer Protection Regulations

The five main offences under the CPRs relating to unfair commercial practices are:

- *Regulation 8* – where a trader will be guilty of an offence if he knowingly or recklessly engages in a commercial practice which contravenes the requirements of professional diligence and the practice materially distorts, or is likely to materially distort, the economic behaviour of the average consumer with regard to the product.

- *Regulation 9* – where a trader will be guilty of an offence if he engages in a commercial practice which is a misleading action. It is an offence to provide price indications which become misleading after they have been given. The Interim Guidance suggests examples, such as price indications in newspapers or magazine advertisements which should apply for a reasonable period unless otherwise stated in the advertisement. Depending on the circumstances, this reasonable period is suggested to be the longer of either seven days or the length of time until a new issue is published.

- *Regulation 10* – where a trader will be guilty of an offence if he engages in a commercial practice which is a misleading omission.

- *Regulation 11* – where a trader will be guilty of an offence if he engages in a commercial practice which is aggressive.

- *Regulation 12* – where a trader will be guilty of an offence if he engages in an unfair commercial practice set out in Schedule 1 of the CPRs.

Schedule 1 of the CPRs includes certain prohibited practices which may also be relevant for our purposes. These include:

- *Item 5* – known as 'bait advertising', whereby a product is advertised for a specific price, but only a small minority of the products are planned to be available at the reduced price, and it is likely that demand will exceed supply. To refrain from breaching the Regulations, the trader must ensure that it is made clear in the advertisement that limited numbers are available.

- *Item 6* – known as 'bait and switch'. This practice involves the trader issuing an invitation to supply a product, with the intention from the outset of supplying a different product to the consumer. The example provided in the BERR Guidance is that of a trader advertising a television for £300. When consumers request to see the product, the trader shows them one which is faulty, and instead refers them to a different product.

- *Item 20* – which prohibits a trader describing a product as 'gratis', 'free' or 'without charge', for example, if the consumer has to pay anything other then the unavoidable cost of responding to the commercial practice and delivery or collection of the item. Advertising a free gift to consumers, but later telling consumers that to claim the free gift they must pay a fee would breach the CPRs. At some point the use of the phrase 'buy one, get one free' may be considered by the courts to fall under this prohibition, but currently the OFT, BERR and CAP have indicated that 'buy one, get one free' promotions are still perfectly legitimate, provided that there has been no artificial increase in the price of the relevant product during the promotion. This may change.

Traders should therefore be vigilant to ensure they do not operate any prohibited practices as identified in Schedule 1.

The BERR Guidance highlights important regulations contained in the CPRs, specifically in relation to pricing indications, and these include:

- *Regulation 5(4)(g)* – which prohibits traders from misleading consumers about the price of a product or the manner in which the price is calculated. The BERR Guidance provides useful examples of such practices, for instance in relation to price comparisons, the BERR Guidance recommends that if no price comparison is intended, traders should avoid words or phrases which, in their everyday context and use, are likely to give consumers the impression that a price comparison is being made.

- *Regulation 5(4)(h)* – which prohibits traders from misleading consumers as to the existence of a specific price advantage.

- *Regulation 6(4)(d) and (e)* – which prohibits the omission, in the case of an invitation to purchase, of information on the price or any related charges, where this would be likely to cause the consumer to take a different transactional decision.

DEFENCES

There is a due diligence defence under Regulation 17 of the CPRs which relates to offences for misleading actions or omissions, or for aggressive commercial practices and for a limited selection of the 31 prohibited practices. There is also a defence of innocent publication of an advertisement for these same offences under Regulation 18. There is no defence to a breach of the general prohibition under Regulation 8, but to be guilty a person is required to have knowledge or to have been reckless as to the breach. Agencies are liable for a breach of the CPRs as well as advertisers.

ENFORCEMENT AND SANCTIONS

Local Trading Standards Services, OFT and the Department of Enterprise, Trade and Investment in Northern Ireland (and the Lord Advocate in Scotland) are under a duty to enforce the CPRs.

Both civil and criminal sanctions are possible following breaches of the CPRs. Civil action may be commenced under Part 8 of the Enterprise Act 2002, by applying for an enforcement order. A breach of the enforcement order could lead to a term of imprisonment up to two years and/or an unlimited fine.

The penalty for breaching the criminal offences identified in the CPRs will be a fine not exceeding the statutory maximum on summary conviction, which at the time of writing was £5000, or an unlimited fine and/or imprisonment for a period up to two years on indictment.

PRICE INDICATIONS IN SPECIFIC CIRCUMSTANCES

Bureaux de change[1]

Any person who operates a bureau de change and gives an indication to consumers of an amount in one currency which he will or may buy from, or sell to, a consumer in exchange for an amount of sterling, must state various information including the relevant exchange rate, the currency values or denominations to which that rate applies and the rate or amount of any commission or other charge payable. If a buying rate is given, the corresponding selling rate must also be given (and vice versa).

Package holidays[2]

Any descriptive matter, such as a holiday brochure, concerning a package holiday must not contain anything misleading about the price or other conditions applicable to the holiday. An organiser is liable to compensate consumers for any loss suffered in consequence of a breach of this rule. All holiday brochures must indicate in a legible, comprehensible and accurate manner the price of the package holidays offered for sale. There are also specific rules relating to price revisions and alterations.

PRICE MARKING ORDER[3]

The Price Marking Order 2004[4] ('Order') came into force on 22 July 2004, revoking the Price Marking Order 1999[5]. The Order has a substantial effect on how retailers and advertisers mark the price of their goods.

Traders are obliged to indicate the selling price of products in accordance with the provisions of the Order. They are required to indicate the selling price of the products including VAT and all other taxes in addition to the unit price of the product if that product is sold from bulk and required by weights and measures legislation to be marked with quantity, or made up in a quantity prescribed – subject to the exceptions set out in Regulation 5 (3) of the Order. Unit price is the final price for one kilogram, one litre, one metre, one square metre or one cubic metre of a product. All prices should be expressed in sterling.

The Order provides that where the trader wishes to sell products at less than the selling or unit price previously applicable, he may comply with his obligations by merely indicating by a general notice or other visible means that the products are for sale at a reduction. The details of the reduction should be prominently displayed, unambiguous and legible. This applies to all forms of advertising: the current sale price and the original price both need to be shown.

The Order does not require advertisements to show a selling price, but some advertisers might choose to include one. If they do, the advertisement must also show a unit price where one is normally required under the terms of the Order. However, selling and unit prices are always required when an advertisement is inviting consumers to conclude a distance contract, as opposed to merely seeking to encourage them to visit another retail outlet where prices will be displayed. Examples of advertisements that invite consumers to conclude a distance contract

are mail order advertisements in newspapers and goods sold direct from the internet. Catalogues do not fall within the definition of advertisement and are required to show selling and unit prices as relevant. Where unit pricing would not be useful to the consumer or would be confusing, then an exemption from unit pricing only may be allowed. The exemptions include advertisements with brief exposure times (e.g. radio and television) and advertisements in small shops.

REGULATORY CODES

The British Code of Advertising, Sales Promotion and Direct Marketing (CAP Code), is applicable to non-broadcast advertising, and contains general rules requiring substantiation for all claims made in advertisements and the prohibition of misleading claims. Rule 15 of the CAP Code contains specific rules dealing with statements about prices as follows:

> '*15.1* Any stated price should be clear and should relate to the product advertised. Marketers should ensure that prices match the products illustrated.
>
> *15.2* Prices quoted in marketing communications addressed to the public should include VAT and other non-optional taxes and duties imposed on all buyers. In some circumstances, for example where marketing communications are likely to be read mainly by businesses able to recover VAT, prices may be quoted exclusive of VAT or other taxes and duties, provided prominence is given to the amount or rate of any additional costs.
>
> *15.3* If the price of one product is dependent on the purchase of another, the extent of any commitment by consumers must be made clear.
>
> *15.4* Price claims such as 'up to' and 'from' should not exaggerate the availability of benefits likely to be obtained by consumers.
>
> *15.5* A recommended retail price (RRP), or similar, used as a basis of comparison should be genuine; it should not differ significantly from the price at which the product is generally sold.'

The Committee of Advertising Practice has also produced 'Help Notes' giving practical guidance on 'Retailers' Price Comparisons' and 'Lowest Price Claims and Price Promises'. The Ofcom Codes for television and radio advertising contain similar rules.

James Lowe, DLA Piper

Notes

1   Price indications (Bureaux de Change)(No 2) Regulations 1992, SI 1992/737
2   The Package Travel, Package Holidays and Package Tours Regulations 1992, SI 1992/3288 (as amended)
3   It is unclear at this stage what effect the Consumer Protection Regulations will have on the Price Marking Order, if any.
4   SI 2004/102
5   SI 1999/3042

Privacy: direct marketing and digital

INTRODUCTION

irect marketing campaigns can increase brand awareness and create valuable marketing databases. Such databases must be created and used in accordance with the applicable legislation, guidance and codes in the jurisdiction in which the campaigns are being conducted. This chapter explores some of the issues that direct marketers in the UK should consider before, during and after the launch of unsolicited direct marketing campaigns in the UK.

APPLICABLE LEGISLATION AND CODES

The considerations derive mainly (but not exclusively) from the provisions of the Data Protection Act 1998 (DPA) and the DPA guidance issued by the Information Commissioner, the Privacy and Electronic Communications (EC Directive) Regulations 2003 (Privacy Regulations) and Information Commissioner guidance and the British Code of Advertising, Sales Promotion and Direct Marketing (CAP Code). In addition, marketers should be aware of the Direct Marketing Association (DMA) Code of Practice, the Electronic Commerce (EC Directive) Regulations 2002, the Consumer Protection (Distance Selling) Regulations 2000 and the Consumer Protection from Unfair Trading Regulations 2008 (CPRs). This chapter is not intended to be a detailed analysis of all the relevant legislation, guidance and codes but is intended to highlight the main practical considerations that marketers should bear in mind when planning the launch of an unsolicited direct marketing campaign and collating, acquiring or renting a mailing list for such purposes.

CAMPAIGN MEDIUM

Different considerations apply to different mediums of unsolicited direct marketing campaigns. We look at the considerations applicable to mailshots, telemarketing (whether by making live telephone calls or by using automated calling systems), faxes, emails and text, picture and video messages in turn. There is also a summary table on page 229 as a quick reference guide.

TARGET AUDIENCE

The considerations for some of the mediums listed above differ according to whether the campaign is targeted towards individuals in their personal/private capacity as opposed to individuals in their business capacity.

Marketers should familiarise themselves with the terms *'individual subscribers'* and *'corporate subscribers'*. This terminology is used in the Privacy Regulations and is applicable to the sending of unsolicited direct marketing material by live telephone calls, fax, email, text/picture/video message and voicemail/answerphone message (other than by automated calling systems).

The term 'subscriber' refers to the individual/entity that pays the bill for the use of their line for the supply of their telephone/fax/email service. The term 'individual subscriber' is used to refer to residential subscribers, sole traders or non-limited liability partnerships in England, Wales and Northern Ireland. 'Corporate subscribers' are corporate bodies such as limited companies in the UK, limited liability partnerships in England, Wales and Northern Ireland or any partnerships in Scotland. Schools, government departments and other public bodies are also 'corporate subscribers'.

SENDING UNSOLICITED DIRECT MARKETING MESSAGES

We look first at the considerations applicable to the sending of unsolicited direct marketing messages, and later in the chapter we look at the considerations applicable to the collation of databases for use in unsolicited direct marketing campaigns.

In respect of all marketing, regardless of the medium, marketers in the UK must comply with the DPA in relation to any personal data, such as names and addresses, that they process. One of the main 'principles' in the DPA is that marketers must process personal data fairly and lawfully and in compliance with at least one of certain conditions. Broadly speaking, and in a direct marketing context, this means that a marketer needs to ensure that recipients know the marketer's identity and the purposes for which their personal data is being processed and the marketer should either:

- obtain the consent of the recipient to be sent direct marketing material; or
- be able to demonstrate that use of the recipient's data is necessary for the marketer's legitimate interests, provided that such use is not unwarranted by reason of prejudice to the rights and freedoms or legitimate interests of the recipient.

Other principles include that personal data must not be retained for longer than necessary, must be kept up to date and must only be used for the purpose for which it was obtained. In addition, the DPA expressly provides individuals with the right at any time by written notice to ask for their personal data not to be used for the purposes of direct marketing.

As noted above, a detailed analysis of the DPA is beyond the scope of this chapter.

SENDING MAILSHOTS

The DPA is the underlying legislation applicable to direct marketing campaigns so, for example, before sending out mailshots, marketers should check their databases to see if anyone has contacted them directly to opt-out of receiving unsolicited mailshots. Marketers should also, as a matter of best practice, check all addresses against the Mailing Preference Service (MPS) before sending any mailshots. If any addresses are listed on the MPS then mailshots should not be sent.

However, if the address is not registered with the MPS, and the recipient has not previously opted out of receiving messages, the advertisers are able to send direct mailshots to these addresses without first seeking consent. Good practice would suggest that it is better to have targeted marketing to an audience who has opted in to receive communications from an advertiser, and 'junk mail' is one of the most hated elements of society (see BBC programme *Brassed Off Britain*), but it is legitimate to send unsolicited mailshots provided that the relevant checks have been made.

There are additional considerations, mainly derived from the Privacy Regulations and the CAP Code, which apply to campaign mediums other than mail (e.g. telemarketing (whether by making live telephone calls or by using automated calling systems), faxes, emails and text, picture and video messages).

TELEMARKETING

The considerations for telemarketing vary according to whether the marketing is being conducted by means of an automated calling system or by live calls. The considerations for live calls in turn vary according to whether or not the marketer intends

to leave a voicemail message or not. These are looked at next. Before doing so however, mention should be made of the fact that it is a criminal offence under the CPRs to make persistent and unwanted solicitations by telephone 'except in circumstances and to the extent justified to enforce a contractual obligation'. In practice this means that any marketer who markets products by telephone to consumers, who does not make a record of a request from such a consumer to be removed from the contact list, and who calls back such a consumer, would be committing a criminal offence.

Marketing by automated calling systems

An automated calling system is referred to in the Privacy Regulations as a system which is *'capable of automatically initiating a sequence of calls to more than one destination in accordance with instructions stored in that system'* and which transmits *'sounds which are not live speech for reception by persons at some or all of the destinations so called'*. An example of a marketing recording transmitted using an automated calling system is the recording sent out by the Scottish National Party (SNP) just before the 2005 General Election. The recording included the following words from Sir Sean Connery:

> *'... if Scotland matters to you, then make it matter in Westminster. Vote for the SNP and get Scotland's voice heard in London. I thank you for listening.'*

Consent must be given by recipients to receive messages sent out by such systems. In this case the recorded message was sent out to voters who had not given their consent to receiving it and formal enforcement action was taken by the Information Commissioner's Office (ICO) against the SNP.

All marketing messages sent using automated calling systems must include the identity of the caller and a contact address or freephone number to enable the subscriber to opt-out of receiving future messages.

Marketing by making live calls (and not leaving a voicemail)

The same rules apply to both residential and business telephone numbers, and the main dos and don'ts for marketers are summarised in the table below.

DO	DON'T
Identify the caller and, if asked, provide a valid business address or freephone number at which the caller can be contacted	Make a telesales call to any number listed on the Telephone Preference Service (TPS)/Corporate Telephone Preference Service (CTPS) unless the subscriber has overridden the registration by consent
Ensure that any sub-contractor call-centre staff identify the organisation on whose behalf they are making the call	
Check marketer databases	Make a telesales call if the subscriber has told the caller not to call

Marketers need to note that TPS/CTPS registrations take 28 days to come into force. It is therefore possible to make calls to a number on the TPS/CTPS register in that 28-day period (provided that the marketer has not received an opt-out request in relation to that number).

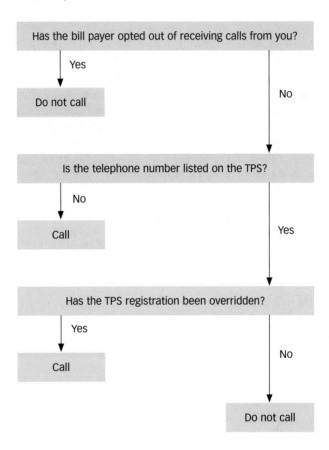

Marketers may find the flow diagram above helpful because it highlights some of the main provisions of the Privacy Regulations which are applicable.

Marketing by making live calls and leaving a voicemail
The rules are the same as those for electronic mail (see page 219).

SENDING FAXES

Fax is one of the mediums in respect of which the rules differ according to whether the recipients are individual subscribers or corporate subscribers. The main considerations for the sending of unsolicited direct marketing by fax are summarised in the table below, although it should also be noted that as for telephone marketing (see

page 214) it is a criminal offence under the CPRs to make persistent and unwanted solicitations by fax 'except in circumstances and to the extent justified to enforce a contractual obligation'.

DO	DON'T
Include the name of the business being promoted and a valid address or freephone number on each fax	Send an unsolicited marketing fax to an individual subscriber unless they have consented to receive it
	Send an unsolicited marketing fax to a corporate subscriber if that subscriber has requested the marketer not send such faxes
	Send an unsolicited marketing fax to any number listed on the FPS register unless the subscriber has overridden the registration by consent

The flow diagram on page 218 highlights some of the main provisions of the Privacy Regulations and CAP Code which are applicable here.

The same 28-day rule applies to the FPS as it does to the TPS/CTPS.

CONSENT

Some of the sections above refer to the need for marketers to obtain consent from recipients before sending them unsolicited direct marketing material. This would

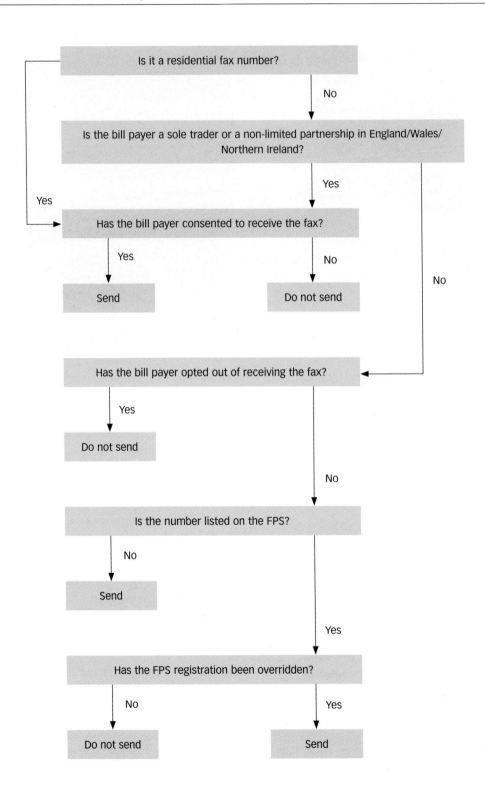

therefore seem to be a convenient place to stop and explore the issue of consent further.

In broad terms, consent must be freely given, specific and informed and there must be some form of communication whereby consent is knowingly indicated. The ways in which valid consent can be obtained can vary. 'Opt-in' tick boxes such as *'tick here to subscribe to our email newsletter'* are often used by marketers to obtain consent to send out unsolicited direct marketing emails, text messages and faxes. Opt-in tick boxes must not be pre-ticked.

However, although opt-in tick boxes provide the most unambiguous evidence of consent, consent does not have to be obtained by means of an opt-in tick box. It may be obtained by clicking an icon, sending an email, subscribing to a service or entering a prize promotion. It is important to understand that, whilst as a general rule, valid consent to receive unsolicited direct marketing material will not be obtained from someone just because they have failed to object to receiving such material (i.e. a failure to 'opt-out' is not an 'opt-in'), in certain circumstances a failure to object can constitute part of the mechanism by which valid consent can be obtained. The following example is an illustration of this:

> *'by submitting this registration form, you will be indicating your consent to receiving email marketing messages from us unless you have indicated an objection to receiving such messages by ticking this box ☐'*

This is illustrated further in an ASA adjudication concerning unsolicited text messaging on behalf of Carphone Warehouse. Carphone Warehouse used an external list provider to send out text messages on its behalf. The list provider had compiled its list from data collected in a National Shoppers' survey. The complainant contacted the ASA to complain that the text message had been sent without his consent. The National Shoppers' survey stated alongside the request for a mobile phone number *'some reputable companies may prefer to communicate offers to you on your mobile phone'*. Carphone Warehouse argued that this was an adequate mechanism of obtaining consent from shoppers to receive marketing material on their mobile phones. The ASA agreed and stated that:

> *'...although the data-owners had not provided a tick box that stated that the respondent gave explicit consent, because the survey stated that some companies might send offers via mobile phone alongside the question that asked for respondents' mobile phone numbers, customers who filled in their mobile number would be aware that in doing so, they were likely to receive offers by text message.'*

The ASA therefore agreed that the complainant had provided his explicit consent to receive offers on his mobile phone.

SENDING EMAILS

All marketing emails (whether unsolicited or solicited) should contain a valid email address to which requests can be sent to opt-out of receiving future such emails.

The sender's identity should also be clearly stated in the 'from' field of all marketing emails.

Different considerations apply to the sending of emails according to the target audience of the email campaign. Therefore, before sending unsolicited direct marketing emails, marketers should consider whether they are targeting individuals at their home email addresses, individuals at their work email addresses (in relation to personal not work related goods or services) or individuals at their work email addresses (in relation to work related goods or services).

Individual subscribers

Unsolicited direct marketing material must not be sent to individual subscribers by email unless those recipients have consented to receive such material (see above) or unless they satisfy the following criteria ('soft opt-in exemption'):

- the recipient's email address was collected in the course of a sale or negotiations for a sale of a product or service;
- the sender only sends promotional messages relating to their similar products and services;
- when the address was collected, the recipient was given the opportunity to opt-out (free of charge except for the cost of transmission) which they did not take; and
- the opportunity to opt-out is given with every subsequent message.

Negotiations for a sale

The ICO's guidance states that the soft opt-in exemption applies whether or not a sale is completed. Collection of an email address as part of an entry into a competition to promote a marketer's products or services may be deemed to be collection of an email address 'in the course of negotiations for a sale', provided that it was clear to the entrant at the time of entry that the entrant's email address would be used in subsequent marketing. However, it should be noted that the ASA takes a stricter view, which is that in respect of data collected from sales promotions, marketers should send one email only asking for explicit consent to use the data for unsolicited direct marketing purposes. The ASA's view is that the marketer should not send any future marketing unless the consumer responds with permission to do so.

Similar products and services

The key intention behind this criterion is that recipients should not receive email marketing communications about products and services that they would not reasonably expect to receive.

Opt-out opportunity

An opt-out opportunity such as 'tick here if you do not want to receive details of our special offers by email ☐', or an unsubscribe option, should be provided.

The criteria set out above are best understood in the context of an example. Consider a company which collects email addresses from consumers when they place an online order for a product. In this situation the consumer's email address will be obtained in the course of a sale and, if the online order form contains appropriate data protection wording (which provides an opt-out opportunity such as a tick box so that the consumer can opt-out of receiving future direct marketing emails), then that company can send unsolicited direct marketing emails to that consumer about its other similar products in the future, provided an opt-out opportunity is included in each subsequent email. If, on the other hand, they sent an email promoting a new but different product or service from that originally sold to the consumer, the email would have been sent without consent.

Criminal offence

In the same way as for tele-marketing and fax marketing (see pages 214–217) it is a criminal offence under the CPRs to make persistent and unwanted solicitations by email 'except in circumstances and to the extent justified to enforce a contractual obligation'.

Business email addresses

Unsolicited direct marketing material must not be sent to individuals at their business email addresses without consent or without the benefit of the soft opt-in exemption, unless the emails concern business products. CAP's view is that recipients who are being marketed to in their private capacity should be protected as if they were being contacted at their private email addresses/mobile numbers[1]. See section 'Viral email campaigns' (page 223) for an example of an ASA adjudication on this point.

ENFORCEMENT ACTION – EMAIL MARKETING

There have been a few publicised examples of action taken under the Privacy Regulations and a large number of ASA adjudications under the CAP Code, examples of which are set out below.

Privacy Regulations

In late 2005 Nigel Roberts sued Media Logistics (UK) Limited for breaching the Privacy Regulations by sending him unsolicited direct marketing emails about car hire and fax broadcasting. This was the first time that an individual obtained a judgment against a company for breach of the Regulations. The action was brought in the Colchester County Court and Roberts obtained judgment against Media Logistics. The action itself was an undefended small claims action and damages of £300 were settled between the parties without the need for a damages hearing, so the case has limited use as a precedent but does serve as an illustration of how consumer awareness of the Regulations has increased, and is a warning to marketers of the adverse publicity that such a case can generate. A case was also brought in Edinburgh's Sheriff Court in early 2007, where the claimant won £750 in damages plus legal costs. Both the individuals involved in these cases have set up websites with information on how consumers can bring action under the Regulations.

ASA adjudication – no consent

The first adjudication on this topic concerned emails sent by a seminar provider called the Training Guild. The emails were headed *'Business Seminars – Telesales & Selling Skills Made Easy'*. The complainant claimed that (1) the subject field of the email did not make it clear that the email was a marketing communication and (2) the complainant had not provided his consent to receive such an email.

The ASA did not uphold the first ground but did uphold the second. In relation to the second ground, the Training Guild had argued that it had bought a list of email addresses which they believed were business email addresses, and furthermore they believed that the list had been compiled on the basis of an opt-in to receive information about business development topics by email. However, the ASA held that the email address was in fact a personal one not a business address and that the Training Guild had failed to ensure that the complainant had provided his consent to receiving unsolicited marketing emails at that address.

It is the marketer's responsibility to ensure that recipients have consented to receive such emails. Reliance on representations given by a seller of a mailing list will not necessarily suffice. Marketers must check the integrity of any mailing lists that they buy.

ASA adjudication – no clear indication of a marketing communication

The subject fields of emails need to make it clear that the email is a marketing communication. The email in the Training Guild adjudication above satisfied this requirement, but emails such as the one below would not satisfy the requirement:

'Subject: FW: Useful information this time of year'
Message of the email:

> *'Hiya, With most of you all going on holiday soon, I just thought this website my boyfriend emailed me about would be useful! Looks like you can save loads on international phone calls. Helen X'*

Further down the page an apparently forwarded original message stated:

> *'Hi Helen, I have just been told about this website where it tells you how to make cheap phone calls, it looks pretty good and we don't even need to register with them. I will be able to call you every day when you are on holiday as it will only cost me the same as ringing you when you are here! The website is here: http://www.pd-dial.com Anyway, must get on with more work, take care babe Steve.'*

This email was the subject of an ASA adjudication against Phone Direct. The email was held to be misleading in its format and content because it was not clear that it was a marketing communication. It should be noted that such a campaign is one of the automatically unfair commercial practices outlawed under the new Consumer Protection from Unfair Trading Regulations 2008.

Viral email campaigns

As email has become a more 'traditional' delivery platform, marketers have become increasingly innovative both in terms of content displayed and additions through the techniques used to expand the target audience. Perhaps the most obvious example of this is the explosion of viral marketing. Guidance on viral email campaigns is contained in both the ICO guidance on the Privacy Regulations and in a CAP Help Note which is accessible on the CAP website. The important message to take from the CAP Help Note is that advertising virals are not exempted from the CAP code 'merely by having originated on a website or by being forwarded-on by consumers'.

'Recommend a friend' email campaigns are typically campaigns where a marketer sends a marketing email to Mr X in which they ask Mr X to (1) forward the email to his friends or (2) provide contact details for his friends.

'Send this email to your friends'

In this first scenario, as a matter of good practice, the email should state that Mr X should only forward the email on to people that would be happy to receive them. Marketers should also be wary of offering incentives to Mr X to forward emails on to his friends.

'Insert here the email addresses of friends who would also like to receive details of this competition'

In this second scenario, the marketer should ask Mr X for confirmation that his friends have consented to receiving emails from the marketer. Marketers should also check their suppression lists to check that Mr X's friends are not listed and tell Mr X that they intend to let his friends know how they got their details.

ASA adjudication – 'tell a friend'

In 2006 the ASA upheld a complaint concerning a viral email marketing campaign. The campaign related to an email which stated 'your e-mail address has been entered into the www.who-remembers-me.com 'tell a friend' link by one of your friends in order for us to send you a short note recommending this web-site as they feel it may be of interest to you'. The complaint was two-fold: (1) the complainant challenged whether his email address had been entered into the 'tell a friend' link by one of his friends and (2) the complainant claimed that the email was unsolicited and sent without his consent.

The ASA upheld both grounds of complaint. The marketer was unable to reveal details about who submitted the complainant's email address and the ASA was therefore concerned that the marketer had not shown that the email address was provided by a friend. The ASA added that they queried why a 'friend' would wish to remain anonymous if he/she was confident that the recipient would want to receive such emails. The marketer claimed that the email was sent to a business email address and that this eliminated the need to obtain consent from the recipient to receive it. The ASA held that this was not the case – the email did not relate to business products so, despite the fact it was sent to a business address, consent was needed.

There will always be some risks attached to 'Recommend a friend' marketing in any event. For example, this type of marketing is open to abuse by unscrupulous competitors or consumers bearing a grudge, who may hand over the contact details of 'friends' who are not in fact friends and who would object to their contact details being handed over. Those 'friends' may forever associate the marketer with unsolicited email marketing.

SENDING TEXT MESSAGES

The same considerations for the sending of unsolicited emails apply to the sending of unsolicited text messages.

In particular, all marketing text messages (whether solicited or unsolicited) should contain a valid address to which requests can be sent to opt-out of receiving future such messages. The ICO guidance suggests, for example, 'PJLtd2STOPMSGSTXT'STOP'TO' followed by a 5-digit short code. In this example the sender's identity is clearly stated as required.

ASA adjudication – opt-out opportunity

Here is an example of an ASA adjudication which illustrates the need for an opt-out opportunity in a text message where the soft opt-in exemption is applicable.

> *'Get sports alerts & more. Text active to 2020 2 set up...'*

The recipient of this text message had signed up to a mobile phone contract in 1998. As part of the signing up process, the recipient had consented to receive marketing communications. The marketer therefore argued that there was no justification for the complainant to argue that he had not consented to receive the unsolicited 'sports alert' text message. However, the ASA held

that since text message marketing was not established in 1998, the recipient had not provided his consent to receive unsolicited direct marketing material by text. If the marketer had wished to rely on the soft opt-in exemption he would have had to provide an opt-out opportunity in the 'sports alert' text. This was not provided and hence the marketer had not complied with the CAP Code.

ASA adjudication – no consent

One of the first adjudications on alleged breaches of the CAP Code in relation to text message marketing concerned a text message which stated that the recipient had won a £400 prize, and which invited the recipient to incur telephone charges of 10p per minute to claim the prize. The complainants objected that the text message had been sent unsolicited. The complaints were upheld and the ASA told the marketer not to send out unsolicited text messages and advised CAP of the problem with the marketer.

Similarly complaints were upheld in relation to a text message which stated that the recipient had won a video camera phone which could be claimed by calling a premium rate number. The ASA considered that the text message breached the CAP Code because the marketer had not shown either that the recipient had given his consent to receive text marketing or that he was an existing customer. The ASA told the marketer to ensure that they obtained the explicit consent of consumers before marketing by text message in future, unless they were marketing similar products to their existing customers and gave an opportunity to object to more marketing on each occasion.

ASA adjudication – opt-in tick box not always necessary

A further complaint concerned the following text message:

'FOR FANTASTIC FREE HANDSETS, INC UP TO 6 MONTHS FREE LINE RENTAL OR A FREE DVD PLAYER, CALL CARPHONE WAREHOUSE ON....T&CS APPLY...'

In this situation the ASA concluded that marketers had obtained the explicit consent of consumers to receive direct marketing by text message. The promoter had used an external list provider to send the messages on its behalf and the list provider had compiled its list from information gathered in a National Shoppers' survey. One of the survey questions asked the respondents to provide their mobile phone numbers and alongside this question, the following wording appeared 'some reputable companies may prefer to communicate offers to you on your mobile phone'. As discussed previously, a tick box is not the only method by which individuals can provide their consent to receive marketing material by text message. The ASA considered that, by providing their mobile phone numbers, customers would be aware that they would be likely to receive marketing offers by text message and therefore concluded that the data owners had obtained explicit consent.

SUMMARY – EMAIL AND TEXT MARKETING

Marketers may find the checklist on page 229 useful in relation to the requirements of the Privacy Regulations and the CAP Code on sending unsolicited marketing emails and texts.

In addition the flow diagram on page 228 highlights some of the main provisions of the Privacy Regulations and CAP Code which are applicable to these types of campaigns.

ASA adjudication – text message content

Although most adjudications upheld against marketers in relation to the sending of unsolicited marketing text messages have come as a result of them falling foul of the direct marketing rules, there have been other problems associated with delivering content through this media. Unlike traditional printed media where marketers can paint a picture and visually expand a concept, a text message can be somewhat blunt (as a result of the need to limit the number of characters within a message) and furthermore, until the general public feel more comfortable receiving marketing materials on their mobiles, recipients can, depending upon the precise circumstances, be confused or surprised by a marketing message. Both these factors contributed to a complaint being upheld against a computer games company in 2001.

The message *'Please report to your local army recruitment centre immediately for your 2nd tour of duty. Commandos 2 on PC, It's More Real Life - out today...'* was received by an ex-member of the British Army. A complaint was made by the recipient on the grounds that the message served to cause undue fear and distress.

The ASA, in upholding the complaint, felt that in the circumstances, the text message could distress recipients. This adjudication serves to highlight the need for marketers to think carefully about the media in which they choose to deliver their message. There is something intrinsically personal about the content stored on a mobile phone and, as a result, a consumer's reaction to receiving a text message will undoubtedly be very different to reading a similar (or even the same) message in a newspaper, for example.

Picture/video/voicemail marketing

The requirements for email/text message marketing also apply to picture and video marketing and marketing by voicemail/answerphone message.

Aside from the issues highlighted above, it is worth noting an adjudication by the ASA in 2003, which serves to reinforce the need for marketers to recognise and appreciate the personal nature of voice messaging as a delivery mechanism. Consequently, marketers must ensure that their message cannot be easily confused or serve to shock or distress any unsuspected recipient.

A voice message advertisement was sent to mobile phones to support the release of the Tom Cruise film, *Minority Report*. The message started with laboured breathing and Cruise asking 'Where is the Minority Report?'. Next, the actor screams 'do I even have one!'. Cruise then repeats the question and a female voice softly responds 'no' before the voiceover concludes 'don't miss out on your *Minority Report*. Buy it now on DVD and video'. The ASA received 18 complaints as a result of this message on the grounds that (1) the advertisement was offensive, (2) it was likely to cause undue fear or distress, (3) it was not immediately clear that the message was in fact an advertisement and (4) in many cases recipients had to pay to hear the message. The ASA upheld the complaints on all four grounds.

In summary, the ASA felt that consumers would not immediately recognise the voice as being that of Tom Cruise. As a result, the message could be perceived as menacing and was likely to cause serious or widespread offence and undue fear and distress.

In addition, recipients may never have heard of the film *Minority Report* and, therefore, the fact that the message was an advertisement should have been made clear near, or at the start of the message. The ASA felt that the voiceover referring to the sale of the product should have come earlier to avoid any confusion.

Finally, although consent to receiving this type of message was not in issue, the fact that consumers could incur a cost in accessing it was not made clear. Although the marketer took practical steps in an effort to reduce the need for recipients to pick up the messages after delivery (by calling consumers at 11am on a Monday morning), the ASA advised that marketers should make it clear at the time when consumers were asked to provide their contact details that a cost could be incurred when receiving the requested information.

Bluetooth

At the time of going to press, the ICO's view is that the requirements for email/text message marketing do not apply to Bluetooth marketing. The reasoning given is that Bluetooth messages are not sent using a public communications network and therefore fall outside of the Privacy Regulations which govern such networks. There has been concern that this could give rise to Bluetooth 'spamming', but it is clear that explicit consent is not required for Bluetooth messaging. Advertisers and agencies

Home email/personal mobile

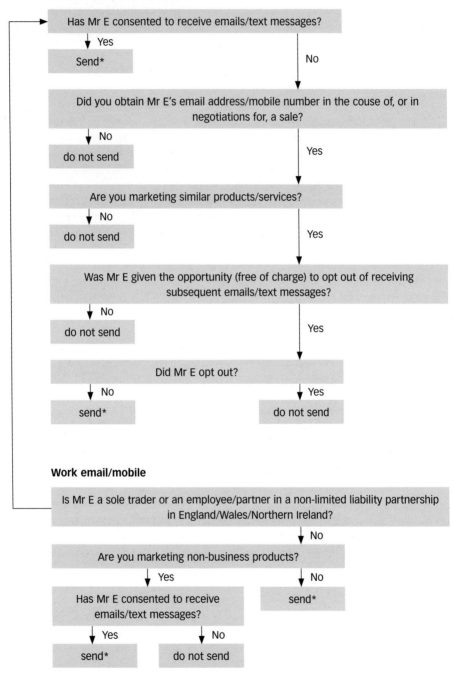

Work email/mobile

*NB: Sender's identity needs to be clearly stated and a valid opt-out address needs to be included. DPA considerations still apply.

must still comply, however, with the other advertising rules relating to the content of such messages and especially the CAP Code. In particular, agencies should ensure that content is always appropriate for children, as it is likely that those under 18 are the most likely to keep their Bluetooth technology enabled all the time.

Summary table

Medium	Consent always needed?		Preference Service check needed?
Post	residential address	no	good practice to check all addresses against the MPS
	business address	no	businesses are not entitled to register on the MPS
Telephone (live calls without voicemail)	residential number/personal mobile number	no	legal requirement to check all telephone numbers against the TPS
	business number/business mobile	no	legal requirement to check all telephone numbers against the CTPS
Automated calling systems	residential number/personal mobile	yes	
	business number/business mobile	yes	
Fax	residential number	yes	
	business number	yes[2]	
		no otherwise[2]	legal requirement to check number against the FPS
Email/text/picture/video/ voicemail message	residential email address/ personal mobile	yes[3]	
	business email address/ business mobile	yes[4] yes[5]	
		no otherwise[4/5]	there is a US-based voluntary email preference service for consumers

COLLATION OF DATABASES FOR USE IN UNSOLICITED DIRECT MARKETING CAMPAIGNS

When marketers collect data for use in future marketing campaigns, e.g. at the point at which a website user subscribes to an online service, they must ensure that the individual knows the identity of the marketer and the purpose for which the marketer intends to use the individual's data. This information can be communicated to the individual by means of a simple statement of use. Such a statement needs to be prominently positioned and marketers should ensure that there is some way of asking individuals to read it before providing any of their details. This is often done by means of a box that must be ticked to show that the individual has read the statement and agrees with it.

Marketers cannot collect names and addresses for one purpose (such as fulfilling an order) and then use such names and addresses for an entirely different purpose (such as sending out unsolicited direct marketing). Thought therefore needs to be given to the precise wording to be used at the point of collection of data from individuals to whom future unsolicited marketing material is intended to be sent.

Marketers need to give careful thought at the outset to the construction of their marketing databases in order to ensure that they are adequate for all intended future marketing purposes. The same point applies to the acquisition or rental of lists (see below).

Marketers need to consider whether they will use different approaches in their marketing campaigns for different mediums (e.g. sending out mailshots to those consumers who have not opted out of receiving them and sending unsolicited marketing emails to consumers who have opted in to receiving them), or the same approaches for all mediums (e.g. sending marketing messages to consumers who have opted in to receiving them, whether by post, email or otherwise). These approaches will govern the way in which a marketer's database should be constructed. Before collecting any data the marketers therefore need to consider the medium by which they intend to conduct future marketing activities.

As mentioned earlier, 'opt-in' tick boxes such as '*tick here to subscribe to our email newsletter* □' are often used by marketers to obtain consent to send out unsolicited direct marketing emails, text messages and faxes. 'Opt-out' tick boxes such as '*tick here if you do not want to receive details of our special offers by post* □' are often used in relation to unsolicited mailshot campaigns and can provide a basis for the marketer to rely on the 'legitimate interests' condition, mentioned on page 212 of this chapter.

BUYING AND RENTING MAILING LISTS

Regardless of the medium of any proposed campaign, if a marketer is buying or renting a mailing list from a third party, they should make the necessary enquiries as to the basis upon which the mailing list was compiled.

The importance of making such enquiries was illustrated in an ASA adjudication in 2004. The marketer (Home Entertainment Corporation plc t/a moviechoices.com) had bought a marketing database of email addresses from a liquidated company. The contract governing the acquisition of this database stated:

> '... the Buyer has agreed to buy a customer list...that contains approximately 216,000 email addresses representing all of the active customers (i.e. customers who have made at least one purchase from the Seller within the period of 12 months immediately preceding the date of this Agreement) known to the Liquidators who have given opt-in consent (which has not been withdrawn and is still current at the date of this Agreement) to receive electronic communications from third parties...'

The complainant received an unsolicited marketing email from the marketer and complained that he had not consented to receive such emails from third parties. The ASA acknowledged that the marketer had bought the database in good faith, but held that they had not seen evidence that the complainant (or any of the other customers of the liquidated company whose email addresses were sold) had provided the liquidated company with consent to pass his email address to a third party. Marketers must therefore ensure that they obtain and maintain evidence of prior consents. As this case has shown, reliance on representations and/or warranties in a contract will not suffice.

Soft opt-in not applicable

The soft opt-in exemption cannot be applied to bought or rented lists. Marketers can only use bought or rented lists if they were compiled on a prior consent basis, i.e. where the individual provided consent to the marketer to receive unsolicited messages.

Opt-out requests

Marketers need to ensure that they have adequate systems in place to deal with opt-out requests and complaints about unsolicited marketing. Opt-out requests should be dealt with promptly. When marketers receive opt-out requests they should suppress the individual's details on their database instead of deleting them. If an individual's details are deleted, it will not be clear from the database that this is as a result of an opt-out request being received.

SUMMARY

Before conducting a direct marketing campaign, a marketer must consider the medium through which the campaign is to be conducted and the legislation, guidance and codes which apply to each medium. Time spent considering such issues before the launch of a marketing campaign will ensure that direct marketers promote their products/services effectively and positively and will result in the collation of valuable databases.

Siân Croxon and Zoe Ham, DLA Piper

Notes

1   Note there is an anomaly between the provisions of the CAP Code and the Privacy Regulations in this area. Despite the fact that the Privacy Regulations allow unsolicited direct marketing emails to be sent to MrA@company.com, without Mr A's consent, the CAP Code only allows such emails to be sent to Mr A without his consent if the emails concern business products.
2   If it is the number of a sole trader or a non-limited liability partnership in England, Wales or Northern Ireland.
3   Unless soft opt-in exemption applies.
4   If the email address/business mobile is that of a sole trader or a non-limited liability partnership in England, Wales and Northern Ireland and if soft opt-in exemption does not apply.
5   If the marketing relates to non-business products.

Pillsbury Winthrop Shaw Pittman LLP Pillsbury Winthrop Sha
Pillsbury Winthrop Shaw Pittman LLP Pillsbury Winthrop Sha
Pillsbury Winthrop Shaw Pittman LLP Pillsbury Winthrop Sha
Pillsbury Winthrop Shaw Pittman LLP Pillsbury Winthrop Sh

3.11

Sponsorship and major events

INTRODUCTION

Sponsorship is an increasingly popular form of 'below-the-line' advertising which enables sponsors to raise the profile of its corporate name or brand by association with another, like-minded party which has a package of rights (the 'Rights Holder') to, for example, an event, venue, merchandise, television or radio programme, team or personality (the 'Sponsorship Target'). The Olympic Games, the FIFA World Cup, FA Premier League, programmes such as *Big Brother*, and so on, are all examples of very high-profile Sponsorship Targets. The award of the Olympic Games to London in 2012 has already attracted some major sponsors (paying handsomely and helping raise money the London Organising Committee of the Olympic and Paralympic Games (LOCOG) says it needs to help pay for the cost of the Games). It has also raised debate about 'ambush marketing' (see page 240).

Sponsorship differs from traditional advertising; while the latter is often accused of being valuable only in itself, Sponsorship Targets can, in some circumstances, benefit third parties by making available to them funding, products or services that would not otherwise be obtainable. Sponsorship effectively embraces consumers by bestowing benefits on the Sponsorship Target, say a football team or its stadium, with which those consumers already have an existing emotional relationship. Further, endorsement by a Sponsorship Target, in the form of a famous personality, can be as powerful as a recommendation from a loyal friend. It is this aspect of sponsorship that makes it an attractive proposition to companies wishing to acquire kudos with an identifiable group of consumers (Tiger Woods and Nike, David Beckham and Gillette, Kate Moss and Rimmel).

The way in which a sponsor associates itself with the Sponsorship Target will depend upon its nature. Similarly, the way in which the Rights Holder is remunerated may vary depending upon what rights to the Sponsorship Target it grants to the sponsor.

RECENT NEWS, OLYMPICS LAWS AND SPONSORSHIP TRENDS

At the time of writing, the Beijing Olympic Games 2008 and forthcoming London Olympic Games 2012 have attracted a lot of media attention, not just about the athletes or the political demonstrations, but also concerning the sponsorship deals which are vital to the economic viability of the games. For example, the *Daily Telegraph* reported[1] Sir Keith Mills (the vice-chairman of LOCOG, responsible for staging the Games and organising the funding), saying that deals would cost a sponsor a minimum of £50m. That is not surprising when you consider that LOCOG has committed itself to raising £2bn to help finance the event, 35% of which is to come from sponsorship deals. The high price has not, however, stopped key market players from wanting to be officially associated with the Olympic 2012 brand: to date, Adidas, British Airways, BT, EDF Energy, Lloyds TSB and Deloitte have signed up.

Even though protection already existed for the Olympic Games brand images (i.e. the Olympic Symbol (Protection) Act 1995), which prevented ambush marketers (i.e. those without a formal association with the Games) from using the word 'Olympic', using the Olympic rings and other symbols as well as trade mark and copyright law, the Government wanted to ensure the London Games had the toughest anti-ambush laws in the world, so any official sponsor was assured its investment would not be diluted. So, in order to protect official sponsors the Olympic and Paralympic Act 2006 introduced new restrictions and protections (see page 241).

As regards trends, a well-established US sponsorship trend that has become much more fashionable this side of the Atlantic is that of stadium/venue naming rights deals. In the UK, Arsenal play at the Emirates Stadium, Bolton play at the Reebok Stadium, and The Spice Girls played at London's newest entertainment hub

(the revamped Millennium Dome), the O_2 Arena. In the US it has been common for many years for significant revenues for a club to be generated by long-term stadia naming rights deals. This now seems to be the way things are headed in Europe.

However, although sponsorship trends come and go, the key questions and the ones that any sponsor should consider before entering into a deal remain the same, namely:

- what am I getting for my money?
- what exactly are the rights being offered?

WHAT'S IN IT FOR THE SPONSOR?

The main attraction for any sponsor is the opportunity to raise its corporate image or brand profile and enhance its reputation by association with the Sponsorship Target through a comparatively inexpensive form of media exposure, thereby transferring the ideals of the Sponsorship Target to the sponsor's corporate image or brand profile.

WHAT'S IN IT FOR THE RIGHTS HOLDER?

From the perspective of the Rights Holder, sponsorship is usually viewed as a means of raising finance to support the Sponsorship Target and, typically where a representative body or sports authority is concerned, may even present an opportunity for the Rights Holder to bind its members to present the 'united front' it may not otherwise have had.

THE PACKAGE OF RIGHTS

The rights on offer will determine what the sponsor will actually get for its money. Accordingly, attention to detail is the key.

Understandably, the rights granted under the sponsorship agreement would preferably be as broad as possible from the perspective of the sponsor (so as to maximise exposure) and as narrow as possible from the perspective of the Rights Holder, who will be aiming to maximise its remuneration by carving up the rights it has to offer to attract a number of different sponsors.

Accordingly, the Package of Rights can be a fairly complex matter; the larger the event and the greater the global dimension of its scope, the deeper the attendant complexities and potential for conflict and confusion. It is not uncommon to find different sponsors potentially stepping on each other's toes. For example, at each Olympic Games a sponsor can find that, although he has written a multi-million pound cheque to the host city organiser to be an 'Official Partner' in return for exclusive marketing rights to a specific sector, the International Olympic Committee (the IOC, responsible for organising each Olympic Games with the host city) has separately already concluded a multi-million pound sponsorship deal on a worldwide scale with someone else operating in a similar market sector, as the IOC sells sponsorship packages on a global basis whereas the rights being offered by the host country are for the host country only (something that is often missed by sponsors when signing up for national sponsorship packages).

In the case of the London 2012 Games, for example, EDF Energy have exclusive marketing rights for the utility services sector and are listed as an Official Partner; however, General Electric are an IOC sponsor and are accordingly listed by LOCOG as a Worldwide Partner for the 2012 Games.

Sole sponsorships

The level of sponsorship will vary depending on the nature of the Sponsorship Target. 'Sole' sponsorships are typically offered on a small scale, for example, sponsorship of a school football team by a local newspaper would probably be offered on a sole basis, with no other sponsors involved. On the other hand, a prestigious international football tournament would undoubtedly be the subject of a multi-sponsor format, with varying levels on offer to potential sponsors. In any agreement, the class of sponsorship on offer should be clearly defined.

Multi-sponsor formats

Multi-sponsor formats require careful organisation to achieve optimum returns. 'Primary' sponsors will have paid considerable amounts to acquire rights similar to those of a sole sponsor, and their intention will be to have their names associated with the event in question, while 'secondary' sponsors associated with the same event will have fewer rights and pay less for the privilege, and 'official suppliers' may be appointed merely to supply their own merchandise or services for the event. The needs, expectations and desires of each of these types of sponsor must be carefully managed in order to balance and safeguard the interests of all the parties involved.

By way of an example, sponsorship opportunities offered by a major sports event may include rights to: the whole tour; individual tour dates; venue(s); teams; individuals; corporate hospitality; event programmes; security; travel arrangements; broadcast rights, etc. (although broadcast rights may not fall within the control of the Rights Holder). Even in relation to these opportunities, the Rights Holder may decide to sub-divide the rights further. For example, the corporate hospitality aspect may be broken down into sponsorship of the cocktail reception, individual courses, after-dinner speakers and so on.

This is not to say that the sponsorship opportunities will be divided up equally, and where there are a number of sponsors, each will want details of where it falls in the hierarchy.

Exclusivity

Certain aspects of the Sponsorship Target may offer exclusive rights. These rights may apply to the whole Sponsorship Target or just in relation to specific areas. Sole sponsors always have exclusivity by definition.

Even where the rights on offer are not exclusive, most sponsors will want some kind of assurance from the Rights Holder that the latter will not grant any identical or similar rights to a third party in respect of the same products or services supplied by the sponsor, i.e. they will want exclusivity within their category.

It is important to ensure that, by granting exclusive rights, the Rights Holder does not breach competition laws, e.g. by preventing, distorting or restricting competition in any way. Similarly, extra care must be taken to avoid accusations of abuse if either party holds a dominant position in its market.

Conditional arrangements

Where a significant level of investment by the sponsor is at stake, the sponsor may make certain elements of the sponsorship remuneration dependent upon the achievement of specified goals, or the substantiation of claims made by the Rights Holder.

For example, the sponsor may want an indication of the minimum expected numbers of visitors to a website, attendees at an event or viewers to a television programme. Perhaps it wants a guarantee of publicity across certain targeted newspapers or specified radio channels. It may want a firm assurance that nominated celebrities turn up at an event or that the venue itself is available. Similarly, where the sponsor's products are a key element of the arrangement, the sponsor will be looking for guarantees relating to the placement of its products or other indicators of brand.

If any of these factors are crucial to the sponsor, as opposed to just being on its 'wish-list', they should be made clear in the sponsorship agreement, which should contain provisions that cater for the withholding of funds, repayment of all or part of the sponsorship fees or some other form of appropriate compensation.

THE SPONSORSHIP AGREEMENT

Whether you are a sponsor or a Rights Holder, it will be of the utmost importance to enter into a written agreement that clearly sets out the nature of the relationship and the rights and obligations of each party, whatever type of Sponsorship Target is in question. A sponsorship agreement is equally important whether you are sponsoring the Olympics, a television programme or a local sports event. There is a checklist of important issues which should be considered in any agreement at the end of this chapter.

Common requirements

Parties to a sponsorship agreement are likely to have certain requirements in common. For example, each party will typically want the right to use the other party's logo and brand names, in conjunction with its own if appropriate, for promotional and publicity purposes.

Bearing in mind the close associations that are likely to be made between sponsor and Rights Holder, it is not unusual to require guarantees and undertakings relating to each party's reputation and protection of its image.

Assurances likely to be sought by Sponsor

As well as requiring the rights to use the logo and marks of the Rights Holder, where appropriate, a Sponsor will wish to ensure that it maintains control over the use of its own logo and marks, e.g. relating to size, colour, location and the surroundings in which they are to be delivered etc. If it is a primary sponsor, it will certainly want the right to use any event logo, and will want to ensure that no other rights are granted which may undermine its status. Almost all sponsors will wish to be able to use any promotional materials generated by the sponsorship opportunity, e.g. photographs and other publicity materials and perhaps even any data collected, such as the names and addresses of participants, in which case particular regard should be had to the UK's Data Protection Act 1998 or any other relevant legislation (see Chapter 3.10).

One of the bonuses of the appointment may entitle a Sponsor to presentation rights, e.g. at sporting events, together with complimentary tickets or free products, entitlement to all of which should be set out in the sponsorship agreement for clarity.

Depending on the nature and outcome of the Sponsorship Target, the sponsor may wish to be granted an option to sponsor further rights relating to the subject of the agreement, e.g. for its own post-event marketing and advertising purposes, films, videos etc.

Assurances likely to be sought by the Rights Holder

Clearly the Rights Holder will only grant rights to those it perceives to be reputable sponsors, nonetheless it should still reserve the right to vet and, if necessary, prevent further usage of any sponsorship materials supplied by the sponsor.

Similarly, where the Rights Holder is subject to certain rules and regulations, e.g. industry standards, it must obtain assurances from the sponsor that it will comply with the same.

Remuneration

While a prime objective of the Rights Holder will be to raise finance for itself, the manner in which it is remunerated will largely depend on the nature of the rights granted under the Sponsorship Target.

In relation to one-off events, fixed amounts are commonly payable up front or in arrears, while tours or rolling events may be payable in instalments or on a periodic basis. Going one stage further, certain arrangements may make remuneration conditional on the Rights Holder achieving certain specified targets, for example, in the event that the Rights Holder secures personal appearances by nominated celebrities or gains publicity for the Sponsorship Target in the national press or on television, etc.

The Sponsor's products or services may also be offered as well as, or in lieu of, payment.

Finally, where the Rights Holder's trademarks or other intellectual property rights are used, e.g. in relation to merchandising deals, it may also be entitled to royalty payments.

Intellectual property rights

As previously discussed, while each party will normally reserve to itself its own intellectual property rights, granting limited rights of use to the other party, ownership and rights of use of any intellectual property rights generated as a result of the sponsorship deal should be addressed in the sponsorship agreement. Accordingly, ownership and use of the following intellectual property should be dealt with either within the agreement or under a separate licence:

- background intellectual property;
- intellectual property created or commissioned by one party to the agreement during the period of the agreement; and
- intellectual property created jointly by the parties during the period of the agreement;

although of course the final outcome will largely depend on the negotiating strengths of the parties. This aspect will be particularly important where the intellectual property is created outside the UK, where the parties cannot rely on certain implied terms of ownership, and where it is likely that such intellectual property will still be used after the event itself has come to an end.

Another aspect to consider is whether or not any intellectual property to be used is still subject to the moral rights of the author. If so, and this may be the case where an individual has been commissioned to create a work, a waiver in respect of the same should be obtained by the commissioning party and covered by the appropriate warranties and indemnities in the sponsorship agreement.

If the Sponsorship Target is to have its own logo or mark or if a composite logo, made up of both the sponsor's mark and the Rights Holder's mark, is to be created, the parties should ensure they take steps to register such logo or mark to ensure they are protected, particularly where merchandising is involved. Similarly, they should ensure adequate and appropriate use of copyright and trademark notices are applied where such logos and marks are used.

RELIANCE ON THIRD PARTIES

One aspect of sponsorship, which is often overlooked, is the necessary cooperation of third parties in the Sponsorship Target to ensure that it takes place. Accordingly, a sponsor needs to obtain an assurance from the Rights Holder that it has the capacity to grant the rights and bind any relevant third parties to the terms of the sponsorship agreement, particularly when they are indispensable.

The ability to bind third parties is particularly important when the Rights Holder represents a group or association, e.g. a sporting body. While it may be an easy task to clarify whether or not that sporting body's Rules of Association confirm its ability to bind its members, i.e. the teams, its ability to bind individuals within those teams is less likely and will require further investigation. If necessary, the sponsor should insist upon proof of any existing contractual arrangements, or that secondary contracts with the third parties are entered into.

A prime example of where things can go wrong was demonstrated in the Aprilia[2] case. A sponsor who had relied on the Spice Girls staying together during a sponsorship arrangement to promote a range of scooters was understandably upset when

Geri Halliwell announced her decision to leave. In this particular case, the sponsor was eventually entitled to recover all of its losses on the basis of misrepresentation. However, had Aprilia had the foresight to make its sponsorship conditional upon maintenance of the line-up of the group for the duration of the promotion, the costly litigation might have been avoided.

It would also be prudent to make checks with any association to which the Rights Holder itself belongs to ensure it is not itself going to be subject to other sponsorship arrangements or to hidden restrictions.

AMBUSH MARKETING

Ambush marketing refers to a company's attempt to capitalise on the goodwill, reputation, and popularity of a particular event by creating an association without the authorisation or consent of the necessary parties. Some popular indirect ambush techniques include buying commercial time prior to and during event broadcasts, sponsoring the broadcasts of events rather than directly sponsoring the event, sponsoring individual teams and athletes, and using sporting events tickets in consumer giveaways, sweepstakes, or contests. Purely defined, ambush marketing does not involve counterfeiting or the illegal use of trademarks, trade names, or symbols. Companies simply develop a creative advertising campaign around the event, never use the event logo, trademark or trade name, and capitalise by association with the event without paying for 'official sponsor' status. When effectively employed, ambush marketing is not illegal and is therefore difficult for legitimate sponsors and event holders to combat.

Ambush marketing may take the form of: unauthorised merchandising; blanket advertising in the vicinity of the event; broadcast sponsorship (which will probably be entirely separate from the event sponsorship); independent sponsorship deals with teams and team members; or even interference with a broadcast such that images in and around the Sponsorship Target are altered to impose alternative brands and logos.

A classic example of ambush marketing took place at the 1996 Atlanta Olympic Games, where Linford Christie appeared wearing blue contact lenses with a white Puma logo in the centre, upsetting the official sponsor, Reebok. The photo of Mr Christie, and in particular his startling branded eyes, appeared on the front pages of newspapers and in lead television news items all over the world (much to Puma's delight no doubt).

Similarly, Nike embarked on a successful ambush marketing campaign during Euro 2000, where Adidas was the official sponsor. Nike put a huge photograph of Edgar Davids on the side of a building next to a venue giving the impression that Nike was an official sponsor.

Some countries have stepped in and try to deal with the 'problem' through legislation. A fairly recent South African law has gone a long way to crack down on it; this now designates certain events which are subject to restrictions such that ambush marketing activities at such events would be a criminal offence. At the cricket World Cup in South Africa in 2002, advertising for anybody other than sponsors was prohibited by legislation not just in the arenas (as is usually the case), but also anywhere within a specific radius around the arenas. This may be regarded as a restriction on the freedom to advertise, but it shows the lengths the organisers of large events will go to in order to protect their sponsors.

New Zealand has recently enacted new legislation called the Major Events Management Act 2007 (MEMA). The Act introduces strict association right restrictions to help protect any major event organiser holding an event in New Zealand. However, the concern is that major event holders now have too much power, resulting in a lack of fair competition for local business and increased sponsorship fees because of the total monopoly such event holders now have in many parts of the world.

As mentioned above, the UK has now arguably gone one step further to become one of the world's leading countries in terms of tough restrictions on ambush marketing. With LOCOG tasked with raising significant sums from sponsors to help pay for the cost of the London Games, a key concern was how to ensure sponsors would hand over huge cheques, given the ability of competitors to 'ambush'.

Some of the major advertising provisions are covered below.

LONDON OLYMPIC GAMES AND PARALYMPIC GAMES ACT 2006

The Act creates a new right, the London Olympics Association Right (LOAR). This gives LOCOG the exclusive right to authorise persons to use and exploit any visual or verbal representation (of any kind) which is likely to create in the public's mind an association between the London Olympics and a person or that person's goods/services.

The concern for many was that this is very wide, and possibly too wide. What exactly is an 'association'? An association can include suggesting to the public there is a contractual or commercial relationship or a corporate connection between the advertiser and the London Olympics.

The Act's further provisions did not give much comfort to those who felt the general exclusive right was already too wide. The Act lists various words ('games', 'Two Thousand and Twelve', '2012' and 'twenty twelve') which, used in conjunction with certain others ('gold', 'silver', 'bronze', 'London', 'medals', 'sponsor', 'summer'), will be treated as implying an association in the absence of contrary evidence. This list can be extended.

For example, a travel agency or airline that wishes to advertise 'come to London in 2012' could be breaching the association right. Much depends on the overall impression of the advertisement and whether LOCOG view it as falling within their fairly wide net. The LOCOG guidance published to date, cites some examples of what would be prohibited. LOCOG's Brand Protection Guide, which explains the new rules and all its other brand protection rights such as OSPA and trade-mark law, can be found on its website.[3]

Advertisers not interested in becoming an official sponsor (for financial reasons or tactical ones, Nike notoriously likes to pursue an 'edgy' or 'cool' image and is often in the 'unofficial sponsor' camp) should be aware the 2006 Act is now in force, and even legitimate commercial references to the Games have been prevented by LOCOG requiring suppliers to enter into contracts under which they agree not to refer to the Games in any marketing or self-promotional material.

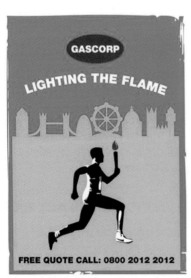

An advertisement which creates an association with London 2012 through the use of images – not permitted under LOAR.

Tough new rules also come in to restrict advertising in the vicinity of Olympic venues, and street trading activity in public places and on private land to which the public has access. In fact the Secretary of State has, under the 2006 Act, the power to make regulations to control these activities.

There are also restrictions on the unauthorised sale of Olympic tickets in a public place by an unauthorised person or in the course of business (i.e. to outlaw ticket touting). The prohibition is widely defined with 'sale' including offering to sell, exposing a ticket for sale, advertising and offering or giving a ticket in return for goods or services.

Care should certainly be taken and specialist advice sought before running campaigns in any way connected with the Olympics and/or the sports represented.

CONFLICTING SPONSORSHIP RIGHTS

If an advertiser sponsors an individual player, it should ensure that it is fully aware of what rights it has under the sponsorship agreement. While an advertiser may, for example, sponsor David Beckham, this does not necessarily carry with it the right to refer to or to portray the entire England team in an advertisement, nor necessarily to portray the England team logo. It will almost certainly not entitle you to use the logo for a major international event such as the World Cup.

There is another potentially difficult issue for international sporting events: conflicting rights of the official sponsors with the sponsors of individual players. If the Rights Holder enforces a ban on any advertising within the arenas, other than that by official sponsors, this will be an issue for individual players if they want to wear, say, baseball caps with the logos of their individual sponsors. Technically to do so would breach the Right's Holder's regulations. What a Rights Holder would do in these circumstances is difficult to predict but it may, for example, prevent the individual player from wearing any item with the conflicting individual sponsor's logo during pre- or post-match interviews.

REGULATORY CODES OF PRACTICE

There are a number of regulatory Codes of Practice that may apply to parties to a sponsorship agreement.

Non-broadcast media (including the Internet)

Non-broadcast sponsorship must comply with the British Code of Advertising, Sales Promotion and Direct Marketing (the 'CAP Code') which is administered and adjudicated by the Advertising Standards Authority (ASA) and which requires all advertisements to be 'legal, decent, honest and truthful'. The CAP Code sets out special rules and restrictions in relation to certain sector-specific advertising (e.g. betting and gaming, children, tobacco) and applies equally to sponsorship formats.

Sanctions for breaches of the CAP Code may result in adverse publicity, denial of advertising space, removal of trade incentives, disqualification from awards and finally referral to the Office of Fair Trading with a view to instigating legal proceedings under the Control of Misleading Advertisements Regulations 1988 (as amended).

Broadcast media

The Ofcom Code of Programme Sponsorship (the 'Sponsorship Code') contains the regulations for sponsorship of broadcast programmes.

The Sponsorship Code currently sets out two key principles:

- programmes must not be distorted for commercial purposes, e.g. to influence content or scheduling of a programme so as to affect the editorial independence of the broadcaster; and
- a distinction must be maintained between advertising and sponsor credits to ensure that the latter are not used to extend the time allowed for advertising.

Further, it specifically addresses the following issues: categories of advertisers which are prohibited from sponsoring programmes (e.g. tobacco, breath-testing devices, pornography etc.); restrictions (as opposed to prohibitions) on sponsorship by certain industry sectors (e.g. pharmaceuticals, bookmaking); and the prohibition on product placement (defined as the reference to a product or service within editorial material in return for payment or other valuable consideration to any Ofcom licensee or any representative or associate of either).

While the non-commercial section of the BBC is prohibited from allowing advertising or sponsorship of its broadcast programmes, the commercial sections of the BBC will sometimes engage in marketing initiatives around their products and services with other commercial parties, e.g. sponsorship of BBC events and joint promotions, in which case, advertisers should refer to the BBC's Producers' Guidelines.

These Guidelines, a code of ethics for BBC programme makers covering editorial policy in relation to commercially funded BBC channels, include the requirement that any sponsorship should only be for holding the event, and no sponsorship money may go into any production budget or be used for any broadcasting cost.

Rafi Azim-Khan, Pillsbury Winthrop Shaw Pittman LLP

Notes

1   25 January 2006
2   *Spice Girls Ltd v. Aprilia World Service BV [2002] EWCA Civ 15*
3   www.london2012.com/documents/brand-guidelines/guidelines-for-business-use.pdf

SPONSORSHIP AGREEMENT CHECKLIST

Parties
Sponsor
Rights Holder

Conditional arrangements
Sponsorship to be conditional upon:
- attendance by designated celebrities;
- availability of venue;
- use of office facilities;
- number of attendees/website hits etc.;
- appointment to board of any management board; and
- television coverage, celebrity endorsement etc.

Sponsor's rights
Set out in schedule, e.g.:
- approval/control of staging of event;
- entitlement to use sponsor's name in Sponsorship Target etc.;
- entitlement to use Rights Holder's name and logo in connection with event;
- whether exclusive or non-exclusive;
- merchandising rights;
- any associated advertising rights or other rights of publicity (if necessary, deal with sponsor's right to lay cable for its own filming purposes etc.);
- permitted designations, e.g. title sponsor or official supplier;
- allocation of free tickets, availability of hospitality areas etc.;
- restrict appointment of other sponsors without consent or limit to non-competitors; and
- rights should comply with any applicable regulatory code.

Broadcast agreements:
- live-for-free terrestrial, or pay-per-view, satellite, cable etc.;
- governing body should try to control copyright in broadcast by negotiating for a full assignment to it with an exclusive licence of copyright back to broadcaster; and
- broadcast sponsorship should be dealt with as sponsor will not want a competitor involved.

Sponsor's obligations
Sponsor must:
- comply with confidentiality requirements;
- pay the sponsorship money;
- pay any prize monies etc.;
- co-operate with Rights Holder regarding media and publicity etc.;
- supply any products or services;
- not bring Rights Holder into disrepute;
- comply with regulatory codes etc.; and
- all sponsorship materials to be approved by Rights Holder.

Rights Holder's obligations
Rights Holder must:
- register event if necessary;
- keep to the agreed format;
- promote and publicise event;

- provide and circulate regular press releases with accreditation of sponsor;
- credit sponsor;
- ensure all persons concerned attend functions etc.;
- provide press conferences;
- provide all necessary facilities etc. (specify, e.g. insurance, referees, event venue etc.);
- not bring sponsor into disrepute;
- use sponsor's products;
- indemnity for breach of warranty;
- limit advertising space around event to prevent ambush marketing;
- where appropriate, permit all advertising to be approved by sponsor;
- comply with regulatory codes etc.; and
- achieve any specified target, e.g. celebrity endorsement.

Remuneration

Consider:
- fixed fee payable in advance/arrears;
- instalments;
- periodic payments;
- conditional payments;
- non-monetary payments;
- royalties;
- conditional fees; and
- compensation for the sponsor in the event of non-achievement of crucial targets, the subject of conditional fees.

Duration

- specify, and allow 'run-on' time if linked to specific number of events which may overshoot;
- allow the Rights Holder to appoint a new sponsor in the event of termination; and
- consider granting the sponsor an option to renew.

Intellectual property rights

Deal with:
- ownership of, and rights to use: (i) background IP; (ii) IP generated by either party under the sponsorship agreement; and (iii) IP developed by the parties jointly;
- sub-licensing;
- goodwill;
- moral rights;
- include an obligation to register any event logo;
- rights to use event logo/other joint IP post-termination;
- provide indemnities and warranties; and
- if necessary, set any licences out in separate agreements, particularly if they are to survive termination of the sponsorship agreement.

Warranties

Rights Holder to warrant that:
- it can bind clubs, team members etc.;
- material agreements with venues, individuals etc. have been concluded;
- it owns, or has the right to use the rights;
- it has all necessary insurances;
- there are no conflicting arrangements with the sponsor's competitors; and
- it is not itself subject to any commercial arrangements likely to conflict with the spirit of the agreement.

Termination

- upon notice;
- material breach (specify what constitutes material breach throughout agreement);
- insolvency;
- cancellation;
- if either party ceases to exist; or
- loss of a venue, endorsement or celebrity.

Consequences of termination

Upon termination:

- Rights Holder reserves right to appoint another sponsor;
- sponsor to cease associating itself with the event; and
- sponsor to remove any facilities, hoardings etc. from the venue within a reasonable time.

Additionally, upon early termination:

- repayment of sponsorship fees.

Advertising Institute of Practitioners in Advertising Institute of Practiti
Advertising Institute of Practitioners in Advertising Institute of Practiti
Advertising Institute of Practitioners in Advertising Institute of Practiti
Institute of Practitioners in Advertising Institute of Practiti

3.12

Tobacco advertising

INTRODUCTION

Arguably, tobacco advertising has seen some of the best work ever produced by advertising agencies. The Hamlet cigar television advertisements and the Benson & Hedges and Silk Cut poster campaigns, for example, are to this day well remembered for their creativity and effectiveness.

However, the debate about the effects of advertising cigarettes and other tobacco products was in due course won by the health lobby and, after a number of years of increasing restrictions, a complete ban has now been introduced on the advertising and promotion of tobacco products.

The driving force behind the commitment was a belief that a ban on advertising would reduce consumption of tobacco by 2.5% in the long term, and in the process public health would be protected and the costs to the National Health Service associated with smoking would be reduced.

After a careful consultation process, the Tobacco Advertising and Promotion Act (the Act) received royal assent on 7 November 2002.

The Act itself is very short, it only has 22 clauses, but it packs a significant punch. It is very wide-ranging and covers direct advertising, promotion, brand-sharing and sponsorship. The ban is broadly defined and includes a prohibition on any advertisement that has the purpose or effect of promoting a tobacco product.

NON-BROADCAST ADVERTISING

The Act introduced a complete ban from 14 February 2003 on advertising and promoting tobacco products in non-broadcast media, including posters, newspapers, magazines and the internet.[1] From 14 May 2003 tobacco advertising was also banned for on-pack promotions, direct marketing and free distributions of tobacco products.[2]

The Act establishes strict liability for compliance for all those involved in the publication of the advertisement. It is not just the advertisers who are held responsible; publishers of the material and editors of newspapers and magazines containing tobacco advertising are also culpable,[3] and it includes advertising agencies.

There is a defence where the publisher or editor did not know that the material contained promotional material for tobacco products, but that is clearly a very narrow defence and is unlikely to afford much protection.

Sponsorship

The Act also banned sponsorship of cultural and sporting events by tobacco companies.[4] The ban applies only to commercial sponsorship agreements. Tobacco companies may continue to donate money to support events but the company's products cannot be endorsed in the process. Any promotional material for such events may only refer to the tobacco company's name.

Tobacco sponsorship of 'global sporting events' was permitted until 31 July 2005 in order to enable certain events to find new sponsors. Global events are defined as events where the sponsorship is more than £2.5m and the events take place in at least two continents and three sovereign states. This exemption was included specifically for Formula One motor racing and the World Snooker Championships. Both these events have now found new sponsors.

Point-of-sale advertising

Under section 4(3) of the Act, point-of-sale tobacco advertising was made subject to separate regulations. Point-of-sale advertising covers all places where tobacco products are sold, including shops, pubs, clubs, aircraft, vending machines and websites.

Under the Tobacco Advertising and Promotion (Point of Sale) Regulations 2004, which came into force on 21 December 2004, only one static, single or multiple advertisement, measuring no more than A5 in size, is permitted at any point-of-sale outlet. Moving images and use of sound or smell are all prohibited. Furthermore, 30% of this space must include the health warning 'Smoking Kills' or 'Smoking seriously harms you and others around you', as well as the NHS Smoking Helpline telephone number. Strict guidelines about the font size, colour and style are included in the Regulations.

MIDDLE TAR as defined by H.M. Government
H.M. Government Health Departments' WARNING: CIGARETTES CAN SERIOUSLY DAMAGE YOUR HEALTH

The point-of-sale advertising may only include a name or emblem of the tobacco product and the price and size of that product. It is not permitted under the Regulations to include an image of the product or any other words.

Such restricted point-of-sale advertising applies strictly to the actual place where the tobacco products are stocked and sold within the retail outlet, and is not permitted in any other part of the retail outlet. If a retail outlet has more than one area where it sells tobacco products, advertising may only occur in one of the areas.

Cigarette vending machines will be permitted to include images of the cigarette packets which correspond to the packets for sale in the machine, but no other imagery is acceptable. The images must be no larger than life size and also must include a health warning similar in text and size to one of those that the packet itself must carry.

Brand sharing

The Act also introduced a ban on brand sharing,[5] but again this was enacted under separate regulations, the Tobacco Advertising and Promotion (Brandsharing) Regulations 2004, which came into force on 31 July 2005.

These Regulations state that the use in any non-tobacco advertisement of any feature which promotes a tobacco brand is prohibited if the effect of using that feature is to promote tobacco products. Exceptions are included within the Act which allow companies who have used these features prior to September 2002 for non-tobacco advertising. Dunhill, which was involved in the luxury goods business before it moved into tobacco, will therefore be able to continue with its range of branded products, provided that such advertising does not promote its tobacco range in any way.

The stance taken by the UK on this point is much stricter than that adopted in Europe.

Sanctions

Breach of the provisions of the Act is a criminal offence, enforced by local trading standards officers. The ultimate sanction is imprisonment and/or unlimited fines for serious breaches. Advertisers and agencies should always bear this point in mind: individuals within the organisations can be held *criminally* liable if they publish any tobacco advertising in contravention of the Act.

BROADCAST ADVERTISING

The Act does not cover advertising on television or radio, but advertising of tobacco was banned under the European Union 'Television Without Frontiers' Directive in 1989.[6]

The terms of this Directive are reflected in the self-regulatory Ofcom Codes on Advertising Standards.

The Code for radio advertising states simply:

> *'Advertisements for tobacco products (including cigarettes, cigarette tobacco and paper, cigars and pipe tobacco) are prohibited.'*

The Code for advertising on television is similar but deals specifically with brand sharing. It states:

'3.1 Advertisements for products or services coming within the recognised character of, or specifically concerned with the following are not acceptable:

…

> *(d) all tobacco products. Also non-tobacco products or services which share a brand name with a tobacco product where these are prohibited by law from advertising in other UK media.*

…

3.2 No advertisement may indirectly publicise an unacceptable product or service'.

Notes in the television Code state that no advertisement is acceptable if it publicises an unacceptable product, such as tobacco products, by referring viewers to a website or publication where the product is promoted.

Furthermore, the Code specifically states that there must be no references to tobacco products or smoking in advertising which might be of particular interest to children or teenagers.

In essence, there will be very few occasions where any reference to smoking in television advertising will be acceptable. The only likely exceptions are in health-related public service advertising and in advertisements for forthcoming films which include incidental images of smoking in the clips.

EFFECT OF THE BAN

Immediately after the ban was introduced, there was no discernible sign of a significant reduction in the amount of tobacco consumption. Tobacco consumption only dropped from 53.5 billion in 2003 to 52 billion in 2004,[7] for example. A greater fall has been apparent after the introduction of a ban on smoking in public places, which came into force in July 2007.

The most significant effect for advertisers has been the inability to launch new brands onto the market place. The most notable of these were Mayfair rolling tobacco and the new '555' cigarette brand.

Manufacturers of tobacco products have therefore complained that the real impact of the ban has been to make the industry anti-competitive by impeding choice. The ban on advertising favours the strong, established brands and penalises the weaker brands. Since the ban has been introduced, the relative market share positions of the brands have stayed more or less the same, whereas new brands have been prevented from gaining any share in the market at all.

LEGAL PROMOTION OF TOBACCO PRODUCTS

The Act did include some exemptions to the rules, which allow advertisers and their agencies to be a little creative in coming up with ideas for marketing their products, but the avenues open to them are limited.

Exemptions

The Act itself contains a number of exemptions from the provisions which can be exploited:

- the advertising and promotion of tobacco products is permitted in business-to-business communications where both parties work within the tobacco trade, and in publications circulated solely within the tobacco industry;

- a tobacco manufacturer or seller is entitled to respond to requests for information about the products from consumers. Thus it would be legal to send a brand magazine to a customer who has requested information. However, it is only permitted to send this information once, and no further promotional material may be sent out again unless a further request is made;

- advertising can be carried in publications for which the UK is not the principal market. This exemption does not include in-flight magazines. It does apply, to an extent, to the internet (see over);

- certain advertisements are permitted in specialist tobacconists. A specialist tobacconist is defined as a retail outlet where over 50% of the sales are cigars, snuff, pipe tobacco and smoking accessories. These tobacconists are permitted to advertise their products in the shop or fixed to the outside of the shop. However, these advertisements must not be for cigarettes or hand-rolling tobacco: only advertisements for other products on sale in the shop are permitted, such as cigars or pipe tobacco.[8]

PR

Although consumer-focused public relations activity is banned, there is little which can be done to prevent corporate PR activity. Most tobacco companies are investing in improving their corporate image. It is also still permitted for tobacco companies to sponsor or support events by name, even though it is not permitted for them to promote their products.

Furthermore, the law cannot prevent 'private' parties. Tobacco companies may organise such parties specifically to market to guests, but how the party is organised and marketed will have to be undertaken very carefully. It should also be remembered that free distribution of tobacco products is banned under the Act.

Packaging

Design of packaging is clearly going to become an increasingly important element in the battle for the tobacco companies to differentiate their brands from one another. The use of colours and packaging to indicate superior filtering systems, light cigarettes and smoothness has already commenced. Limited-edition packs are another way the tobacco companies will no doubt seek to attract consumers.

The problem remains, however, that the restrictions on advertising mean it will be difficult to lure customers to new products.

The internet

Internet marketing is included in the ban under clause 2(3) of the Act. There will no doubt be a serious problem in enforcing such a ban due to the very nature of the internet. Tobacco companies are entitled to print their corporate internet addresses on packs and if consumers contact them via the site the company may respond to any requests.

The tobacco companies are not permitted, however, to carry branded advertising on the home pages of their websites and any other advertising on the website is to be restricted to pictures of products for sale.

Furthermore, the Government does not wish to prevent the electronic retailing of tobacco products, and therefore have indicated that supermarkets and other retailers who legitimately stock tobacco products are allowed to offer them for sale on the internet.

The use of viral emails for advertising is also a grey area. Advertising agencies should note that the ban on tobacco advertising extends to viral emails. The reality is, however, that once in cyberspace control of such emails is lost and the powers to prevent such campaigns are limited. However, it is highly likely that brand owners will be assumed to have been involved in the creation and initial publication of branded viral emails, and they (and their advertising agencies) will be held responsible. There has, as yet, been no prosecution, but advertisers should be very wary of considering using this route for advertising their tobacco products.

Finally, it is not an offence under the Act for a person who does not carry on business in the UK to publish a tobacco advertisement on a website which can be accessed in the UK. Foreign retailers of tobacco (who do not trade in the UK) can

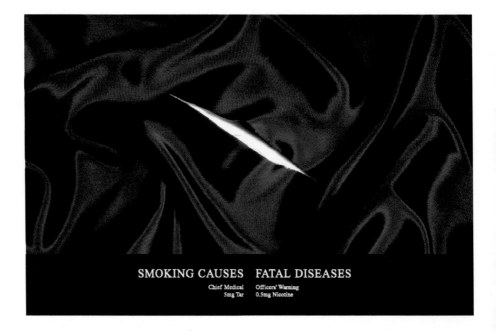

SMOKING CAUSES   FATAL DISEASES

Chief Medical   Officers' Warning
5mg Tar   0.5mg Nicotine

legitimately advertise on their websites, and the UK Government is powerless to prevent people accessing it here.

CONCLUSION

In essence, despite the exemptions, all advertising and promotion of tobacco products is prohibited. It seems therefore that the halcyon days of beautifully creative and clever cigar and cigarette advertising are well and truly over.

Christopher Hackford, Institute of Practitioners in Advertising

Notes

1   Tobacco Advertising and Promotion Act 2002, clause 2(3)
2   Clause 9 of the Act
3   Clause 3 of the Act
4   Clause 10 of the Act
5   Clause 11 of the Act
6   Directive 89/552/EEC
7   Tobacco Manufacturers Association figures
8   Clause 6 of the Act

Silkin Lewis Silkin Lew

3.13

Usage FAQs

INTRODUCTION

This chapter will deal with issues relating to the use of common, everyday items in advertisements. Some of these require consent, while others do not; this chapter seeks to help agencies decide when to seek permission and from whom.

BADGES

If a badge is to appear reasonably prominently in an advertisement, for instance if it is to be worn by an actor so as to be clearly visible, then permissions may be required in respect of use of any image or design that appears on the badge. The recent High Court case of *The Flashing Badges Company v. Brian Groves*[1] has confirmed that if the design on a badge can exist independently of the badge, then it will be deemed surface decoration and an artistic work. It may therefore be protected by copyright and any use may require the consent of the copyright owner.

On the other hand, if the badge design is integral to the configuration of the badge and cannot be used independently of the badge, then it will be deemed to be a design work and any use through copying will fall within the defence in section 51 of the Copyright, Design and Patents Act 1988, and thus will not usually need to be cleared with the owner of the design right.

Even if the image on the badge does have copyright protection, it may be possible to argue that its inclusion in an advertisement is merely 'incidental,' or insufficiently substantial to infringe. This may be of assistance where the inclusion of the badge is very fleeting or partial, and clearly not central to the commercial purpose of the advertisement. However, the case-law is not clear cut in this area, and the courts may be less inclined to treat the inclusion of copyright works in an advertisement as incidental or insubstantial (given that most advertisements are usually very carefully planned and staged) when compared with, for example, footage shot 'live' for a documentary or news report. If in doubt, the safest option would be to avoid the inclusion, even quite fleetingly, of a badge with distinctive surface decoration, or alternatively to obtain permission from the relevant copyright owner.

Care should also be taken to check that any image on a badge is not a registered trade mark. If it is, clearance from the trade mark owner is advisable to avoid any suggestion that the owner is endorsing or somehow connected with the advertised product or service.

BANKNOTES

The Bank of England holds the copyright to British banknotes. Section 18(1) of the Forgery and Counterfeiting Act 1981 provides that permission must be obtained from the Bank of England before an image of a British banknote may be legally reproduced. Consent is required whether the front or back of the banknote is reproduced, whether the note is still legal tender or not, and for all possible reproductions including modified or distorted versions. Although it does not allow banknote reproductions on articles for sale, such as T-shirts, the Bank will clear the use of banknotes in advertisements subject to certain conditions which it has published.

The following pre-conditions must be met before permission will be granted for reproducing the images of banknotes in broadcast and non-broadcast advertisements:

1. Reproductions must be one-sided, i.e. nothing should appear on the reverse which might give the impression that it is a genuine banknote. This condition will not apply quite so strictly for television commercials.

2. Reproductions (partial and entire) must differ in size from actual banknotes. If smaller, they must be at most two-thirds as long *and* at most two-thirds as wide. If larger, they must be at least one-and-a-half times as long *and* at least one-and-a-half times as wide.

3. Reproductions may not appear in an offensive context (for example, in conjunction with violence or pornography).

4. The Queen's image should not be distorted (other than by enlargement, reduction or slant).

5. In addition, reproductions of banknotes must meet *one* of the following criteria:

    a) the reproduction is shown on the slant, not flat to camera. In this case the distortion must be such that right angles are reduced to angles of 70° or less, or increased to angles of 110° or more; or

    b) the reproduction is printed on a material clearly different and distinguishable from paper; or

    c) the colours on the reproduction differ distinctly from the main colours on any of the current series of Bank of England banknotes; or

    d) in the case of a partial reproduction of a banknote, at most 50% of the total surface area of one side of the original banknote may be reproduced; or

    e) if the reproduction is flat to camera it must be overprinted with the word 'SPECIMEN' twice in solid black capital letters, once from the bottom-left corner to the top-centre and again from the bottom-centre to the top-right corner of the banknote. The word SPECIMEN must be not less than one-third of the length of the reproduction in length, and not less than one-eighth of the height of the reproduction in height. This applies whether the entire banknote is reproduced or just part.

For images of banknotes to be included on CD-ROMs or on the internet, just points 3, 4 and 5e must be observed before permission can be sought.

In order to seek permission to reproduce banknotes, advertisers should contact the Notes Reproduction Officer of the Bank of England[2], or visit the Bank of England's website[3] and submit the online Banknote Reproductions Application form. The site indicates that a response can usually be expected within five working days.

(See also the entries in this chapter on Coins, page 264; Postage stamps, page 269; and Royalty and the Crown, page 272).

BUILDINGS (EXTERIORS AND INTERIORS) AND SCULPTURES

Although buildings are protected as copyright works (assuming that the copyright has not expired), UK copyright legislation provides a specific exemption allowing buildings to be reproduced in drawings, photographs, films and broadcasts without the permission of the copyright owner (section 62 Copyright Designs and Patents Act 1988), provided that they are permanently situated in a public place or in premises open to the public.

The same section also permits drawing, painting, photographing or filming sculptures and works of artistic craftsmanship, such as furniture and ironwork, in similar circumstances. Thus, merely using the outside of a building in the UK as the backdrop for an advertisement will not in itself usually raise any copyright issues. In the case of sculptures and works of artistic craftsmanship, however, there could still be a claim for 'passing off' by the creator of the work, particularly if they have a reputation which is associated with a particular work or style of work. There is also a danger of complaint under the Codes if you feature a private building prominently in an advertisement (see below).

If agencies are shooting in the interior of a building, however, it is important to note that section 62 does not apply to the inclusion of any photographs, paintings or other graphic works situated within the building, so permission from the relevant copyright owner would usually be required to feature these. The same would be true if the exterior of the building had any such items displayed on it. Agencies should avoid showing any brand logos on buildings.

In some circumstances it is possible to argue that the inclusion of copyright works in the background of advertisements is merely 'incidental', or insufficiently substantial to infringe, although this is rare in an advertising context (given that most advertisements are usually very carefully planned and staged). This defence may be of assistance where the inclusion of copyright works is very fleeting or partial, and clearly not central to the commercial purpose of the advertisement. If in doubt, the safest option would be to avoid the inclusion of any such works, or to obtain permissions from the copyright owners of those works that are included.

It is also common for the owners of buildings to impose specific contractual conditions upon filming, particularly of interior shots. If it is necessary to make arrangements with the owners for access, then it is likely that accepting such contractual terms will be unavoidable, and these will take precedence over any copyright exceptions. From the advertiser's point of view, it therefore makes sense to ensure that such an agreement includes a full release for the use of the location. Sports stadia frequently impose restrictions on the commercial filming inside the stadium.

The CAP Code contains a provision which urges advertisers to obtain written permission before 'referring to or portraying members of the public or their identifiable possessions'; such possessions can include both buildings and land provided that the owner can be identified from them. However, there is an exception for the use of 'general public locations', while for private locations it is usually possible to manipulate any images of buildings or land to render them sufficiently unidentifiable.

CARS

There are specific rules set out in the CAP and BCAP Codes for the advertising of motor vehicles, with which car retailers need to comply. This section, however, discusses the issues facing other advertisers who wish to feature cars or other motor vehicles in their advertisements.

There are a number of potential issues that could arise when the images or brands of motor vehicles are used (either deliberately or incidentally) in advertisements.

Copyright

While mass-produced articles such as cars do not usually attract copyright in terms of their three-dimensional shape and configuration, hand-built or customised cars might be protected as 'works of artistic craftsmanship'. Some designer marques, such as Lamborghini, may also argue that their iconic and limited-production designs are 'artistic works' and therefore covered by copyright protection. There is no case law on such claims, but agencies should seek permission before using customised cars or designer marques.

There is also the potential for copyright to protect aspects of 'surface decoration' applied to mass produced cars, including some logos. If a motor vehicle has particular graphics or logos incorporated into its paintwork which will be visible in the advertisement, then permission should usually be sought for its use or the logos and badges should be removed or blurred, or the shot should be taken so that the logos are obscured. The manufacturers' badges or logos usually appear at various places on a car, on the bonnet, steering wheel and hub of car's wheels.

Trade marks

The manufacturer's name and logo, and the name of the model of the vehicle used, are almost certain to be registered trade marks. Trade mark issues will obviously not apply if the badges and logos have been removed because of the copyright issues (see above). If they have not been removed, in most cases it will be clear that the vehicle's brands and trade marks are not being used as trade marks for the advertised product – they are included simply because they are part of the vehicle – and thus the trademark is not infringed. If the advertisement is comparing different makes of car, then the rules of comparative advertising will apply (see Chapter 3.2).

The owner of the car brand may feel aggrieved if their brand is being associated with the product or service in the advertisement but their permission has not been sought. The owners of very well-known brands may object to the use of their trade marks if they can show that such use takes unfair advantage of, or is detrimental to, the distinctive character of their mark. (This would be most likely to be the case if the advertisement showed the car in a negative light, or implied that the brand owner endorsed the advertised product.) While it is not always clear-cut whether the use of trade marks in such circumstances is infringing, the safest option would always be to avoid the marks/logos appearing in the advertisements.

Design rights

There are a variety of design rights that attach to the external shape and appearance of motor vehicles. The law is not fully tested in this field, but it seems that the rights are only infringed when the design is incorporated in, or applied to, another traded 'product' (so merely photographing, filming or broadcasting images of the vehicle is unlikely to infringe design rights). If a three-dimensional model of a car is made, then an infringement of the design rights in the original design will occur unless permission is obtained. (See also Chapter 1.3.)

Passing off

Even if the registered trade mark is not visible in the advertisement, if the motor vehicle is clearly recognisable as being of a particular make then 'passing off' may be an issue. To have the advert withdrawn or to claim damages, however, the car manufacturer would have to show that its goodwill or reputation was being damaged by the advertisement through customers becoming confused, for example, into thinking that there was some connection between the vehicle manufacturer and the advertised product. It is highly unlikely that this would be the case if the car was only briefly and incidentally part of the background of the advertisement and passing off is therefore not usually an issue for agencies. (See also Chapter 1.4.)

Regulatory considerations

Clause 5.4.3 of the BCAP Code states that '*Advertisements must not discredit or unfairly attack other products or services ... either directly or by implication*'. Clause 20.2 of the CAP Code includes similar provisions. It is therefore essential that advertisements featuring identifiable cars or other motor vehicles do not show them in a denigratory light. This will include featuring, for example, crashed cars or broken-down cars. It is common practice in such cases to ensure that the car used in these situations is not identifiable, and in many cases this may require the creation of a generic car, especially for television commercials.

COATS OF ARMS

Coats of Arms in England and Wales derive from the Crown, but control is delegated to the Kings of Arms, who are members of the Royal Household and regulate the devising of new arms by ensuring that each design is unique.[4]

Coats of arms are the property of the person or family to whom the arms were granted by the Crown. They are governed by the Law of Arms, which is not part of common law, and so the normal courts do not generally regard coats of arms as either property or as being defensible by legal action. Instead, the Court of Chivalry has exclusive jurisdiction over the Law of Arms. It does not sit very often, the last time apparently being in 1954 to hear the case of *Manchester Corporation v. Manchester Palace of Varieties*[5] in which a theatre was successfully sued for using the arms of the Corporation without permission. It does still have jurisdiction, although it is doubtful now whether the court is likely to sit again.

None of this is to suggest that coats of arms can be used with impunity. Where possible they should be cleared with the rights owner, not least because other IP rights could be infringed in unauthorised use, such as copyright (particularly if the coat of arms is relatively modern), passing off or defamation. It would also be wise to check whether any coats of arms that you intend to use have been registered as trade marks.

(See also the entry in this chapter on Royalty and the Crown, page 272.)

COINS

The UK coinage is technically protected by Crown Copyright, but the Crown has delegated the administration of such permissions to the Royal Mint and the Royal Mint has waived its right to charge a royalty fee for the use of coin images or designs in flat form, providing the image or design does not form an integral part of a commercial product (for example, a coin reproduced on a T-shirt).

Agencies should follow the provisions below when using coins in advertisements:

- the reproduction of the coin should be reproduced in a faithful likeness and shown in good taste (in respect of which the Royal Mint relies upon the good sense of the advertisers and agencies);

- parts of the designs used on the coinage should not be reutilised out of context. However, showing part of a coin will usually be acceptable, providing it is clearly recognisable as part of a coin and good taste is used;

- the 'Heads' (Queen's effigy) side of a coin, or the 'Tails' side if it shows the Royal Arms, must also be a faithful reproduction of actual currency in circulation, and must be shown unaltered;

- technically, permission to use the Queen's effigy requires permission of the Lord Chamberlain (see Royalty and the Crown page 272), so agencies are advised to use the Tails side when featuring coins. However, it is generally acceptable to feature both Heads and Tails when featuring a pile of coins.

It is however an offence under section 19 of the Forgery and Counterfeiting Act 1981 to make a coin that resembles a UK coin in shape, size and substance, in connection with a scheme intended to promote the sale of any product or the supply of any service, unless the Treasury has previously consented in writing to such sale or distribution.

(See also the entries in this chapter on Banknotes, page 258; Postage stamps, page 269; and Royalty and the Crown, page 272.)

CROWDS/PASSERS-BY

(This section assumes that the passers-by or members of the crowd included are not people with a public reputation. For detailed coverage of the use of celebrities in advertising, see Chapter 3.1.)

The BCAP Code provides that *'with limited exceptions, living people must not be portrayed, caricatured or referred to in advertisements without permission'*. Thus the consent of all living individuals, not just celebrities, is normally required and best practice would be to obtain it by way of a signed release. One of the specific exceptions to this general rule under the BCAP Code, however, is for *'advertisements where the appearance is brief and incidental, for example in a crowd scene'*. The inclusion of a passer-by who is caught on camera only briefly and incidentally would probably also benefit from this exception.

The CAP Code (which applies to all non-broadcast media including the internet) has a slightly less stringent approach. It states that *'Marketers are urged to obtain written permission before referring to or portraying members of the public or their identifiable possessions...[or] implying any personal approval of the advertised product'*. However, again an exception is made: *'the use of crowd scenes or general public locations may be acceptable without permission'*. The CAP Code rules are reasonably lenient in respect of crowd scenes or passers-by, and indeed use of individuals without consent.

There are also some more general legal rules to bear in mind. In particular, data protection and rights of privacy under the Human Rights Act may arise when individuals who are identifiable from the photo or footage are included without their consent, even if purely 'incidental' to the message of the advertisement. The case law regarding data protection and privacy protection in such circumstances is still not fully developed, particularly in the advertising context, but the overall trend in recent years has been towards increasing court recognition for the rights of private individuals to have their private life respected, although currently the damages awarded in such cases are minimal and generally speaking the taking of a photograph of an individual in a public place in the UK is not an actionable breach under the Data Protection Act.

If an advertisement has to be shot in a place open to the public, it is therefore advisable to use signs to warn people away if they do not wish to be caught on camera. Anyone who does appear sufficiently prominently to be identifiable should be asked for their written consent, or agencies should edit the image(s) in order to remove the relevant individual or render them unidentifiable.

DESIGNER CLOTHES/JEWELLERY

Three-dimensional articles that have been mass-produced do not usually raise copyright issues when used in photographs, films or broadcasts (although care should be taken if any trade mark is visible or a distinctive product 'get-up' is clearly recognisable).

Greater caution is needed with hand-made 'haute couture' clothes or designer jewellery, particularly if they are one-off items. These are likely to be treated as 'works of artistic craftsmanship' and so qualify for copyright protection.

It may be possible to argue that the inclusion of copyright works in the background of photographs, films or broadcasts is merely 'incidental,' or insufficiently substantial to infringe. This may be of assistance where the inclusion of copyright works is very fleeting or partial, and clearly not central to the commercial purpose of the advertise-ment. However, the case-law is not clear cut in this area, and the Courts may be less inclined to treat the inclusion of copyright works in an advertisement as incidental or insubstantial (given that most advertisements are usually very carefully planned and staged). The safest option would be to obtain permissions from the copyright owners of any one-off designer clothing or jewellery that is to be included.

If the clothes or jewellery are protected as works of artistic craftsmanship, then their creator will also have moral rights to be identified as such (if this right has been asserted) and to object to any derogatory treatment. Derogatory treatment includes distortion or mutilation of the work, or other treatment that is 'prejudicial to the honour or reputation of the author'. In theory, this could give the designer grounds to prevent an advertisement being shown if his or her design is being associated with products or services that might be detrimental to his or her reputation.

The more prominent the use of the clothes or jewellery, and the more recognis-able their brand or origin, the more likely it is that the relevant designer would be aggrieved by any use in an advertisement without permission (particularly if they feel that being associated with the advertiser may be damaging to their brand's reputa-tion). To avoid any dispute arising, it would therefore be prudent to obtain a written release from the relevant designer in such circumstances.

FICTITIOUS NAMES AND TESTIMONIALS

It is common practice to make up a fictitious name for use in an advertisement (whether in respect of an individual or a business) in order to lend a greater air of reality to the content. Although this might seem to avoid the numerous pitfalls associated with using the names of real businesses or people (in particular celebrities: see Chapter 3.1), simply making up a name is not necessarily the panacea that one might think.

For example, if the name turns out to be that of a real person or business and it is used in a defamatory context (i.e. it unjustifiably damages the reputation of the person or business: see Chapter 1.5), then the advertiser may be liable for defamation even though it had no intention of referring to the real person or business in question. Equally, if the name chosen is that of a real individual or business and they have a registered trade mark or significant goodwill in the name, then the lack of intention on the part of the advertiser will not necessarily prevent legal action being taken for trade mark infringement (see Chapter 1.2) or passing off (see Chapter 1.4).

It is therefore prudent when using made-up names to conduct a trade mark search, and potentially also to search Companies House or directories for relevant business names or individual's names, in the geographical territories at which the advertisement is aimed.

Advertisers may also be tempted to make up endorsements or testimonials for their products or services, and to associate these with fictitious names in order to make the endorsements seem more realistic. This practice is specifically addressed by the CAP Code which makes it clear in rule 14.4 that fictitious testimonials should not be presented as if they are genuine, although ASA decisions seem to indicate that fictitious testimonials that can be seen as 'dramatisations' of consumer opinion (if not of particular individuals) will be acceptable as long as they are representative. Likewise the BCAP Code, rule 5.4.4, provides that: '*Testimonials or endorsements used in advertising must be genuine and be supported by documentary evidence. Fictitious testimonials must not be presented as genuine. Any statement in a testimonial that is likely to be interpreted as a factual claim must be substantiated.*'

If the advertiser does not make up a fictitious name, but uses the name of a fictitious character already made popular by others (for example, a character from a book, film or television programme), then permission will almost certainly be necessary. There is no copyright in a mere name, but many popular characters are protected by trade marks in order to optimise income from merchandising opportunities. Even if not registered as a trade mark, an action in passing off may arise if the public perceive there to be an endorsement by the creators of a character where there is none and a licence has not been granted.

FLAGS

Flags of state and state emblems are generally free from copyright, not least because of their age. Care should be taken over any flag of modern design, however, in case copyright still subsists and is enforceable by the designer or commissioner of the flag's design.

In addition, flags cannot be registered as a trade mark by virtue of Article 6 of the Paris Convention for the Protection of Industrial Property 1883, which states that any flag or emblem that has been communicated to the international bureau of the World Intellectual Property Organisation by any State party to the Paris Convention is prohibited from registration as a trade mark in any other state that is party to the Convention.

However, great care should be taken before using foreign national flags in advertisements and marketing materials if the materials are to be widely disseminated around the globe (for example on the internet). Many countries have rules and regulations specifying how their national flag should be used in order to protect its honour and reputation. In some countries these rules include a blanket ban upon the use of the national flag in advertisements or other commercial contexts (for example the United States of America and The Philippines).

The use of the UK's Union Flag and the national flags of England, Scotland and Wales are unregulated and can be used freely, although obviously they should not be used in a manner that is likely to cause serious or widespread offence.

Care should also be taken not to use flags in a misleading way on marketing materials and packaging for food and other products subject to country-of-origin rules.

The European Union flag of twelve yellow stars against a blue background (which it shares with the Council of Europe, an entirely separate institution) may be used with permission, on condition that the proposed usage will not be confused in the mind of the public with the European Union or Council of Europe. Further, the emblem may not be used in connection with an activity that runs counter to the aims and principles of the EU or Council of Europe. Permission is unlikely to be granted if the European emblem is used in conjunction with a company's own logo, name or trade mark.

Control of usage of the flag is shared between the European Commission (on behalf of the EU) and the Council of Europe to ensure that usage of the flag retains dignity and reflects the values of the Union and Council. Requests for permission to use the flag/emblem should be addressed to the European Commission.[6]

Commercial use of the United Nations flag and emblem is regulated by section 2(a) of General Resolution 92(I), which places an obligation on Member States of the United Nations to take legislative steps to prevent usage of the emblem for any commercial purposes. It specifies that any commercial use of the seal must be authorised by the Secretary General of the UN.

(See also entries for Red Cross, Red Crescent, page 270 and Royalty and the Crown, page 272.)

MAPS

Maps are protected by copyright as a type of artistic and/or literary work, except for those that are so old that the copyright has expired. In the United Kingdom, most official maps and road atlases are based upon the mapping conducted by the Ordnance

Survey, a government agency. Ordnance Survey maps are subject to Crown copyright, the administration of which has been delegated to the Director General of Ordnance Survey. Ordnance Survey has not waived its copyright in its maps and permission should always be sought before reproducing them.

Advertisers proposing to feature a substantial extract from an Ordnance Survey map will need a publishing licence, the cost of which is based (in the case of print advertising) on the amount of mapping used and the number of copies of the publication printed. Separate permission is required for any reprint or new publication. Given that other publishers (for example Philips) use Ordnance Survey maps as the basis for their own maps and road atlases, any reproductions of their material will require both the permission of that publisher and also Ordnance Survey.

For publications that contain 'redrawn mapping' at a scale of 1:1,000,000 or less, a licence fee may not be payable, provided the mapping is sourced from 1:1,000,000 scale Ordnance Survey mapping with a similar specification to Ordnance Survey's MiniScale® dataset.

Advertisers may copy Ordnance Survey mapping that is out of copyright (copyright persists for 50 years from the end of the calendar year in which maps are first published), but should contact Ordnance Survey[7] for confirmation that the mapping is over 50 years old.

Agencies can create their own maps, but these must be their own work and not copied or traced from existing mapping.

OLYMPIC SYMBOLS

Use of Olympic symbols, insignia and words are all heavily protected. Chapter 3.11 deals with this in detail.

POSTAGE STAMPS

The copyright in all designs for British Postage Stamps is owned by Royal Mail Group Ltd. Certain stamps are also registered as trade marks (for example the Penny Black). Written permission for the reproduction of stamps should be obtained from the Royal Mail.[8]

The Royal Mail insists that stamps must be reproduced faithfully in every detail and in their entirety (for example showing the Monarch's head, the stamp value and the stamp's perforations). When showing stamp images they must not be obscured or partly covered with another object or illustration. However, if a number of stamps are to be shown it is acceptable for some to be partly covered by others. Stamps or stamp-related imagery must not be altered in any way to suit the purposes of the advertisement, nor must their use impact negatively upon Royal Mail or the stamp's designers.

Stamp or stamp-related imagery must also carry the following acknowledgment close to the reproduction of the stamp image on all printed material:

[name of stamp] ©Royal Mail [year of creation of stamp].
All rights reserved.
Reproduced with the permission of Royal Mail.

In order to protect new designs, the Royal Mail insists that stamps must not appear in any media including philatelic, local or national press, electronically or on the internet more than 20 weeks before that stamp issue goes on sale.

If permission is to be granted, a signed, written agreement will be required and a fee or royalty may be payable.

If reproducing material for commercial use incorporating the profile or portrait of HM the Queen, or other members of the Royal Family, you must observe the rules laid down by the Lord Chamberlain's Office. (See the entry for Royalty and the Crown on page 272).

QUOTATIONS

The use of substantial verbatim quotations without permission from works such as books, plays, journals and newspapers may constitute copyright infringement unless the amount quoted is very small, or covered by a fair-dealing defence (or the copyright has expired – see Chapter 1.1 for further details). The moral rights of the author may also be infringed. By and large, though, the use of short quotations in advertising is possible.

The same principles also apply to using spoken words that have been recorded in films, sound recordings or broadcasts. In the latter case, there may be two copyright owners, both the speaker and the maker of the recording, but again a single line from a film is unlikely to be an infringement.

The common example of using quotations in advertisements of excerpts from published reviews of new books, films, CDs, etc. on promotional materials will be fine, provided that such quotes are kept very short, i.e. a line or two.

Another common example of the use of quotes is quoting a famous line from a film, such as 'I'll be back' or 'Go ahead, make my day'. Very short excerpts from a film script such as this would usually be perfectly acceptable if used by themselves and without any other reference to the film. Agencies should always be aware, however, of the rules on parodies set out in Chapter 1.1 on copyright (see page 11). There is no hard and fast rule as to the amount of material that can be quoted without infringing. This is because the courts will look at the quality as well as the quantity of material that has been reproduced before deciding whether the amount taken is 'substantial' and thus infringes. Usually it is safe to assume that one line is legitimate, but agencies should take care if using more than this. Long quotations from poems and even shorter song lyrics may infringe, especially if the poem or song is itself very short.

RED CROSS, RED CRESCENT

Agencies should avoid using the Red Cross and Red Crescent emblems, either in advertisements or when creating logos for clients.[9] The 'Red Cross' and 'Red Crescent' terms and associated emblems are protected by the Geneva Convention Act 1957. Use of these marks is restricted, making any unauthorised use of the words or emblems 'Red Cross' or 'Red Crescent' (or misleadingly similar symbols) a criminal offence with a penalty of a fine up to £5000. The guilty party will further be ordered to forfeit any goods in connection to which the infringing symbol was used.

If an advertiser's logo featuring a red cross or red crescent symbol was registered as a trade mark before the passing of the 1957 Act, it is a defence for the owner of the registered trade mark to show that his use of the design or wording was lawful.

(See also the entry in this chapter on Flags, page 267.)

ROAD SIGNS

Road signs are the subject of Crown Copyright. However, any road signs determined by the Traffic Signs Regulations and General Directions 2002 (the majority of them) are covered by a government waiver. The waiver means that agencies and advertisers are free to reproduce and use road signs in any advertising provided that the signs are not used in a misleading or derogatory manner.

The Department for Transport may object when signs are used on advertising material and sited on the roadside where they could be mistaken for a traffic sign. Agencies should ensure that their choice of media for advertisements featuring road signs is not likely to confuse motorists; particular care should therefore be given to roadside billboards and bus shelters.

The reproduction of a sign should also not imply the advertiser has official status or that it, or its product, is endorsed by government.

If there is any doubt over whether the use of a road sign will comply with the waiver, a 'click-use' PSI Licence should be obtained from the Office for Public Sector Information. There is no charge for the PSI Licence, and they last for five years.[10]

In addition, the City of Westminster Council has recently purportedly acquired the copyright in the famous red and black rectangular designs of central London street signs. All products incorporating the street signs must therefore now be licensed and failure to acquire a licence could leave advertisers liable to civil enforcement or criminal prosecution. It is debatable whether their featuring in an advertisement would infringe the copyright, and no cases have yet been brought in this respect.

ROYALTY AND THE CROWN

Generally the use of royal images for advertising purposes in any medium is prohibited. The commercial use of all royal images is governed by rules issued by the Lord Chamberlain's office. Royal images may only be used when advertising a book, newspaper, magazine article or television documentary that is itself about a member of the Royal Family, and only if express approval has been obtained from the Lord Chamberlain's office. All necessary permissions must also have been obtained from copyright holders (i.e. in the photographs, etc.).

It is also not permitted to use photographs of any member of the Royal Family visiting a firm's premises or trade stands or being publicly involved with the firm, in order to advertise the firm's business activities.

Strict provisions also apply to the use of the Royal Arms, Royal Crown and emblems which are personal to members of the Royal Family. Enquiries should be made in writing on a case-by-case basis, with details of the intended advertising use and context, to the Deputy Comptroller, Lord Chamberlain's Office.[11] More general advice can also be obtained from this office.

Royal warrants are awarded to 'tradesmen' (not professionals, media, government or places of refreshment or entertainment) based upon a minimum of five years supply to the relevant member of the Royal Family. A warrant gives the holder the right to display the Royal Arms on advertising, premises, packaging, stationery and

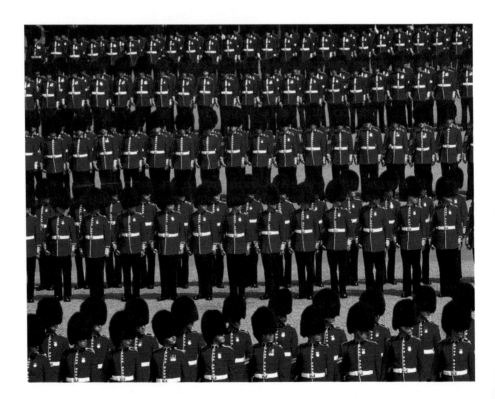

vehicles with the statement 'By appointment to…' H.M. the Queen, H.R.H. the Duke of Edinburgh or H.R.H. the Prince of Wales, as the case may be. Royal warrants are again administered by the Lord Chamberlain's Office[11], which issues very particular rules about how the Royal Arms should appear.

The above rules are reflected in sections 13.4 and 13.5 of the CAP Code, which state that '*Members of the Royal Family should not normally be shown or mentioned in marketing communications without their prior permission. Incidental references unconnected with the advertised product, or references to material such as books, articles or films about members of the Royal Family, may be acceptable. The Royal Arms and Emblems should be used only with the prior permission of the Lord Chamberlain's office. References to Royal Warrants should be checked with the Royal Warrant Holders' Association.*'

However, there have been a number of cases in which complaints about look-alikes, impersonators and cartoon images of members of the Royal Family have not been upheld by the ASA, and so humorous references to royalty may be acceptable provided they are not likely to cause offence.

(See also the sections of this chapter on Banknotes, page 258; Coins, page 264 and Postage stamps, page 269.)

UNIFORMS

Under the Chartered Associations (Protection of Names and Uniforms) Act 1926, any association incorporated by Royal Charter can apply for an Order in Council to be made to protect the name of the association and any uniform with distinctive markings or badges used by the association.

Where such an Order has been made, use of the uniform, badge or marking without the permission of the association is prohibited. The associations which enjoy the protection of such an Order are the St John Ambulance, the Royal British Legion, the Royal Life-Saving Society, the Scouts, the Girl Guides and the NSPCC. Therefore, any advertisement involving the reproduction of a uniform or badges belonging to one of these associations will require the consent of the relevant organisation.

Under the Uniform Act 1896, which is still in force today, it is unlawful for any person who is not serving in the Forces to wear any military uniform without the permission of the Crown. There is, however, an exemption for the wearing of uniforms or dress as part of a stage play, music hall or circus, or in the course of bona fide military representation. This exemption is likely to cover most advertising uses. However, it should be noted that any civilian contravening the Act, or who while wearing a uniform or any mark distinctive to a regiment brings contempt on the uniform or emblem, will be liable to a fine.

The Police Act 1996 states that any person who with the intent to deceive impersonates a member of the police force or special constable will be guilty of an offence. The same applies to anyone who wears a police uniform in circumstances which would be likely to give the appearance so nearly resembling a police officer as to deceive. The offence requires an intention to deceive, and therefore use of uniforms within an advertisement is unlikely to fall foul of this section. However, when using

uniforms in public (for example for filming) it is suggested that it would be prudent to inform the local police station.

Agencies are generally urged, when recreating police or other emergency service uniform, to create a generic copy of the uniform which does not feature an identifying police force (or other) badge or logo.

Brinsley Dresden, Lewis Silkin and
Christopher Hackford, Institute of Practitioners in Advertising

Notes

1   *The Flashing Badges Company Ltd v. Brian Groves [2007] EWHC 1372Ch*
2   Email: banknote.reproductions@bankofengland.co.uk
3   www.bankofengland.co.uk/banknotes/reproducing-banknotes.htm
4   For further details see: www.college-of-arms.gov.uk.
5   *Manchester Corporation v. Manchester Palace of Varieties [1955] 2 WLR 440*
6   European Commission
    Secretariat-General
    Directorate E-1 — Institutional Matters
    Rue de la Loi /Wetstraat 200
    B-1049 Brussels
    Tel. (32-2) 296 26 26
    Fax (32-2) 296 61 40
    email: embl@ec.europa.eu
7   Customer Service Centre
    Ordnance Survey
    Romsey Road
    SOUTHAMPTON
    SO16 4GU
    email: customerservices@ordnancesurvey.co.uk
8   Requests for permission can be submitted by email to stamp.team@royalmail.com or by completing the online form to be found on the 'Reproducing Stamps' page of the www.royalmail.com/ip section.
9   Further information is available at: www.ifrc.org/who/emblem.asp.
10 To register for a PSI Licence go to www.opsi.gov.uk/click-use/system/online/pLogin.asp or contact OPSI.
11 Lord Chamberlain's Office, Buckingham Palace, London SW1A 1AA. For more general advice, the office is also contactable by phone: 020 7930 4832

Silkin Lewis Silkin Lewis Silkin Lewis Silkin Lewis Silkin Lewis Silkin Lewis Silkin Lew
Silkin Lewis Silkin Lewis Silkin Lewis Silkin Lewis Silkin Lewis Silkin Lewis Silkin Lew
Silkin Lewis Silkin Lewis Silkin Lewis Silkin Lewis Silkin Lewis Silkin Lew

4.1

Client/agency contracts

INTRODUCTION

The most important legal relationships that any agency enters into are the contracts with its clients. These govern both the income derived from the client, and everything else that can make the difference between a profitable piece of business or an over-serviced account. The contract provides a road map for the relationship from cradle to grave, preventing the uncertainty that flows from having a binding contractual relationship without any evidence of the terms intended to govern that relationship.

Why does this matter? When the relationship is going well, it probably doesn't. While there is sufficient goodwill between the parties, any ambiguities can usually be resolved amicably enough. The problem comes when there is a dispute between the parties, such as an allegation that a handling charge has been applied to third-party production costs which the client expected to be charged at cost. Such problems often arise on termination of the relationship. For example, the agency may believe that there is a six-month notice period, while the client believes that the notice period should be just one month.

Since 1998, the Institute of Practitioners in Advertising (IPA), the Incorporated Society of British Advertisers (ISBA) and The Chartered Institute of Purchase and Supply (CIPS) have been encouraging their respective members to complete signed, written client/agency contracts based on, or adapted from, their agreed suggested terms ('Suggested Terms').

The Suggested Terms are often referred to colloquially as 'the standard form contract', but in fact they do not lay down a single set of terms and conditions but a range of options for parties to choose from. An agreed set of terms would have given rise to a straightjacket that would not have been appropriate for all circumstances, and it would also have been anti-competitive, giving rise to complex legal problems.

WHAT HAPPENS IF YOU DO BUSINESS WITH NO WRITTEN AGREEMENT?

Despite the best efforts of the trade associations, it is still not uncommon to find agencies and clients doing business together without signed, written contracts. Sometimes, there is a written agreement that has never been signed, creating uncertainty about whether the parties had completed their negotiations and actually intended to enter into a binding legal relationship on those terms. In other cases, there is not even a single draft contract that sets out the terms and conditions. In that instance, if a court needs to establish the basis on which the client and agency

originally entered into their relationship, it may look for evidence in minutes of meetings, copies of correspondence, and even by taking evidence under oath from the individuals concerned. The process of gathering such evidence in the course of pretrial proceedings will be time consuming and expensive.

In the absence of a signed, written contract, a client may also try to argue that there is not even an existing contractual relationship, particularly if it is attempting to terminate the contract without the requirement for payment during a defined period of notice. In fact, the parties will almost inevitably have entered into a binding contractual relationship as a result of their actions before the time when the dispute arose.

Although under English law there are some contracts that are only binding if they have been committed to writing, these are the exception to the general rule that a contract is formed by an offer, acceptance and consideration (which normally takes the form of payment). Examples of these exceptions include the transfer of ownership of land, and perhaps of greater relevance for these purposes, the transfer of the legal interest in a copyright work.

However, the general rule is that a contract will come into existence when there has been an offer, acceptance of that offer and some consideration. For example, the agency may have 'offered' to provide its Services at a pitch. The client then 'accepted' that agency's offer, perhaps by letter or in a meeting. The 'consideration' will be the agreement to pay the fees. Evidence of the existence of this contract will therefore be matters such as the approval of advertising created by the agency and payment by the client of the agency's invoices.

In some ways, this is the worst of all situations. There is a contractual relationship but considerable uncertainty about its terms, such as the duration of the appointment, the Services to be performed, the arrangements for fees, and the ownership of intellectual property rights in the advertising created by the agency. From the agency's point of view, the uncertainty about the length of the term and the duration of any notice period are the ones that are likely to be most dangerous. From the client's point of view, the absence of a written document signed by the agency which transfers ownership of copyright will be the major headache, particularly if the client wants to continue to use advertising created by the agency after termination of the contract. By virtue of section 90(6) of the Copyright, Designs and Patents Act 1988, copyright can only be transferred by an instrument in writing, signed by the assignor, which in this case would mean the agency, although there may be implied licences governing the client's right to use the advertising.

There are also a number of terms that are implied by statutes into client/agency relationships if they have not been excluded by virtue of a written agreement, such as an obligation on the agency to supply its Services using reasonable skill and care. The Unfair Contract Terms Act 1977 (UCTA) may also impact on the relationship. For example, in a badly drafted contract which purports to exclude liability of all kinds, UCTA will operate to make the exclusion clause unenforceable, as it prohibits any exclusion of, or limitation on, liability for death or personal injury caused by negligence. Any clause that attempts to exclude liability for fraud or fraudulent misrepresentation will also be unenforceable.

In the absence of a signed contract, for whatever reason, agencies should ensure that their invoices contain the following wording, as this will assist in arguing that standard terms of trading will apply, and all agencies ought to have such standard terms of trading ready and available for inspection.

'In the absence of a signed contract to the contrary our standard terms and conditions apply to the services and products provided, which may also be the subject matter of this and future invoices. Standard terms and conditions of business are available from the Company on request.'

THE MOST IMPORTANT CLAUSES OF A CLIENT/AGENCY CONTRACT

This chapter is not going to consider every clause of the Suggested Terms, which can be found by IPA members, in various forms on the IPA website at www.ipa.co.uk. Instead, we shall focus on the more crucial and controversial clauses which cause the most dispute during contract negotiations, and why they are important.

Term of the appointment

Agencies should try to ensure that there is a minimum fixed initial period for the contract, particularly when agencies are on a retainer. This is to ensure that an agency is adequately rewarded for all of its work. Most creative and media planning work is carried out at the beginning of the relationship, whereas fees are usually spread over the course of a year or more. If the client terminates the contract half-way through that year, then the agency will not have been properly remunerated.

The notice period and the fee must be considered in conjunction with the term. It is not in the best interests of either party to have a 12-month contract with the ability to terminate on one month's notice. Both parties must have the right to terminate, but only on reasonable notice, probably six months, in order to ensure that when the appointment ends, there is enough revenue to cover the agency while it re-assigns its staff, or if necessary, discusses TUPE arrangements with any new agency. (See also TUPE section, page 283.)

The Commencement Date specified in the contract should be the date on which the agency started to provide its Services, which will often be reflected in any invoicing arrangements. If that was some time ago, that does not matter. By contrast, however, the date on the front cover of the contract should be the date on which the last party signs the contract, and should not be backdated, or for that matter, post-dated.

Scope and territory

It is in the interests of the agency for the scope of the appointment to be set out with as much clarity as possible, stating the accounts to be included in the appointment and the countries where the agency's work can be used. This will then mean that if the client wishes to instruct the agency to produce work for other accounts, or to use the work in other countries, the agency can demonstrate that these matters are not covered by its fees, and that it should therefore be paid additional sums. These definitions will also be relevant when interpreting the exclusivity clause, as it may be possible to confine the restrictions placed on the agency to the accounts, rather than the whole range of products and Services provided by the client to its customers.

The Services

The reference in the body of the contract to the Services to be provided by the agency to the client is often by way of a brief cross-reference to a schedule to the contract. The schedule would then set out clearly and in detail all the services to be provided by the agency. The importance to the agency of getting this right cannot be exaggerated. The contents of the schedule will determine what the agency is supposed to be providing under the contract, what it is liable for, what it is being paid for and also what it can legitimately charge extra for.

Exclusivity

An exclusivity clause is a clause whereby the agency agrees not to provide Services to a competitor of the client, and also whereby the client agrees not to use any other agency to provide advertising services.

An agency should not accept a narrowly-worded, or generally-worded, clause which requires the agency not to provide similar services to any competitor of the client's goods or services. An exclusivity clause ought to be reasonable, and so it should refer to named direct competitors only.

In an ideal world, the exclusivity should also apply to the client, so that the agency remains the sole provider of advertising services to the client during the term.

Remuneration

It may be obvious, but remuneration is one of the most important clauses in a contract. The client is entitled to expect that the remuneration set out in the contract will cover everything that falls within the ambit of the contract, while on the other hand, the agency is entitled to ask for additional remuneration if the client wants to vary the terms and conditions of the contract by adding further services, accounts or territories. The agency must therefore avoid a general right for the client to add further obligations upon the agency at its sole discretion, through wording such as 'and such other Services as the client may specify from time to time' when describing what services are being provided.

The Suggested Terms include some remuneration options, but that is all they are, options. The manner in which an agency structures its fees, commission and/or payment by results will vary and every contract must be considered separately.

Audit

If the agency can enter into a contract with no audit provisions at all, then there is no obvious reason why it should not do so. Even if it has nothing to hide, preparing for an audit is a time-consuming and disruptive exercise that is unlikely to yield any benefit for the agency.

If a client insists on including audit provisions, then the agency probably has little practical alternative but to agree. The focus of the negotiation should then shift to seeking to protect the agency from the worst excesses of some of the more overzealous auditors, for whom the process is more about what they can achieve for their own benefit, rather than what they can achieve for the client.

The Suggested Terms do include a reasonable audit clause which agencies are recommended to use in place of more onerous ones which clients may propose.

Copyright and other intellectual property rights

The intellectual property clause will unquestionably be one of the most controversial clauses in the contract. The industry bodies were unable to agree a compromise clause and so produced a 'Handbook of suggested clauses' dealing with the ownership and licensing of intellectual property. Intellectual property in creative materials, computer software and code and planning materials may well be the agency's greatest asset: the value of a client company can be increased substantially with a successful advertising campaign and it has been estimated that 60% of a company's value is 'goodwill', or 'intangible assets'. These assets are often created or underpinned by the work produced by advertising agencies.

Given the value of intellectual property rights, agencies are encouraged therefore to:

- resist a client's demands for an automatic assignment to the client of all intellectual property rights in materials produced by the agency on creation;
- licence their work to the client for a limited period, in the same way that photographers do. This would give agencies the chance to be rewarded in the future if their concept proves to be successful;
- ensure, at the very least, that any assignment is made only at the end of the term and conditional on the fulfilment by the client of all their obligations under the contract, including those in relation to payment and notice period. In that way, the agency is at least being paid for the work it has produced;
- ensure that third-party intellectual property rights are adequately dealt with in the contract.

This is a complex area and one that ought to be addressed at the early stage of a client relationship when commercial terms are being discussed, so that fees and commissions can reflect what is agreed concerning intellectual property rights.

Insurance

The insurance provisions in the Suggested Terms should not require any significant amendment. The agency should avoid any obligation that requires it to provide the client with a copy of its insurance policy, as this may be prohibited by the policy itself. If evidence is required, this should be in the form of written confirmation from the insurer that the insurance is in place on suitable terms and that the premiums are up to date.

Agencies should not agree to name the client on the insurance policy. To do so increases the cost of the premium and, unless that client agrees to pay any increase, this is unfair and should be refused.

The agency should ensure that the level of liability that it accepts under the limitation of liability provisions does not exceed the level of its professional indemnity (PI) insurance. Crucially, the agency must also ensure that any contracts with sub-contractors contain insurance obligations and limitation of liability provisions that reflect those that it accepts itself under the client/agency contract. Otherwise, if the client suffers a loss as a result of a breach by the sub-contractor, the debt owed by the agency to the client may be greater than the amount that it can recover from the sub-contractor.

Warranties and indemnities

Agencies should read through any warranties and indemnities in a contract with care. Indemnities must be limited only to acts or omissions on the part of the agency. Agencies should especially beware of providing an indemnity to the client for events due to the client's own negligence or omission. Do not agree to indemnify a client for breaches of contract which are beyond the agency's control.

Indemnities should also be tied to a limitation of liability clause (see below).

Limitation of liability

This clause is one of the most important in a client contract, yet is frequently missing altogether from many client contracts. There are complex laws that govern the enforceability and extent of limitation of liability clauses, which are generally interpreted on a presumption against the party seeking to rely upon them, so they need to be drafted carefully. Agencies ought to ensure:

- the limit on liability for direct losses is set at a level that does not exceed the agency's PI insurance;
- to exclude liability for indirect or consequential loss. In practice, there can be considerable debate about whether particular losses are direct or indirect, but to ensure compatibility with the agency's PI insurance, it should usually exclude losses of this type.

Clients may also suggest that their own liability to the agency should be subject to a limit. This may be seen as pedantic, as most of the potential liabilities arising from the performance of the contract will fall upon the agency. If, however, the client is giving a warranty about the accuracy of the information that it provides, for example, backed up by an indemnity, then it is not wholly unreasonable for it to seek to limit that liability. It is essential that any such limit be expressed to be in addition to the client's liability to pay for fees and expenses in accordance with the contract.

TUPE

The Transfer of Undertaking (Protection of Employment) Regulations 2006 (TUPE) provide an employee(s) with the right to transfer his/her employment, on the same terms and conditions, from an incumbent agency to a successor agency, when the client decides to change its agency. TUPE also applies to situations where the client decides to bring the services back in-house. The general effect of TUPE is to transfer any employees who are dedicated to working on the client account, together with any liabilities, such as unpaid bonus, holiday pay and grievance claims etc. in relation to those employees, to a successor agency.

Often one of the primary reasons that a client wishes to change agency is to obtain 'new blood' and fresh thinking on the account. In these circumstances, the last thing the client wants is to end up with the same staff working on the account, which is the effect of TUPE. Therefore, it is not unusual to find in clients' standard contracts attempts either to contract out of TUPE altogether, or to mitigate the effects of TUPE by requiring the agency to give indemnities protecting the client and any successor agency from unfair dismissal or discrimination claims over which the agency has no control. These clauses are extremely unreasonable and could prove to be financially catastrophic for an agency losing a piece of business if enforced.

The first thing to note is that the parties cannot contract out of TUPE. It is a statutory employee right and as such overrides anything to the contrary in a contract. Secondly, if an employee is dismissed in connection with the transfer, either beforehand or afterwards, he/she will have a claim for automatic unfair dismissal (unless, for example, the dismissal is on the grounds of redundancy). Quite apart from the extortionate costs (legal, management time and reputation) involved in defending tribunal claims, the maximum unfair dismissal award is £72,900 and there is no limit on the amount of compensation that can be awarded in discrimination claims.

In view of the duties and potential liabilities imposed by TUPE the Suggested Terms seek to strike a fair balance between the parties. In essence, the Suggested Terms aim to ensure that, on the one hand, an outgoing agency agrees to comply with the provisions of TUPE upon termination of the contract and to accept responsibility for any employment claims arising prior to the date of termination of the contract, while, on the other hand, a successor agency takes on responsibility for any claims that are made by transferring employees arising out actions taken after the date of transfer.

Further information regarding the IPA/ISBA TUPE Protocol and a practical 10-step guide to handling TUPE transfers can be found by IPA members on the IPA website at www.ipa.co.uk. Agencies are always encouraged to seek legal advice in this area.

Governing law and jurisdiction

A clause that specifies both the laws that will govern the contract and the place where any dispute will be resolved is a standard feature of most contracts. If the client and agency are based in different countries and there is no such clause in the contract, the resulting confusion can be difficult to resolve.

An agency based in the United Kingdom should be very hesitant about agreeing to a governing law other than that of England and Wales (or Scotland, if applicable). If the client is based abroad, generally speaking it may be useful to agree that the jurisdiction of the courts of England and Wales is exclusive.

CONCLUSION

Agencies can demonstrate greater sophistication and confidence if they have carefully tailored agreements ready to provide clients from the outset of negotiations. New business directors, finance directors and those appointed to negotiate terms must be familiar with standard contract terms to protect their agencies from unreasonable obligations and liabilities, to demonstrate professionalism and to manage risk.

Brinsley Dresden, Lewis Silkin

Advertising Institute of Practitioners in Advertising Institute of Practiti
Advertising Institute of Practitioners in Advertising Institute of Practiti
Advertising Institute of Practitioners in Advertising Institute of Practiti
Advertising Institute of Practitioners in Advertising Institute of Practiti

4.2

Pitch protection

In the previous chapter, it was demonstrated how important it is to agree the terms of a client/agency contract once an agency has been appointed. However, legal issues should not be forgotten in the pre-appointment stage either. In particular it is very important to clarify intellectual property (IP) rights and confidentiality from the outset in order to avoid problems later.

The Institute of Practitioners in Advertising (IPA) and Incorporated Society of British Advertisers (ISBA) have worked together to recommend best practice in the pitch process. Not all advertisers will be familiar with the suggested best practice guidance, and it is therefore always worthwhile for agencies to reiterate to them some of the recommended principles. It is in the best interests of both the advertiser and the agencies pitching that the pitch is conducted properly and professionally.

Furthermore, in a business environment in which intellectual property is becoming more and more valuable, it is also important that all parties understand the intellectual property rights that arise during the pitch process and with whom those rights vest.

The IPA Pitch Protocol, which is available on the IPA website, covers confidentiality issues, the retention of all IP rights in materials produced by the agency, possibility of pitch fees and sets out a list of questions which should be dealt with by the parties before the pitch process commences. The protocol includes a draft pitch agreement and there is also an online facility to register pitch work with the IPA.

This chapter deals with the most important legal issues of the pitch process, namely confidentiality, protecting an agency's IP in the materials created for a pitch, fees and the Transfer of Undertakings (Protection of Employment) Regulations (TUPE).

PITCH AGREEMENT

Confidentiality

An agency should not wait, or expect a client to provide a confidentiality (or non-disclosure) agreement. They should take the initiative and send their own tailored pitch agreement incorporating a mutual confidentiality clause[1].

In a pitch process, both parties will be disclosing confidential information. The client will obviously be disclosing information about its new products, its marketing plans and its budgets. The agency will be disclosing its fees and rates, and its ideas and other creative assets. All of this needs protection in order to prevent either party doing mischief. Any client who refuses to agree a mutual confidentiality agreement should be viewed with care, as it could suggest that they intend to use the pitch process as an exercise to glean information about fees, or simply as a hunt for new creative ideas.

By agreeing a mutual confidentiality agreement, however, the client is provided with comfort that the agency will not disclose any sensitive trade secrets to third parties and the agency is given some comfort, albeit limited, that its ideas will not be passed to another agency to develop. The IPA has a mutual non-disclosure agreement available for members to use.

Protecting intellectual property

As explained in Chapter 1.1, English law provides that copyright will automatically exist in all literary, artistic, musical and dramatic work. Thus copyright will automatically subsist in the designs, drawings and illustrations an agency presents at a pitch. However, there is no sure fast way of preventing ideas or designs from being used by clients determined to copy them. A confidentiality agreement goes some way to protecting ideas, but it is not a cast-iron guarantee: an agency would have to sue a potential client for breach of contract, and this may not always be desirable or successful.

Most situations, however, arise out of ignorance rather than a deliberate attempt to misappropriate agency work. Agencies should therefore try to guard against this. The following steps are primarily aimed at deterring advertisers in the first place from using work without consent, by reiterating from the outset that the ideas and materials the agency is presenting are not only confidential, but also protected by copyright. If a dispute arises, the following steps may also help satisfy the court that the agency ideas and material in question were original, belong to the agency and that this valuable commodity was misappropriated.

Agencies should:

- clearly state in the pitch agreement that the intellectual property in agency materials remains vested in the agency;

- ensure all material submitted is clearly labelled with a copyright sign '©' and the name of the agency and a date. Any artwork presented at a pitch should include a statement along the following lines 'This artwork is protected by copyright which belongs to [agency name]. It must not be used, copied, reproduced or disclosed to any third party without the explicit written permission of [agency name]';

- ensure that a date is included on all material produced during the pitch. Keep a record of who produced it and conserve all working drafts. With web-based designs and ideas it is useful to keep downloaded versions;

- consider registering the work created online with the IPA Pitch Protection Scheme. This simple registration system records the agency details, the client and product or service, the date of production of the ideas and materials, and the key concepts. The agency may then also attach relevant material to the online registration form.

All registrations on this system receive an 'IPA Certificate of Registration' which can be attached to the work submitted on a pitch, thereby reinforcing even further the agency's rights in the material and putting the advertiser on notice of the agency's intellectual property rights and of how seriously this issue is taken.

Pitch fees

Some pitches include a fee payable by the client to the agency for the pitch. This is particularly the case where clients wish to have the copyright of all artwork produced during the pitch assigned to the client. Agencies should decide whether the fee offered represents a fair and reasonable estimation of the value of their creative work before deciding whether to participate. There is a danger that once an agency is paid a fee the client will require or assume there will be an assignment of intellectual property in work created, but really a fee ought to represent time spent and not the total value of the idea. This may be much more valuable.

TUPE

The application of TUPE in commercial contracts was discussed in the previous chapter. The implications of TUPE, however, should also be considered during the pitch stage. It is possible, under TUPE, that the successful agency in a pitch will inherit employees from the previous agency.

It is therefore advisable for all agencies pitching to find out as much information as possible about potentially transferring employees in the early stages of the pitch. This will have an influence on their costings and also on whether they decide to continue the pitch. A request for information about the incumbent agency and any potential employee transfers, should the pitching agency win the business, is very wise and demonstrates good business acumen.

CONCLUSION

The pitch process is often seen by agencies not to be the time to raise legal issues, in the mistaken fear that this will repel a potential client. However, it is essential if rights are to be protected from the perspective of both the agency and the client that the issues referred to above are tackled up front. As with later contract negotiations, agencies need to have the confidence and understanding necessary to insist upon what are nothing more than equitable commercial practices.

Marina Palomba, Institute of Practitioners in Advertising

Note

1   IPA Suggested pitch agreement terms available for members.

Television Commercials Production Contract

INTRODUCTION

Since 1955, when the first television commercial for Gibbs SR toothpaste was aired in the UK, television advertising has become one of the principal connections between advertisers and a mass audience. The UK has an enviable reputation for producing commercials of the highest quality and ads for brands like Hovis, PG Tips, Smash and Heineken have embedded themselves and, more importantly, the products they were selling, in the national consciousness.

However, the actual procedure of making a commercial is a complex one. Shooting a 'film', as it is known in the business, is probably one of the most expensive activities that an advertising agency will undertake on behalf of its client. Scripts and costs will vary but the process is complex, frequently conducted under time pressure and involves a considerable degree of artistic, and therefore largely subjective, input.

Fortunately, the UK television production industry is among the finest and most professional in the world, and the combination of knowledgeable and experienced production company directors and producers and equally informed agency television departments has meant that it is the norm for commercials (7,500 of which are made each year) to realise the advertisers' vision of them, and be delivered on time. The job of the agency television department and the production company is to make an outstanding advertisement for their mutual client.

The role of the contract is to facilitate this through clarity of responsibility and, should the unthinkable arise and a commercial become the subject of a dispute, to provide a mutually acceptable process whereby this is resolved – fairly, quickly and without recourse to the courts. Fortunately, the occasions on which recourse to the disputes procedure has been necessary have been infrequent in recent years.

The current contract, which is endorsed by the Advertising Producers Association (APA), the Institute of Practitioners in Advertising (IPA) and the Incorporated Society of British Advertisers (ISBA), was formally adopted in July 2003 and was subsequently updated and re-launched in the summer of 2004. It is a blueprint for the industry and is used across much of Europe and the rest of the world.

THE PURPOSE OF THE CONTRACT

The 2004 contract breaks the process of making a commercial down into two separate, though related, parts.

- *The Production and Insurance Specification (PIBS)* – sets out all the information specific to the production under consideration and assigns responsibilities between the agency and production company for the job. This forms Part 1 of the arrangement;
- *The Contract (or Part 2 of the procedure)* – sets out the terms that apply to every commercial produced under it.

Although Part 2 is entitled 'Contract' both Part 1 and Part 2 are contractual documents and the rights and obligations of the parties are defined by both documents taken together.

Although the advertising agency is working for a client in arranging and contracting for the production of a commercial, it is important to note that in this context, the agency is a principal in law. In consequence, the advertising agency is liable to the production company in respect of its contractual obligations as principal, rather than as an agent for the advertiser.

THE PRODUCTION OF COMMERCIALS CONTRACT

Paradoxically, the contracting process is best explained by taking Part 2 of the contract first and then running through the contents of Part 1, the PIBS.

Part 2: the Contract

This chapter will consider the most important clauses only.

Responsibilities *(Clause 1)*
This defines the commercials to be made by reference to the PIBS, the script and the cost estimate, in order that the production company is clear about what film it is making and the agency is clear about what film it is getting. The production company will also produce a treatment for the script – an explanation of how it will bring it to life on the screen. This is not a contractual document but it assists in ensuring the parties share a vision of how the commercial will look.

Payment *(Clause 5)*
Production companies and agencies agree a fixed price for the production and contract in advance of the commercial being produced, and that sum is written into the contract.

It shows the production company's fee, referred to as the mark-up, which is a percentage of the costs of the production. The production company is then responsible for producing the commercial for that fixed price; it cannot invoice the agency for extra costs it incurs because, for example, an unforeseen problem arises. The contract provides exceptions; if the agency requires the production company to do additional work e.g. by changing the script, or the agency defaults in its obligations e.g. in providing actors, and such results in additional costs. Half the budget is payable no later than seven days before the shoot and the balance after the shoot as set out in the contract.

The position is different for 'fast track' production (those defined as commercials which are to be completed within 21 days of the contract being signed), where 75% of the budget is payable no later than seven days before the shoot.

Copyright and other rights *(Clause 12)*

It is essential that the agency ensures it obtains all the necessary rights needed to comply with its obligations to the client. Thus, provided the agency pays for the commercial, this agreement provides for the assignment of copyright in the commercial by the production company to the agency. The agency can then use the commercial and any image from it in any media, anywhere in the world.

However, there is an important exception for animation. The agency may use the commercial (or clips from it) in any audio-visual media, anywhere in the world, but copyright in the animation remains with the production company. Thus, if the agency wants to use a still from it, e.g., in some other advertising or in merchandising, it may only do so if it agrees a fee for such use with the production company. It is very important a client understands the restrictions that will always exist with using commercials indefinitely, whether because of animation rights, or artists and models performance rights.

The PIBS provides a shopping list for agencies so that they have the option of agreeing the price for a particular use of animation at the outset. They can agree that such fee is payable on first use. The clause also provides that agencies and production companies are responsible for obtaining copyright clearance on third-party material they include in the commercial.

Postponement or cancellation at agency's request *(Clauses 13 and 14)*

The agency may postpone production, but must pay the production company any extra costs which arise as a result of the postponement. Similarly, the agency may cancel the production of the commercial, but it will then be obliged to pay the production company the costs it has incurred, plus producer's and director's fees and mark-up, in sums to be agreed.

Insurance *(Clauses 16–18)*

The insurance clause is very important. It may be that this clause needs amending if the client wishes to insure. The usual clause, however, provides that the agency indemnifies the production company and insures itself against specified items and vice versa.

If weather is unsuitable for filming a commercial on a planned shoot day and the shoot day has to be extended, or another shoot day is required as a result, the extra day is referred to as a 'weather day'. The client is responsible for that additional cost. In contractual terms, the agency is responsible for paying that cost to the production company and the agency is entitled to recover that cost from the client. Weather day insurance is available. The premium will depend upon the type of weather to be insured against i.e. the definition of 'unsuitable' weather in respect of the commercial being shot and the likelihood of that weather occurring at that location at that time. However, weather insurance premiums are typically 30%–40% of the cost of a weather day, so it is not unusual for clients to opt not to buy cover and take the risk of having to pay for a weather day themselves. The production company is responsible for the additional cost of sets built outside prior to the commencement of the shoot if the agency asks and pays for the production company to insure against that. The production company is also responsible for additional costs as a result of it not being able to reach the location because of adverse weather.

Disputes procedure *(Clause 23)*
Under this contract, the agency and the production company agree that any dispute will be dealt with by mediation or arbitration, rather than going to court. The aim of this is for industry disputes to be determined by representatives of the industry who have a good understanding of it. Further, in most circumstances, mediation provides a quicker, cheaper and more flexible method of determining disputes. This issue is dealt with in a little more detail in Mediation (see page 306).

Part 1: the Production and Insurance Briefing Specification (PIBS)

Moving on to consider the first part of the agreement, the PIBS records the details particular to the commercial being shot as part of the agreement between the agency and production company; it is as much part of the contract between them as Part 2, the Contract.

The PIBS is set out in such a way as to operate as a checklist to assist the parties in ensuring that every element of production of the commercial is attributed as a responsibility to either the agency or the production company.

The PIBS deals with the following:

Section A
This contains spaces to insert information as to duration of the commercial, formats required and critical dates.

Section B: Insurance
The purpose of this clause is to ensure that all the different types of insurance that might be required are considered. If they are appropriate to the production, the production company and agency must make clear who is responsible for which elemants of the insurance. A quotation is best obtained from a specialist broker.

The section details the different areas that need to be insured:

- non-appearance insurance
- employer's liability insurance and workers' compensation
- commercial producer's Indemnity Insurance
- personal accident insurance
- negative insurance
- vehicle insurance
- all risks loss or damage to agency props and wardrobe
- weather insurance
- special requirements insurance
- evidence of insurance in effect.

Section C: Time critical information
This clause provides an opportunity for the agency to identify whether the shoot could be postponed because of force majeure (rather than being cancelled).

Section D: Animation
See clause 12 of Part 2 (page 303) in respect of animation copyright.

Section E: Agency approvals
Agencies should use this section to identify those elements of the production where the agency specifically requires approval before the production company proceeds.

Section F: Currency/exchange rate fluctuations
This clause sets out the procedures for commercials being shot outside the UK. The method adopted is for the production company to identify what part of the quote they must pay out in foreign currency and what exchange rate is used. The production company fixes the exchange rate on the day the production is confirmed by forward-buying the currency. The price agreed is varied to reflect the actual cost to the production company of forward-buying the currency and that adjusted figure is inserted in clause 5 of Part 2.

Section G: Checklist
This section is a checklist of other items that may be required as part of producing the commercial, with the opportunity to say that they are inapplicable, or the responsibility of the agency or of the production company.

Section H: Additional contractual requirements
Any additional terms specific to each case can be inserted in this section.

Section I: Payments
It is important to set out clearly in this section when the price, agreed in clause 5 of Part 2, is due to be paid. For overseas shoots, and other shoots that are front-end cost heavy, it is appropriate for the parties to consider accelerating payment of the second 50%. For example, the parties could agree that half of the second 50% (i.e. 25% of the total fee) will be paid immediately following the last shoot day.

Section K: Showreels
The agency commits to endeavour to get licences in favour of the production company to use the commercials to promote itself, in the same terms as the agency gets such rights for itself.

Section L
This section provides that the agency should issue the contract, Part 2, to the production company by the day following verbal/written confirmation.

DISPUTES

Fortunately, disputes in commercials production are comparatively rare, but when they do crop up – even with the procedures outlined in the contract – they are time consuming and emotionally draining.

As such, invoking the formal dispute procedure is a step only usually taken as an 'action of last resort', when informal discussions have broken down and neither side can see a way forward.

The rationale of an industry disputes procedure

Given that the sums involved in production disputes are comparatively small in commercial law terms, it is clearly desirable to avoid recourse to the courts. In these circumstances, the procedure outlined in clause 23 of the contract, was designed to provide a totally confidential, fair and rapid means of resolving disagreements.

In the first instance however, the IPA and APA will, if asked, investigate whether an informal intervention from them can help resolve the problem, and recent experience has shown this to be an effective means of resolving some potential disputes, by tackling the issue before the parties' positions become ingrained.

Recognising the need for administrative expertise in the actual process of mediation and arbitration, it was agreed to place the process of the arrangement into the hands of professional mediators/arbitrators, who would work alongside knowledgeable representatives of the industry to determine a fair and reasonable outcome. To this end, the Centre for Disputes Resolution (CEDR) has been appointed to carry out this role.

Mediation

In mediation, the parties are invited to work towards a mutually agreeable solution via a professional mediator. The respondent may decline to participate in mediation and proceed directly to arbitration, but a resolution achieved via this process can benefit the parties by reducing administration costs and avoiding the potentially damaging effects on commercial relationships by allocating blame. It is a confidential process, unlike court proceedings. However, should this route prove unfruitful, or if the respondent requires it, a dispute can move to formal arbitration.

Arbitration

Arbitration is more similar to court proceedings. The parties in the standard contract agree to CEDR appointing an arbitrator, who in turn administers the procedure to a strict timetable. Evidence of claims and defences are exchanged between the parties and they put their case at a hearing before a tribunal made up of a panel of mutually acceptable representatives from the film production industry, advertising agencies and advertisers (one per sector) under the chairmanship of the CEDR arbitrator.

CONCLUSION

As will be gathered from all the above, making a television commercial is a highly complex procedure, frequently conducted under considerable pressure. The Production Contract (Parts 1 and 2) acts as a bedrock on which the British advertising industry creates some of the most outstanding and effective television commercials made anywhere in the world.

By providing clarity and certainty in an environment driven by creativity, the contract's value to all parties is immense.

Steve Davies, Advertising Producers Association and
Geoffrey Russell, Institute of Practitioners in Advertising

Advertising Institute of Practitioners in Advertising Institute of Practiti
Advertising Institute of Practitioners in Advertising Institute of Practiti
Advertising Institute of Practitioners in Advertising Institute of Practiti
Institute of Practiti

5

Ethics and advertising

Increasingly, consumers believe that industry, rather than government, should be proactive in both promoting and undertaking environmental and socially responsible business practices, as evidenced particularly by the debate surrounding obesity and the role of advertising of high-fat, salt and sugar foods. Victorian utilitarianism has re-emerged as modern-day altruism where it is unacceptable for big business to pursue purely profit. Indeed, it is not in the best interest of any business to damage its brand image. Enlightened self-interest or corporate social responsibility is positively good for business, good for consumers and good for government.

The marketing communications industry cannot advocate the philanthropy of its client advertisers when falling foul of the same ethical principles itself. In fact the communications industry has done much to ensure that the continuing integrity of marketing communications and ethics should form part of both agencies' own internal processes and the manner in which they operate with competitors and clients.

The industry has a historic reputation for responsible communications and ethical advertising, as is illustrated by some of the issues below, but it requires the continued support, adherence and enforcement of responsible advertisers against those, as in any industry, who seek to circumvent the rules.

Code of ethics

The IPA is a member of the European Association of Communication Agencies (EACA), which brings together the advertising, media and sales promotions agencies across Europe as well as agency associations across the world.

Through the IPA, UK members sign up to the EACA Code of Ethics that sets out the basic principles by which IPA members undertake their business.[1] The Code recognises the obligation to create advertising that is consistent with the social, economic and environmental principles of sustainable development. It also sets out how agencies should act in dealings with the media, the advertisers, suppliers, employees and competitors.

Self-regulation

The marketing communications industry has one of the most successful and effective systems of self-regulation and co-regulation in the world for non-broadcast and broadcast advertising. It is a system that is funded by the advertisers, and one that responsible agencies and advertisers wholeheartedly endorse because it is in the best interest of consumers and the industry alike to ensure the integrity of marketing communications. (See Chapter 2.) However it has come under increasing criticism for not fully extending to the internet. In order to ensure the integrity of marketing communications the 'wild west' of the online world has to change.

Discussions are well under way, at the time of publishing this book, by the Digital Media Group of the Advertising Association, who will be making recommendations to extend the CAP Code to marketing communications on the internet. This will be controversial, but messages which would be unacceptable in traditional advertising media are put on the internet with little or no concern for the protection of the consumer, and both government and NGOs are pointing to these executions and accusing the industry of duplicity.

However, the support of the industry, and funding by advertisers and collection of levies by agencies is paramount to the continued success of self-regulation.

It is noticeable in the UK that there is incredible consumer confidence in the system shown by the sheer number of complaints made and the manner in which they are so effectively and swiftly dealt with. We have yet to see how effective self-regulation on the internet will be.

Media Smart®

The advertising industry has been a long-time advocate of educating children about the media. Media Smart[2] is a media literacy programme launched in 2002 with the objective of providing children with the tools to help them understand and interpret advertising, so that they are able to make informed choices.

Media Smart is an industry-funded initiative designed for primary school children aged 6–11 years old. It is the first UK media literacy programme to run inside the classroom and the home using broadcast and written educational materials. Media Smart programmes are now in eight EU countries.

There is no question that media plays an important role in children's lives today; they watch programmes and advertising via satellite and terrestrial television, the internet, billboards, magazines and newspapers, mobile phones, videos and DVDs. Calls to ban certain types of advertising to children in broadcasting will not prevent young people from exposure to the commercial world, nor should it.

Media Smart provides primary school children with the tools to help them interpret, understand and use information provided in adverts to their benefit. The programme teaches children to question their sources of information and helps them think about the influences on their everyday choices.

The advertising business has a long track record of responsible advertising to children and Media Smart continues this tradition.

Portman Group

The Portman Group[3] is another example of advertisers seeking to act responsibly in relation to a product that can be easily misused. UK's leading drinks manufacturers, who together supply the majority of alcohol sold in the UK, established the Group in 1989.

The purpose of the Group is: to promote responsible drinking; to help prevent misuse of alcohol; to encourage responsible marketing; and to foster a balanced understanding of alcohol-related issues.

The majority of people who drink alcohol enjoy it without causing harm to themselves or others. Unfortunately there is a section of society that misuse alcohol and the best way to tackle this issue is through education, not a ban on advertising.

However, the Group and the advertising industry accept the need for responsible promotions and steps were taken in 2006 to tighten the self-regulatory codes (see Chapter 2). The Portman Group's own Code strictly regulates the naming, packaging and 'below-the-line promotion' of alcoholic products and it has been the lone body advocating moderate drinking for some years.

Can advertising ever be ethical?

Any defence of the advertising industry is bound to sound less dramatic than the criticisms sometimes levelled at it. The fact remains that advertisers are as much controlled by the fickle consumer as they are in control themselves. Brands can be irreparably damaged by even the slightest hint of scandal or consumer whim, and the internet is perhaps the pinnacle of such consumer power and almost self-policing.

Nevertheless, the increasing desire to use the internet as an unregulated media is of concern. So called word-of-mouth and buzz marketing via the internet, social networking sites, blogs and interactive advertising funded sites has led advertisers to think they can get away with misleading advertising. This is not the case. In 2008 the Consumer Protection from Unfair Commercial Practices Regulations wiped away a great deal of old law and brought into force a stricter regime for misleading advertising. This, coupled with an extended CAP Code and above all consumer power with the possibility of damage to reputation, will lead to greater observance by reputable advertisers on the internet.

Buzz marketing

No business wishes to attract the bad publicity experienced, for example, by Walmart and its PR firm, Edelman PR, in the US. Edelman, himself an author of the WOMM (Word of Mouth Marketing Association) Code of Ethics[4], created a fake blog called *Wal-Marting Across America*, ostensibly launched by a pair of average Americans chronicling their cross-country travels. When the bloggers were disclosed as a promotional tactic Edelman was forced to publicly apologise and the brand suffered a huge amount of adverse publicity. But this is not a unique case, and in future advertisers and their agencies will need to realise that 'flogs', 'astroturfing', 'sockpuppets' and other such techniques are illegal, a breach of the Codes and if discovered, the public condemnation will be intense. The golden rule is always 'be transparent'.

Conclusion

As an industry it is essential that advertisers and agencies pay proper deference to the modern phenomena of corporate responsibility and adhere to the rules about advertising being legal, decent, honest and truthful in all media. However, a line has to be drawn between the responsibilities of government and business. Advertisers are not philanthropists nor should they be, that is the work for politicians and preachers or, possibly, philosophers. Advertisers sell products consumers want. Even the best agency will fail to sell a product nobody desires.

The facts are that advertising has endowed modern western society with benefits that should not be undervalued. It provides vital information about the vast number of products available to us, the average supermarket alone stocks over 300,000 products; it stimulates competition, without which we would see prices rise and new products fail; it creates wealth (both directly and indirectly); it entertains and enriches our cultural and creative society and it underwrites the cost of media – estimates suggest that one-third of magazine cover prices and two-thirds of newspapers' cover prices are underwritten by advertising. Free content on the internet is equally funded by advertising.

Calls to restrict advertising, purportedly in the name of the consumer, have become an all too common response to complex social issues that have little or nothing to do with brand advertising. The most important step the marketing communications industry can take in response to the creeping threat to the freedom of commercial expression is to act responsibly, and to communicate the value of advertising to all.

Marina Palomba, Institute of Practitioners in Advertising

Notes

1   EACA Code of Ethics 2004 – www.eaca.be
2   Media Smart www.mediasmart.org.uk
3   Portman Group www.portman-group.org.uk
4   Word of Mouth Association (WOMM) USA www.womma.org/ethics

Appendices

USEFUL WEBSITES

Advertising Association (AA)
www.adassoc.org.uk
Promoting and protecting the rights, responsibilities and role of advertising.

British Board of Film Classification (BBFC)
www.bbfc.co.uk
Responsible for classifying cinema films and videos.

Clearcast
www.clearcast.co.uk
Operates a pre-clearance system for TV advertisements.

Committee of Advertising Practice (CAP)
www.cap.org.uk
A self-regulatory body that devises and enforces the British Code of Advertising, Sales Promotion and Direct Marketing (The CAP Code).

Direct Marketing Association (DMA)
www.dma.org.uk
Promotes the image of direct marketing.

Direct Selling Association (DSA)
www.dsa.org.uk
Trade association for direct selling companies.

History of Advertising Trust (HAT)
www.hatads.org.uk
Encourages the study of advertising and related fields. HAT holds a collection of advertising material from 1800 to the present day.

Incorporated Society of British Advertisers (ISBA)
www.isba.org.uk
The single body, within the UK, to represent advertisers' interests across all marketing communication disciplines.

Institute of Direct Marketing (IDM)
www.theidm.com
Europe's foremost professional development body for interactive and direct marketing.

Institute of Sales Promotion (ISP)
www.isp.org.uk
Dedicated to protecting and promoting the sales promotion industry.

Newspaper Society (NS)
www.newspapersoc.org.uk
Provides legal and advertising control advice for regional and local newspapers.

Outdoor Advertising Association (OAA)
www.oaa.org.uk

Periodical Publishers Association (PPA)
www.ppa.co.uk

Proprietary Association of Great Britain (PAGB)
www.pagb.co.uk
Represents the manufacturers of non-prescription medicines and food supplements which are available to the public for sale over the counter in pharmacies and other retail outlets.

Radio Advertising Clearance Centre
(RACC)
www.crca.co.uk
*Commercial radio's advertising clearance
body.*

INTERNATIONAL WEBSITES

Advertising Standards Canada
(ASC)
www.adstandards.com
Canadian regulator.

Austria: Osterreichischer Werberat
(OWR)
www.werberat.or.at
Advertising self-regulatory body for Austria.

Czech Republic: Rada Pro Reklamu
(CRPR)
www.rpr.cz
*Advertising self-regulatory body for the Czech
Republic.*

Denmark: Reklame Forum (RF)
www.annoncoer.dk
*Advertising self-regulatory organisation for
Denmark.*

European Advertising Standards
Alliance (EASA)
www.easa-alliance.org
*A non-profit organisation to represent the views
of the advertising self-regulatory and industry
bodies across Europe.*

European Association of
Communications Agencies (EACA)
www.eaca.be
*A Brussels-based organisation representing
full-service advertising and media agencies as
well as agency associations in Europe.*

Finland: Liiketapalautakunta (LTL)
www.keskuskauppakamari.fi
*Advertising self-regulatory organisation for
Finland.*

France: Bureau de Verification de la
Publicite (BVP)
www.bvp.org
*Advertising self-regulatory organisation for
France.*

Germany: Deutscher Werberat
www.werberat.de
*Advertising self-regulatory organisation for
issues of taste and decency in Germany.*

Germany: Zentrale zur Bekampfung
unlauteren Wettbewerbs e.V (ZEN)
www.wettbewerbszentrale.de
*Advertising self-regulatory organisation for
issues of misleading advertising and unfair
competition in Germany.*

Greece: Enossi Etairion Diafimisis-
Epikoinonias (EDEE)
www.edee.gr
*Advertising self-regulatory organisation for
Greece.*

The International Advertising
Association (IAA) UK Chapter
www.iaauk.com
*A worldwide business association for all
individuals and enterprises involved in the
branding process.*

Ireland: Advertising Standards Authority
for Ireland (ASAI)
www.asai.ie
*Advertising self-regulatory organisation for
Ireland.*

Italy: Istituto dell'Autodisciplina
Pubblicitaria (IAP)
www.iap.it
Advertising self-regulatory organisation for Italy.

Luxembourg: Commission
Luxembourgeoise pour l'Ethique en
Publicite (CLEP)
www.clc.lu
*Advertising self-regulatory organisation for
Luxembourg.*

Netherlands: Stichting Reclame Code (SRC)
www.reclamecode.nl
Advertising self-regulatory organisation for the Netherlands.

New Zealand: Advertising Standards Authority Inc (ASA NZ)
www.asa.co.nz
Advertising self-regulatory organisation for New Zealand.

Portugal: Instituto Civil da Autodisciplina da Publicidade (ICAP)
www.icap.pt
Advertising self-regulatory organisation for Portugal.

Russia: Reklamny Sovet Rossii
www.advertising.ru
Advertising self-regulatory organisation for Russia.

Slovak Republic: Rada Pre Reklamu (SRPR)
www.rpr.sk
Advertising self-regulatory organisation for the Slovak Republic.

Slovenia: Slovenska Oglasevalska Zbornica (SOZ)
www.soz.si
Advertising self-regulatory organisation for Slovenia.

Spain: Asociación para la Autorregulación de la Communicación Comercial (Autocontrol)
www.aap.es
Advertising self-regulatory organisation for Spain.

Switzerland: Commission Suisse pour la Loyaute (CSL)
www.lauterkeit.ch
Advertising self-regulatory organisation for Switzerland.

Turkey: Reklam Ozdenetim Kurulu (ROK)
www.rok.org.tr
Advertising self-regulatory organisation for Turkey.

USA: The Advertising Review Council (ARC)
www.esrb.org
US regulator.

GOVERNMENT DEPARTMENT LINKS

Department for Business, Enterprise and Regulatory Reform (BERR)
www.berr.gov.uk/cacp/ca
Helps ensure business success in an increasingly competitive world.

Department of Health
www.dh.gov.uk
The DH's aim is to improve the health and well-being of people in England.

Equality of Human Rights Commission
www.equalityhumanrights.com
Champions equality and human rights for all, working to eliminate discrimination, reduce inequality, protect human rights and to build good relations, ensuring that everyone has a fair chance to participate in society.

Financial Services Authority
www.fsa.gov.uk

Information Commissioner's Office
www.dataprotection.gov.uk
An independent supervisory body responsible for enforcing the Data Protection Act and the Freedom of Information Act.

Local Government Association (LGA)
www.lga.gov.uk
Represents all local authorities in England and Wales.

Medicines and Healthcare products Regulatory Authority (MHRA)
www.mhra.gov.uk
Regulates the standards of safety in medicines and healthcare products and grants marketing licences to manufacturers.

Ofcom
www.ofcom.org.uk
The regulator for the UK broadcast and telecommunications industry. Ofcom deals with complaints about TV and radio commercials.

Office of Fair Trading (OFT)
www.oft.gov.uk
A non-ministerial Government Department, plays a front-line role in protecting the economic welfare of consumers and in enforcing UK competition policy.

Office of the Telecommunications Ombudsman (Otelo)
www.otelo.org.uk
Looks at complaints made against telecommunication companies that are members of the Ombudsman scheme.

Phone Pay Plus
www.phonepayplus.org.uk
Regulates the standards of telephone information and entertainment services (e.g. premium rate lines) and ensures adherence to the ICSTIS Code of Practice.

Press Complaints Commission (PCC)
www.pcc.org.uk
An independent organisation which deals with complaints from members of the public about the editorial content of newspapers and magazines.

Trading Standards Central
www.tradingstandards.gov.uk
Consumer rights under the law.

Word of Mouth Marketing Association (WOMMA)
www.womma.org
The official trade association for the word of mouth marketing industry.

INTERNET AGENCIES/ ASSOCIATIONS

European Internet Services Providers Association (EuroISPA)
www.euroispa.org
Voices internet services providers' concerns to politicians and officials at European Union level and influences EU Internet policies.

Interactive Advertising Bureau UK
www.iabuk.net
Establishes standards for the industry.

Internet Services Providers Association
www.ispa.org.uk
Represents internet services providers in the UK.

Internet Watch Foundation
www.iwf.org.uk
An independent body assisting in the regulation of content, particularly child pornography.

London Internet Exchange (LINX)
www.linx.net
A not-for-profit partnership between internet service providers.

Wireless Marketing Association
www.wirelessmarketing.org.uk
Promoting the growth of marketing via mobile phones.

OTHERS

The Advertising Archives
www.advertisingarchives.co.uk
A specialist picture library from 1850 to the present day.

Fax Preference Service
www.fpsonline.org.uk
Available to businesses and individuals to register fax numbers on which they do not wish to receive fax marketing messages.

Mailing Preference Service
www.mpsonline.org.uk
A free service which enables consumers to register their wish not to receive unsolicited direct mail.

Newspaper Marketing Agency
www.nmauk.co.uk
Set up by the national newspapers to represent them to advertisers and their agencies.

Telephone Preference Service
www.tpsonline.org.uk
Helps individuals to make sure their telephone numbers are no longer available to organisations who may telephone with offers and information they do not wish to receive.

The IPA accepts no responsibility for the availability, content or accuracy of the information provided on these sites and accepts no liability for any loss resulting from use of any of these sites or ordering goods and services from any of these sites.

GLOSSARY OF ACRONYMS

AA	Advertising Association
ABPI	Association of the British Pharmaceutical Industry
ABTA	Association of British Travel Agents
AMCO	Association of Media and Communications Specialists
APA	Advertising Producers Association
ASAI	Advertising Standards Authority for Ireland
BERR	Business Enterprise and Regulatory Reform, Department of
BBFC	British Board of Film Classification
BNF	British Nutrition Foundation
BRC	British Retail Consortium
BSI	British Standards Institution
CAA	Cinema Advertising Association
CAP	Committee of Advertising Practice
CECG	Consumers in the European Community Group
Clearcast	Broadcast Advertising Clearance Centre (previously known as the BACC)
COMATAS	Committee for Monitoring Tobacco Advertising and Sponsorship
CTPA	Cosmetics, Toiletry and Perfumery Association
DMA	Direct Marketing Association
DMARC	Direct Mail Accreditation and Recognition Centre
DPR	Data Protection Registrar
DSA	Direct Selling Association
EACA	European Association of Communications Agencies
EASA	European Advertising Standards Alliance
ECLG	European Consumer Law Group
ELSPA	Entertainment Leisure Software Publishers Association
FDF	Food and Drink Federation
FSA	Financial Services Authority
FSA	Food Standards Agency
HAT	History of Advertising Trust
HFMA	Health Food Manufacturers Association
IAA	International Advertising Association UK
IAB	Interactive Advertising Bureau
ICC	International Chamber of Commerce
IDM	Institute of Direct Marketing
IPA	Institute of Practitioners in Advertising
ISBA	Incorporated Society of British Advertisers
ISP	Institute of Sales Promotion
ISPA	Internet Service Providers Association
LACORS	Local Authority Co-ordinators of Regulatory Services
LACOTS	Local Authorities Co-ordinating Body on Food and Trading Standards
LGA	Local Government Association
LINX	London Internet Exchange
MCA	Medicines Control Agency

MHRA	Medicines and Healthcare products Regulatory Agency
MCPS	Mechanical Copyright Protection Society
MOPS	Mail Order Protection Scheme
MOTA	Mail Order Traders Association
MPA	Music Publishers Association
MPS	Mail Preference Service
NAFSS	National Alliance for Food Safety and Security
NCC	National Consumer Council
NFA	National Food Alliance
NPA	Newspaper Publishers Association
NS	Newspaper Society
OAA	Outdoor Advertising Association
OFCOM	Office of Communication
OFGEM	Office of Gas and Electricity Markets
OFT	Office of Fair Trading
PAGB	Proprietary Association of Great Britain
PCC	Press Complaints Commission
PhonePay Plus	Premium Rate Telephone Regulator (previously known as ICSTIS)
PPA	Periodical Publishers Association
PRS	Performing Rights Society
RAB	Radio Advertising Bureau
RACC	Radio Advertising Clearance Centre
SDNS	Scottish Daily Newspaper Society
SFD	Society of Film Distributors
SMMT	Society of Motor Manufacturers and Traders
SNPA	Scottish Newspaper Publishers Association
TMA	Tobacco Manufacturers Association
TPS/FPS	Telephone and Fax Preference Services
TSI	Trading Standards Institute
WOMMA	Word of Mouth Marketing Association

Contributors

The IPA is the industry body and professional institute for leading advertising, media and marketing communications agencies in the UK. Collectively, IPA members handle over 80% of the annual media spend (worth £18bn in 2007).

This book is the result of an idea and the efforts of the IPA Legal Department. **Marina Palomba**, Legal Director, and **Christopher Hackford**, Senior Legal Manager, have co-edited and contributed to the content of the book, which is primarily aimed at agencies and advertisers.

Marina and Christopher advise their IPA member agencies on all aspects of marketing communication law and regulation, and it is their hope that this book will assist agencies in understanding, in a practical way, the important issues which arise in the creation of effective but responsible and legally compliant communications.

Both Marina and Christopher are senior lawyers with many years experience in private practice prior to joining the IPA.

Marina was a partner in the Commercial Litigation Department of a City of London firm acting for clients such as Mohammed Al Fayed, Associated Newspapers and Channel 4. As well as advising IPA members directly, Marina also advises the IPA on most aspects of the law and is a member of CAP (Committee of Advertising Practice regulating non-broadcast advertising) and a Director of BCAP (regulating broadcast advertising). She is a member of the International Bar Association and has both written and lectured on advertising law, human rights and data protection issues. Marina is a Director of Media Smart (the initiative to teach media literacy to 6–11-year-olds). She has the Chartered Institute of Marketing (CIM) postgraduate diploma in marketing. Marina qualified as a solicitor in 1989.

Christopher also worked as a commercial litigator in private practice and was involved in a number of commercial, financial and defamation cases as well as some public international law disputes. He graduated in history from the University of Durham and studied law at the College of Law in London, where he obtained a distinction in his final year LPC exams and qualified as a solicitor in 1997. Christopher also works closely with CAP and he has particular expertise in prize promotions, e-commerce, betting and gambling and the use of celebrities. He is a member of International Trade Marks Association.

Geoffrey Russell is the Director of Media Affairs at the IPA as well as IPA Company Secretary and Secretary to the IPA Council, the Commercials Production Policy Group, the Media Futures Group and the Sponsorship Group. Geoffrey joined the IPA in 2000 from the Radio Advertising Bureau where he was Company Secretary and Director of Special Projects. His marketing and advertising experience includes senior roles with Procter and Gamble, McCann Erickson and AAP Ketchum (now part of Grey Advertising). A former Kitchener Open Scholar in Modern History, he is a graduate of St Catherine's College, Oxford.

Marina, Christopher and Geoff also lobby National and European government on legislation affecting the advertising industry and work closely with government on initiatives such as Creative Britain.

Marina Palomba   marina@ipa.co.uk
Christopher Hackford   christopher@ipa.co.uk
Geoffrey Russell   geoff@ipa.co.uk

Image and film rights, music clearances and talent management

Corbis is a creative resource for advertising, marketing and media professionals worldwide, helping to bring creative work to life with the highest quality photography, footage and rights services. (Corbis provided the majority of the images in this publication.) They offer a pre-eminent collection of more than 100 million creative, entertainment and historic images, a comprehensive footage library, the world's deepest rights and clearances expertise and an award-winning media management solution.

Their network, GreenLight, works with clients on a 24-hour basis, to perform all types of rights clearances, including:

- celebrities and celebrity estates
- music master, mechanical, performance and synchronisation rights
- feature films and television clips
- athletes and sports leagues
- fine art
- properties and landmarks
- derivative works.

The services that GreenLight specifically offers IPA member agencies are:

- free initial consultations on rights clearance projects during regular business hours;
- a response to initial rights clearance requests within one business day of receipt. For questions that require additional research, GreenLight will respond by confirming receipt of the request and project and providing an estimated time for a more detailed response;
- a 10% reduction of the fee normally invoiced to the client for the rights clearances licence(s) (up to a maximum of US $10,000.00);
- an easy form licence agreement for all rights clearance requests, which will include preferred, pre-agreed terms and conditions;
- a full indemnity up to a maximum of $1m US dollars for all rights clearance projects fulfilled by GreenLight;
- free on-site education sessions for IPA agency creative teams, with the aim of increasing their understanding of rights clearances, the role of negotiated rights for iconic material, and the legal ramifications involved.

Lucy Charlesworth   020 7644 7623
Sonia Bouadma   020 7644 7503

LAW FIRMS

 Bates Wells & Braithwaite
SOLICITORS

BWB provides clients, particularly in the sports, arts and social enterprise fields, with practical commercial advice for marketing campaigns across all media. This includes agency contracts, database issues, IP licences, comparative advertising, sales promotions (including terms and conditions and charity-linked promotions), prize draws and competitions, including Gambling Act 2005 requirements and sponsorship agreements.

BWB has special expertise in regulatory law. Rupert Earle has advised the Committee of Advertising Practice and Advertising Standards Authority for many years on regulatory matters, and on the vast range of sector specific advertising legislation, for example, in the advertising of foods, and other more general EU-inspired requirements, particularly the Consumer Protection from Unfair Trading Regulations 2008. His colleagues advise Phonepay Plus.

Rupert also specialises in freedom of expression, freedom of information, privacy and intellectual property litigation, both for and against the media and advertisers. He has defended numerous libel actions for publishers, and trading standards prosecutions for retailers.

Rupert Earle   r.earle@bwbllp.com

collins long   JUST MUSIC and **JUST PUBLISHING**

John Benedict is a Fellow of the Royal Society of Arts and a highly respected music and entertainment lawyer with over 25 years experience in the industry.

Following business affairs directorships at Polygram, Chrysalis and MCA Records, John set up his own specialist entertainment law firm. He was Managing Director of China Records until its sale to Warner, and is co-founder of the specialist multimedia music companies Just Music and Just Publishing, who provide music to the advertising, television, film and games industries, in addition to releasing both physical and digital records.

John is now a Consultant at Collins Long Solicitors, providing specialist advice on legal and business issues within the entertainment industry and representing talent, corporate and independent clients in all areas of entertainment, music and new media law.

He sits on the AIM Rights Committee and New Media Committee and is the author of the *AIM Guide to Survival and Success in the Music Business*. He is a frequent contributor to various industry publications and has chaired a number of conferences about digital music, music and advertising and the future of music.

In addition, John is fully committed to the continued development of the Just Music companies and to their forward-looking approach to the role of music in licensing and branding.

John Benedict: johnbenedict@collinslong.com   www.collinslong.com
Just Music: john@justmusic.co.uk   www.justmusic.co.uk

DLA Piper is a global legal services provider with more than 3,700 lawyers around the world. Lawyers operating from offices in Europe, Asia, the Middle East and the United States provide high quality legal advice to clients in their local market and internationally. DLA Piper's global services are grounded by the strength of its domestic offices and commitment to client-driven services. The firm aims to support the strategic and operational needs of clients, wherever they do business.

The advertising team is an integral part of the Technology Media and Commercial Group which has more than 400 lawyers globally. The team offers all the advantages of a dedicated specialist group of lawyers with a multi-jurisdictional, multi-disciplinary approach. The combination of size, geographical reach and business acumen allows the lawyers to provide a seamless service on the largest and most complex projects, including multi-jurisdictional clearance programmes for all forms of media. They also advise on strategy and enforcement to protect a client's brand and reputation. In addition, the advertising team works in conjunction with colleagues in the Regulatory Group who specialise in the financial services sector and can advise on all types of financial promotions.

The firm's clients include some of the world's leading technology, communications, multinational media and entertainment companies, owners of well-known international brands and patents, sports governing bodies, internet service providers, e-business enterprises, government departments, national regulatory authorities and major financial institutions.

Siân Croxon   siân.croxon@dla.com

lewissilkin

Lewis Silkin is a successful commercial law firm based in the City of London that believes the fastest route to success is investing in relationships with its clients, its people and the markets it serves.

The firm's reputation for the services it provides to marketing services clients comes from combining legal expertise with an ingrained understanding of their business problems. Lewis Silkin advise on agency start-ups, international M&A, employment, acquiring a new HQ, celebrity endorsements, resolving disputes, advertising clearance and regulation, and client/agency agreements.

As the sole UK member of the Global Advertising Lawyers Alliance (GALA), Lewis Silkin can also solve clients' international problems, as well as those closer to home.

Brinsley Dresden   brinsley.dresden@lewissilkin.com

pillsbury

Pillsbury Winthrop Shaw Pittman LLP is one of the world's largest full-service law firms, with market-leading strengths in IP, advertising, media, commercial and technology law. Its lawyers serve clients internationally from key global centres including London, New York, Tokyo and Shanghai. The 2008 Corporate Counsel survey of in-house lawyers at Fortune 500 companies named Pillsbury a 'Go-To Firm' in numerous areas, including IP/brand and litigation. Pillsbury has substantial advertising experience and a rare global marketing law team supporting clients with international campaigns, comparative advertising and IP disputes, major sponsorships, overcoming regulator problems (e.g. large numbers of NAD cases (ASA equivalent in the US)), competitions and sweepstakes.

Rafi Azim-Khan is a Partner in Pillsbury's London office and Head of IP/IT, Europe. Rafi also heads the Marketing Law and e-Business teams. He has been listed as a 'leader' in advertising law since 1994 and one of the 'digital dozen' UK e-commerce specialists. He has advised many well-known agencies and multinational brands on all aspects of advertisement clearance; global product launches (e.g. Red Bull, Coke); headline comparative advertising/IP disputes (e.g. leading ECJ case, global Gillette v. Schick 'razor wars'); sponsorships (e.g. FIFA World Cup); promotions (e.g. UK's first £1m draw); lotteries (e.g. launching UK National Lottery); and overcoming regulator problems (e.g. F1). Rafi has over 15-years worth of rare 'gamekeeper turned poacher' experience, having advised 15 of the top 20 agencies, as well as advertisers, and having previously practiced at the ASA's law firm. He is listed in *Chambers World's Leading Lawyers*, *Legal 500* and *Global Counsel* guides.

Rafi Azim-Khan   rafi.azimkhan@pillsburylaw.com

swan turton

Swan Turton is a leading firm in the advertising and marketing law sector. It advises on all aspects of advertising content, contracts, disputes and complaints. The firm focuses on advising clients in the media, entertainment and creative industries and has particular strengths in the areas of advertising music and talent contracts. The firm's corporate and litigation groups regularly advise clients in the advertising and marketing sector.

Charles Swan is named as one of the leading advertising lawyers by both *Chambers* and *The Legal 500*. He is the Chairman of Adlaw International, a global network of advertising law specialists with members in 20 countries. He advises agencies and advertisers on all aspects of content, on contracts with clients, talent contracts, sales promotion issues, ASA complaints and claims by rights owners and competing advertisers. Charles is the author of the Advertising Industry section in *Copinger and Skone James on Copyright*, the leading work on copyright law.

Jonathan Coad heads the firm's litigation group and acts for a wide range of agencies, media corporations and celebrities. He is recognised as one of the UK's leading defamation and privacy lawyers and as part of his IP practice is also an expert on disputes relating to television formats. Jonathan is co-founder and Director of the International Format Lawyers Association (IFLA).

Charles Swan   charles.swan@swanturton.com

Wedlake Bell

Wedlake Bell is a commercial law firm based in Central London. The firm has a strong advertising and marketing practice within its 20-strong IP and Commercial team. This advises on all aspects of advertising and marketing law including commercial agreements relevant to advertising, sales promotions, sponsorship and branding issues. The team also has a strong dispute resolution capability for pursuing and defending claims in these areas.

The breadth of its services is demonstrated by a range of clients: from FTSE 100 companies, owner-managed private companies, banks and financial institutions, to trade associations and private individuals.

Michael Gardner is the head of Wedlake Bell's IP and Commercial team. He advises clients in relation to dispute avoidance and dispute resolution involving intellectual property matters. He is highly experienced in both pursuing and defending claims in the fields of trade marks, passing off, malicious falsehood, copyright and designs – including Community designs. He also regularly advises on the associated areas of confidentiality, privacy, data protection and malicious falsehood.

Over the years, Michael has gained experience of all aspects of IP dispute resolution, including the use of search orders and other types of interim injunctions.

He lectures regularly on IP topics, such as comparative advertising.

Michael Gardner   mgardner@wedlakebell.com

withers LLP

Withers has a reputable and somewhat unique Art and Cultural Assets Group consisting of a team of specialist lawyers advising art collectors, art galleries and dealers, artists, museums and cultural organisations worldwide, headed up by Pierre Valentin. Prior to joining Withers, Pierre was a senior director and legal counsel at Sotheby's. His legal focus is cultural property, art collections and the international art market. He advises clients on acquisitions and disposals of art, contentious issues including ownership, export and restitution, art fraud, art banking, art investment funds and the taxation of works of art.

Pierre is a trustee of the World Monuments Fund and of the Artist's Collecting Society. He is a qualified mediator, and speaks four languages.

Daniel McClean is an Associate in the Withers' Art and Cultural Assets Group. He has extensive experience of the international contemporary art market having worked as an art curator in London and Tokyo and in a leading private art gallery in New York. Daniel's main focus is advising artists, galleries, collectors and consultants on commercial agreements (including sales, consignment and agency agreements) and on dispute resolution and litigation (including disputes involving ownership, attribution and the recovery of stolen art works). He also specialises in the protection and enforcement of intellectual property rights, and has advised several leading national art institutions on copyright issues.

Daniel has commissioned, edited and contributed to two publications on the relationship between art and law, *Dear Images: Art, Copyright and Culture* (2002) and *The Trials of Art* (2007). He teaches art law on the MA in Art Business at the Sotheby's Institute of Art (London).

Pierre Valentin   pierre.valentin@withersworldwide.com
Daniel McClean   daniel.mcclean@withersworldwide.com

Index